DARK MIRROR

# DARK MIRROR

## AFRICAN AMERICANS AND THE FEDERAL WRITERS' PROJECT

J. J. Butts

THE OHIO STATE UNIVERSITY PRESS
COLUMBUS

Copyright © 2021 by The Ohio State University.
All rights reserved.

Library of Congress Cataloging-in-Publication Data
Names: Butts, J. J., author.
Title: Dark mirror : African Americans and the Federal Writers' Project / J. J. Butts.
Description: Columbus : The Ohio State University Press, [2021] | Includes bibliographical references and index. | Summary: "Shows how Black writers such as Richard Wright, Zora Neale Hurston, and Ralph Ellison participating in the Federal Writers' Project of the 1930s responded to and shaped New Deal programs and ideology"—Provided by publisher.
Identifiers: LCCN 2021009885 | ISBN 9780814214770 (cloth) | ISBN 0814214770 (cloth) | ISBN 9780814258033 (paper) | ISBN 0814258034 (paper) | ISBN 9780814281482 (ebook) | ISBN 0814281486 (ebook)
Subjects: LCSH: Federal Writers' Project—Influence. | American literature—African American authors—History and criticism. | African Americans—Social conditions. | Liberalism—United States—History—20th century. | United States—Race relations—20th century.
Classification: LCC E175.4.W9 B88 2021 | DDC 305.896/073—dc23
LC record available at https://lccn.loc.gov/2021009885

Cover design by Andrew Brozyna
Text design by Stuart Rodriguez
Type set in Minion Pro

# CONTENTS

| | | |
|---|---|---|
| *Acknowledgments* | | vii |
| *List of Abbreviations* | | ix |
| INTRODUCTION | | 1 |
| CHAPTER 1 | New World Symphony: New Deal Civic Pluralism in the FWP Guidebooks | 28 |
| CHAPTER 2 | This Wise Geolatry: Modernization and Urban Planning in the FWP Guidebooks | 48 |
| CHAPTER 3 | Other Than What We Seem: The Folk Histories of Hurston and Wright | 67 |
| CHAPTER 4 | They Seek a City: The Future of African America in FWP Social Histories and Intertexts | 100 |
| CHAPTER 5 | Patterns of Modernity: The Urban Folk, State Power, and Citizenship in Petry and Ellison | 131 |
| CONCLUSION | Irony and Liberalism | 161 |
| *Bibliography* | | 167 |
| *Index* | | 177 |

# ACKNOWLEDGMENTS

Federal Writers' Project authors evinced a love of details and correspondences, coincidences and characters—the stuff of life. The writing of this book has been full of them. At one point while writing, I realized that the East Village café in which I was sitting occupied one of the street-level commercial bays of First Houses, New York's first New Deal public housing project. This soon-to-be-defunct coffee house named Des Moines was for a time a kind of writer's home, one of several waypoints that would serve that purpose between my Brooklyn apartment and various adjunct gigs. The final drafts would be written 1,100 miles to the west in another Des Moines I'd come to call home with its own East Village and legacy of competing visions of modernization.

Throughout this time, I've had generous support. As with all scholarly books, this one owes a debt to the scholarship of others, many of whom are acknowledged in the bibliography. The manuscript and contributing materials benefited directly from comments by Jeff Allred, Crystal Bartolovich, Kristin Bluemel, Matthew Calihman, Debra Rae Cohen, Steven Cohan, Leigh Anne Duck, Eve Dunbar, Susan Edmunds, Tracy Floreani, Jan Goggans, Ayesha Hardison, Yẹmisi Jimoh, Anne Mosher, Bonnie Roos, and Harvey Teres. Editors and reviewers at *The Space Between, African American Review, American Studies,* Cambridge University Press, and The Ohio State University Press have also left their mark. I'm deeply grateful to Ana Jimenez-Moreno, Tara Cyphers, Juliet Williams, Laurie Avery, the editorial and production staff, and reviewers at The Ohio State University Press for their ideas, guidance, labor, and support. A number of other scholars with whom I've had conversations about the project offered insights that helped me move it forward. A non-exhaustive list includes: Lori Askeland, Wesley Beal, Sterling Bland, Kyung-Sook Boo, Robert Brinkmeyer, Claire Buck, Keely Byars-Nichols, Katharine Capshaw, Paula Derdiger, Bruce Dick, Erika Doss, Mary Selden Evans, Matt Garite, Christina Hauck, Lena Hill, Sarah Hogan, Lesley Larkin, Anastasia Lin, John Lowe, Robin Lucy, Steve Pearson, Stella Setka, Karen Skinazi, Cristina Stanciu, Catherine Stewart, Michael Thomas, Myka Tucker-Abramson, Agnieszka Tuszynska, and Michael Williamson. Archival research is one of the great joys of historical scholarship, and thanks to research grants and a sabbatical from Simpson College, I was able to seek help from librarians at the Library of Congress, the Municipal Archives of New York City, the National Archives, the New York Public Library's Schomburg Research Center, the Newberry Library, and special collections at Northeastern University, the University of Rochester, Syracuse University, and Yale University. Along the way, the interest and support of my colleagues and students at Hunter College, Wartburg College, and Simpson College has been crucial, as has the friendship, wisdom, and encouragement of my scholarly kith and kin at the Space Between Society and the Society for the Study of the Multi-Ethnic Literatures of the United States (MELUS).

My family—the Butts, Hendershot, and Licht clans—continued to believe the book would be published while I wrote and rewrote (and then rewrote again), and I'm humbled by their faith and support. Most of all, I'm grateful to Amy for her patience as a listener and acuity as a reader, but especially for her love. This book is dedicated to our children, Hannah and Elias, who remind me every day that we live for a better future indebted to those who came before.

# ABBREVIATIONS

| | |
|---|---|
| AFL | American Federation of Labor |
| APMEW | African Pacific Movement of the Eastern World |
| Bontemps Papers | Arna Bontemps Papers |
| CIO | Congress of Industrial Organizations |
| Conroy Papers | Jack Conroy Papers |
| CPL | Chicago Public Library |
| CPUSA | Communist Party of the United States of America |
| Ellison Papers | Ralph Ellison Papers |
| FAP | Federal Art Project |
| FWP MACNY | Federal Writers' Project New York City Records in the Municipal Archives of the City of New York |
| FEPC | Fair Employment Practice Committee |
| FHA | Federal Housing Authority |
| FSA | Farm Security Administration |
| FTP | Federal Theatre Project |
| FWP | Federal Writers' Project |

| | |
|---|---|
| IWP | Illinois Writers' Project |
| Mangione Papers | Jerre Mangione Papers |
| Moon Papers | Henry Lee and Mollie Moon Papers |
| NAACP | National Association for the Advancement of Colored People |
| NARA RG69 | Federal Writers' Project Administrative Records, National Archive and Records Administration |
| Negro History Group | FWP Negroes of New York Collection, Schomburg Library |
| NLRB | National Labor Relations Board |
| NPB | National Planning Board |
| NRM | New Religious Movement |
| NRPB | National Resources Planning Board |
| PWA | Public Works Administration |
| TVA | Tennessee Valley Authority |
| UNIA | Universal Negro Improvement Association |
| USWPA | United States Works Projects Administration Records, Library of Congress |
| WPA | Works Progress Administration; Work Projects Administration after 1939 |
| Wright Papers | Richard Wright Papers |

# INTRODUCTION

In 1938, *New York Panorama,* the first of the New Deal Federal Writers' Project (FWP) guidebooks for New York City, offered this cautionary note on the nation's future:

> The question of what will ultimately happen to the Negro in New York is bound up with the question of what will happen to the Negro in America. It has been said that the Negro embodies the "romance of American life"; if that is true, the romance is one whose glamor is overlaid with shadows of tragic premonition.[1]

Claude McKay, the Harlem Renaissance poet and novelist, drafted this essay, titled "Portrait of Harlem," which traces the history of Black New York. It was rewritten for publication by emerging literary star Richard Wright and photojournalist Arnold De Mille.[2] Reflecting this transition from one of the leading lights of the Harlem Renaissance to the emergent face of the Chicago Renaissance, the essay heralds a crucial shift in understandings of urban Black space, replacing romance with tragedy. Gone: lively images of Harlem, the capital of

---

1. Federal Writers' Project (hereafter FWP), *New York Panorama,* 151.

2. Rowley, *Richard Wright: The Life and Times,* 543, note 82, cites a July 18, 1938, letter from FWP Director Henry Alsberg to Ruth Crawford that traces the authorship of *New York Panorama*'s Harlem material.

Black America; in their place: the hard-hit slum, the object of sociologists, planners, and writers for a generation to come. "Harlem Is Nowhere," former FWP employee Ralph Ellison would title his 1948 profile of the neighborhood, repeating a street aphorism that captured the social death of its denizens.[3] Like Wright's own 1940 novel of urban entrapment, *Native Son,* the FWP essay anticipates Gunnar Myrdal's influential analysis in his 1944 study *An American Dilemma.* It yokes the fate of the nation to that of the slum, suggesting the latter would be the proving ground of American liberalism, a showcase for its success or its failure.

In *Black Is a Country,* Nikhil Pal Singh highlights the persistent tension between American liberalism's universalist ambitions and its ethnic specificity. Since the founding of the United States, liberalism has provided a framework of inclusion through rights, political representation, and a vision of a community of citizens. At the same time, historical ascendance through colonial and imperial ventures that racialized specific groups in order to make them available for exploitation haunts liberalism. Singh argues that historical shifts in liberalism are "mediated through a series of negotiated compromises around racial boundaries" that recreate the social and civic exclusion of specific groups.[4] For African Americans, Native Americans, and immigrants in particular, this legacy of devaluation and disenfranchisement has continuously undercut liberalism's universalist claims. Whether this is a flaw in liberalism or inherent in its design, a bug or a feature, is a problem this book does not propose to answer. It is enough to recognize that as the structure of liberalism has changed, exclusion based on racial distinction has proven politically and economically useful, historically and geographically malleable, and socially formative, making racial inequity the American liberal nation-state's most fundamental and intractable challenge.

*Dark Mirror* explores one of those momentous shifts in the structure of American liberalism through literary artifacts of the New Deal era written by African Americans. It constructs a conversation around the problems of welfare state modernization, national community, and race by reinterpreting FWP texts and their narrative and documentary intertexts in light of New Deal policies that promoted civic pluralism—a vision of national community that recognized the specific histories of social groups while celebrating their participation in civic and cultural activity—in tandem with plans for modernizing the nation. As the New Deal welfare state raised the possibility of new rights and forms of citizenship, it did so through a pluralist vision of national

---

3. Ellison, "Harlem Is Nowhere," *Collected Essays of Ralph Ellison,* 320–327.
4. Singh, *Black Is a Country,* 25.

inclusion. Simultaneously it advanced a modernist planning and development agenda that, if no less ambitious than civic pluralism, was more monolithic and exclusive in its imagination of America's future.

The incredibly prolific FWP, with its project of describing American space through guidebooks and other documentary texts, offers an important example of how the New Deal's vision of liberal community was constituted and promoted. Liberalism has long depended on public statements delineating temporal, spatial, social, and cultural connections to generate a sense of national coherence. Singh notes:

> Intellectual descriptions of national history, identity, and community help resolve a special problem for the liberal-democratic or "civic" nation: the production and reproduction of a people who recognize themselves as consenting to a common enterprise in advance of the institutional forms that claim their allegiance.[5]

The universalist social descriptions of rights and responsibilities in public proclamations on liberalism are, in reality, performative—seeking to create community while masking its exclusions. Through the performative descriptions of American space and society in FWP texts, we can see how New Deal liberalism challenged socio-civic boundaries while engineering racial inequity. Throughout the century, this contradiction would shape the terms on which welfare state liberalism would operate, including forms of participation in national modernity and of resistance to it.

*Dark Mirror* explores the representation of American urban space and race in these FWP texts and in literary intertexts by Black writers from the late 1930s to the early 1950s. Over the course of this book, I advance several interrelated claims. First, in the FWP guidebooks, a commitment to civic pluralism—blending romantic nationalism, cultural pluralism, and a republican emphasis on participation—is often undercut by a focus on modernization as a cure for social inequity. The New Deal's cultural programs, including the FWP, promoted this inclusionary vision of national community, advancing new understandings of culture that recognized the contributions and innovations of African Americans. However, shaped by racism both explicit and implicit, many of its modernization programs, and particularly those focusing on urban and housing reform, cut African Americans out of the benefits of welfare state expansion. The New Deal's involvement in setting the terms for systemic racial inequity and rights claims is widely acknowledged across the

---

5. Singh, *Black Is a Country*, 19.

political spectrum today, but it remains valuable to see how African American writers participated alongside their White peers in constructing a national vision reconciling pluralism and modernization.

Second, African American writers, many of whom worked for the FWP, developed literary intertexts—fiction and documentary writing that made use of FWP materials, concepts, and forms to challenge New Deal representations of modernization, race, culture, and national community. Lawrence Jackson shows how an "indignant generation" of writers and critics working through political, social, and cultural networks advanced ideas from the interwar period and into the Cold War.[6] The FWP represents a crucial node in these networks, spawning a wide range of intertexts and political diagnoses. Writing against the panacea of New Deal modernization, these intertexts often invoked the New Deal's sociological analysis of the city, while warning against a liberal future without a reckoning over racial inequity. Simultaneously, they utilized FWP work on Black history and culture to highlight political possibilities and restore the presence of African Americans to visions of the national future.

In effect, these writers produced countermodern literary visions, refusing the break with history imagined in FWP guidebook descriptions of state-led modernization. Michel Foucault suggests the idea of countermodernity in "What Is Enlightenment?":

> I wonder whether we may not envisage modernity rather as an attitude than as a period of history. And by "attitude," I mean a mode of relating to contemporary reality; a voluntary choice made by certain people; in the end, a way of thinking and feeling; a way, too, of acting and behaving that at one and the same time marks a relation of belonging and presents itself as a task. A bit, no doubt, like what the Greeks called an ethos. And consequently, rather than seeking to distinguish the "modern era" from the "premodern" or "postmodern," I think it would be more useful to try to find out how the attitude of modernity, ever since its formation, has found itself struggling with attitudes of "countermodernity."[7]

In lieu of defining the term, Foucault instead suggests that modernity is configured in the perceptual break between past and present, enabling the inference that countermodernity refuses this break. Narratives based in countermodern attitudes assert the continuing and efficacious presence of the past,

---

6. Jackson, *Indignant Generation*.

7. Foucault, "What Is Enlightenment?," 38.

at times even to the point of challenging distinctions among past, present, and future.

Countermodern visions depend on their position vis-à-vis shifting dominant narratives of modernity, and they may take many forms, positing their own particular valuations of culture, space, and time. Neither entirely negative nor necessarily utopian, countermodernities highlight alternative, critical understandings of the relationship among past, present, and future. Like the modern visions they challenge, countermodern visions may contain their own blind spots, ambiguities, incoherencies, and contradictions. For example, in asserting the value of agrarian life and natural order against industrial rationalism and positivism, the Southern Agrarians problematically downplayed the dehumanizing realities of chattel slavery and Jim Crow. Despite these failings, countermodern visions can provide an important critical function by highlighting continuities and conflicts that assertions of modernity seek to erase.

Much of this conversation revolved around the status of the Black folk in an urbanizing nation. The folk, as a conception of both people and cultural practices, has long been the companion of national modernity. David Nicholls contends that the folk is a "contested vision of collectivity" rather than a stable cultural phenomenon or social formation.[8] It provides useful cultural pasts and conceptions of community, while marking boundaries between the modern and the premodern.[9] As Robin Lucy argues,

> Much of the writing of this period was concerned with the transition of the folk into a modernity that [Black migration to Northern cities] seemed to represent, as well as the extent to which the particular historical experience and location of African Americans would alter ideas of "cultural development" born out of the European Enlightenment.[10]

FWP intertexts in this study often utilize or interpret African American and African diasporic folk materials to affirm or challenge the New Deal's modern vision, often opening up political alternatives. Writers repurposed research materials and forms from FWP projects to generate literary texts experimenting with folk modalities of coding, prophecy, and allegory. Countermodernity

---

8. Nicholls, *Conjuring the Folk*, 4.

9. See Favor, *Authentic Blackness*; Hirsch, *Portrait of America*; Nicholls, *Conjuring the Folk*; Retman, *Real Folks*, for discussions of how the folk concept was utilized in the interwar era by African Americans and folklorists.

10. Lucy, "'Flying Home,'" 258–259. Lucy draws on Nicholls, *Conjuring the Folk*, 133–134, for this insight.

has many faces in these texts. Among other places, it appears in the "folk history" of Wright's photobook *12 Million Black Voices*; the signifying on Mosaic lore in Zora Neale Hurston's novel *Moses, Man of the Mountain*; and the motif of being "out of history" in Ralph Ellison's *Invisible Man*. In these works, even the ones that take a relatively sanguine view of modernization, the folk becomes a means of complicating and mediating progressive discourses of modernity, reintroducing questions of racial justice irreducible to economic change or reforming the physical environment.

Third, the conversation between FWP and African American literary intertexts had a deeply transformative impact on postwar African American literature, shaping its themes, forms, and political outlook. The FWP was not the only driver of these changes, of course. Shifts in anthropology, sociology, psychology, and folk studies played a role, as did the vigorous cultural debates on the communist-led Left, but all of these intersected with the New Deal cultural programs. However, the FWP's role remains underexplored. FWP work embedded writers in the political discourses and documentary forms of the liberal welfare state. Thematically, conflicting understandings of the city and the particular problem of how to understand Black folk culture and history became dominant, reflecting broader tensions over culture and modernity in FWP work. These tensions shaped well-known novels like *Invisible Man* and Ann Petry's *The Street,* but also relatively unknown documentary books such as Roi Ottley's 1943 study *New World A-Coming,* which used Harlem as a lens for exploring persistent problems in Black communities across the nation and leveraged its description into wartime political pressure on the federal government.

African American writers engaged in a sustained dialogue over modernity, the nation, and pluralism that would shape their political outlook on liberalism and resistance in the years ahead. This book shows how African American literature interrogated claims of inclusion and the shifting terrain of exclusion in the New Deal's reenvisioning and remaking of the modern liberal state. It also demonstrates that, while many of these works offer thoughts on the future of African American political engagement, their outlook reflects the transitional politics of the era. In particular, many intellectuals recalibrated their commitments to the Left in the late 1930s and early 1940s as disappointment and anticommunist pressure mounted. New Deal liberalism offered a popular alternative, promising national renewal through the state, though often falling sharply short of fitting this aim with racial justice. The political shifts of this era yield complicated rhetorical and allegorical stances marked by caution, contingent thinking, and ambivalence. Some writers warned against problems inherent in liberalism, while others embraced the New Deal welfare state as an incomplete if potentially useful development, advocating legal remediation to exclusionary practices. Nearly all of these writers challenged the New Deal's claims that state-led modernization alone would be the pathway to a more just society. Even so, their engagement often echoed key elements of the popular New Deal vision and recast the terms of political conversation on primarily liberal grounds, setting the stage for political claims based in identity, inclusion, resources, and community. At the same time, these writers identified alternate political possibilities, particularly forms of racial nationalism and internationalism that would shape lines of resistance to the postwar welfare–warfare state.

## The Federal Writers' Project

In the depths of the Depression, with World War II on the horizon, the FWP worked to reassure US citizens a bright national future still lay ahead. To do so, it put writers to work on a collective and immensely ambitious project describing American space: the American Guide series—forty-eight state guidebooks; three highway guides; two gargantuan guides to Washington, DC; and two guidebooks to New York City. These books represented the New Deal to the nation while they simultaneously reimagined the nation. Singh suggests that the New Deal provided a coherent vision of a modern community that allowed individuals to see themselves within it, effectively a hegemonic strategy of culture-building paired with relief and infrastructure programs. This vision legitimated an expanded liberalism and proved more popular than the radical Left-wing alternatives that enticed many intellectuals during the interwar years.[11] Alongside other documentary work, the guidebooks served a crucial propaganda function: they gave the New Deal a voice. If FWP guidebooks did not offer the sympathetic appeal of Roosevelt's fireside chats, they nevertheless "carried a double authority," as Christine Bold notes, of "the truth claims of an informational genre and the official sponsorship of the federal government."[12] FWP guidebooks repeatedly reference New Deal programs, making them seem a natural, even native, fit with American history, thereby turning description into prophecy.[13]

---

11. Singh, *Black Is a Country*, 86.

12. Bold, *WPA Guides*, 3.

13. For accounts of the FWP, see Bold, *WPA Guides*; Griswold, *American Guides*; Hirsch, *Portrait of America*; Mangione, *Dream and the Deal*; Penkower, *Federal Writers' Project*; Schindler-Carter, *Vintage Snapshots*; Shaffer, *See America First*; Sklaroff, *Black Culture and the New Deal*; Stewart, *Long Past Slavery*; Taylor, *Soul of a People*.

The FWP also kept a generation of writers at work *as* writers even though, to the chagrin of many FWP employees, the work rarely extended to writing fiction or poetry.[14] As Wendy Griswold argues, the primary aim of the program was practical. Federal One—which included the Federal Art Project (FAP), the Federal Music Project (FMP), and the Federal Theatre Project (FTP) in addition to the FWP—was to provide work relief for unemployed culture workers.[15] Working under the direction of the national office based in Washington, FWP units were set up in each of the forty-eight states and New York City, and these were further divided into subunits with varying degrees of autonomy. This federal arrangement ensured a wide range of employment, even if it was never enough to satisfy writers' unions and advocacy groups. Perhaps only the radical Left or Hollywood can claim such a broad array of literary talent in the 1930s. Certainly, at no other moment in American history have so many authors collaborated so widely, openly, and directly with the state.

The FWP personnel roster was impressive. Heading the national office, FWP Director Henry G. Alsberg was a playwright known for his work with the Provincetown Players and the Neighborhood Playhouse. His 1925 English adaptation of S. Ansky's tale of love, modern ethical dilemmas, and spiritual possession, *The Dybbuk,* had thrilled New York theatergoers while immersing them in forms of Yiddishkeit. While most administrators in the Washington office remain largely unknown today, figures like Katherine Kellock, George Cronyn, Reed Harris, and Jerre Mangione were instrumental in creating and running the project. The list of consultants includes more familiar names: Benjamin Botkin, Sterling Brown, James Weldon Johnson, John Lomax, Lewis Mumford, and Charles Seeger. These figures' preeminence in the fields of African American culture, folklore, and urban studies suggests areas in which the New Deal cultural legacy would be particularly important.

The list of writers associated with FWP units is even more striking. Nelson Algren, Saul Bellow, Arna Bontemps, John Cheever, Jack Conroy, Ralph Ellison, Kenneth Fearing, Vardis Fisher, Zora Neale Hurston, Claude McKay, Philip Rahv, Kenneth Rexroth, Studs Terkel, Margaret Walker, Frank Yerby, and Anzia Yezierska all worked for the Writers' Project. These are merely some of the most recognizable figures. Many FWP writers had ties to the literary

---

14. See Mangione, *Dream and the Deal,* 123, for discussion of some of these complaints. There are a few notable exceptions to the FWP's concentration on nonfiction. In 1937, the FWP published a book of fiction and poetry by FWP writers titled *American Stuff.* The New York City FWP unit also had a unique subunit of talented writers who were allowed to pursue creative work on work relief funds.

15. Griswold, *American Guides,* 15–33.

Left, like Bontemps, Conroy, Ellison, and Wright. Some earned their place in specific literary fields such as children's literature, as was the case with Ellen Tarry, or journalism, like Roi Ottley and Ted Poston. For Maxwell Bodenheim and Claude McKay, the Writers' Project was the twilight of a career. For Yezierska, the "sweatshop Cinderella" of 1920s immigrant fiction, it was a literary rebirth. Others, like William Rollins Jr., a star of the proletarian literary scene, largely disappeared from the public consciousness after the 1930s. For Bontemps and Henry Lee Moon, the FWP was an important transitioning point to careers focusing as much on utilizing institutional power as individual authorial voice. Hurston and Wright wrote their most celebrated novels as FWP employees. And for Algren, Bellow, Cheever, Ellison, and Walker, the FWP experience became a catalyst for brilliant wartime and midcentury literary careers.

As this list suggests, African American writers were represented relatively well in a few FWP units, especially the New York City unit and the Illinois unit based in Chicago. The prominence of so many Black writers in the FWP rosters speaks to their inability to find adequate literary employment elsewhere in the Depression, but Federal One was no jobs panacea. While Lawrence Jackson asserts that NYC's FWP unit "produced an early model of a moderately racially integrated workspace," Catherine Stewart notes that Black writers had difficulty securing FWP jobs in states without major cities.[16] Southern state units were particularly resistant. African Americans were generally shut out of FWP leadership positions unless that position specifically had oversight over material on Black history or culture. Nevertheless, FWP activities supported a number of significant Black writers while providing them time and practice in researching and reporting on Black communities in the nation's metropolises. This would be deeply significant for African American writing in the years ahead, as research into history and culture, ideas about urban space, and documentary forms of writing offered useful possibilities for narrative and ways of reimagining American community.

The guidebook project pragmatically solved a problem of governmental patronage. While public modes of representation—such as murals, sculptures, public concerts and theatrical performances—offered a comparatively clear public benefit for which primary credit would go back to the government, compensation for individual writers producing creative literary works for private consumption was politically unfeasible. Concerns about writers' political convictions made the very existence of the FWP controversial, as many legislators worried about propaganda for communism or racial equality. Other

---

16. Jackson, *Indignant Generation*, 65; Stewart, *Long Past Slavery*, 120–142.

critics worried about the potential for boondoggling, a popular term of the era coined to represent wasteful expenditure on New Deal projects. Working with Jacob Baker, the Civil Works Administration assistant administrator who pushed for a Works Progress Administration (WPA) work relief program for artists, Kellock, who became one of the lead editors for the FWP, devised an innovative solution, although it did not entirely allay suspicions. The FWP would produce a wide range of useful texts: tourist and commercial brochures, ethnic group and folklore studies, and short journalistic pieces, but the primary focus would be guidebooks for each of the states in the model of the expansive European Baedekers.[17] The American Guides would promote nationwide tourism, chronicle local histories, and highlight modern currents. In a pattern set by the national FWP office to enable the guides to serve these functions, they were divided into essays about the economic, social, and political elements of the particular geographic location, descriptions of various locales, and extended narrative "tours" of points of interest. Priced reasonably at $2.50 per volume, within reach of middle-class households, they were marketed heavily and sold relatively well. Many persist in libraries and reprint editions, and have served as sources of information for generations of journalists and scholars.[18]

The guidebooks' role in promoting the New Deal vision of national modernity is perhaps most evident in what many critics have described as a spectacular generic failure due to their complex mission. The unwieldy FWP tomes drown the would-be tourist in excessive information and interpretation.[19] Early proposals for the guidebooks supplemented the pragmatic conception of the guides as work relief and tourist industry pump-priming with a more idealistic rationale. An archived draft prospectus for the *American Guide* stated that the guidebooks "will give to the citizens of the United States an explanation of the cultural values of their country, past and present, and the problems and achievements of the Nation," and cited the value of an increased public "understanding of the measures now being taken along the lines of landreclamation [*sic*], rural rehabilitation, slum clearance, land and city plan-

---

17. The most recent Baedeker guide to the US had been published in 1909. See Bold, *WPA Guides*, 19–36; Griswold, *American Guides*, 15–51; Mangione, *Dream and the Deal*, 29–93, for the best accounts of the origins of the FWP and adoption of the guides as its primary project.

18. See Griswold, *American Guides*, 236–251, for a discussion of FWP distribution and readership. The question of readership is also one of political efficacy. One of the primary charges leveled at proletarian novels was that, as relatively expensive commodities, the group on whose behalf they were written rarely read them. See Foley, *Radical Representations*, 98–109, for a discussion of the problem of audience in proletarian fiction.

19. Griswold, *American Guides*, 226–251, notes that surviving copies bear marks more consistent with reference works than use in travel.

ning, and other public improvements."[20] Bold asserts that the *American Guide* series attempted to represent a cohesive "harmoniously diverse" national community, to allow readers to imagine themselves as part of the wealth of the national heritage, and to instruct readers in the art of being citizens in such a community.[21] Even Kellock, who had warned against muddying the guidebook's touristic orientation with social analysis, stated: "It would seem that an American guidebook could be launched almost as a community project. It would certainly be a tremendous cultural contribution to aid an understanding of American civilization."[22]

As these statements suggest, FWP guidebooks were guides not only to national values but also to change—to modern living and the possibilities of the future. Citizens would see their locale, and by extension themselves, represented in the national project and could envision what the future might look like. The information in the guides, another early prospectus suggested, could facilitate social and spatial transformations, encouraging relocation for environmental, educational, or employment reasons, as well as "vacation-making."[23] By familiarizing people with the United States' varied social and physical geography, the guidebooks could convince them that certain locations or ways of living would have distinct advantages over others. They could encourage citizens to adopt new social and settlement patterns, and see themselves as part of interlinked state, regional, and national communities.

## Remaking a Nation: Civic Pluralism and Modernization

Progressive ideas reconciling community and modernity, while advancing a conception of the state as an active force in provisioning rights grounded the FWP's promotion of a pluralistic vision of national community alongside an

---

20. NARA RG 69, "The American Guide Book: A Directory and Guide to the Cultural and Recreational Resources of America," Central Office Records, Miscellaneous Publicity Materials 1935–41, Box 1.

21. Bold, *WPA Guides*, 18.

22. NARA RG 69, Katherine Kellock. "A Project for Relief Employment of White Collar Workers," Central Office Records, Miscellaneous Publicity Materials 1935–41, Box 1. See also Kellock's critique of guidebook form, NARA RG 69, "Differences in Form and Content of Different Types of Books," Memo to Reed Harris, Central Office Records, Records of Henry G. Alsberg Sept 1935–June 1939, Box 1. As Shaffer, *See America First*, 169–220, has argued, the guidebooks drew on a history going back to St. John de Crevecouer of using geographical description to generate national values.

23. NARA RG 69, "Prospectus: The American Guide," 10, Central Office Records, Miscellaneous Publicity Materials, Box 3.

emphasis on state-directed planning and modernization.[24] Civic pluralism reflected both the Progressive intellectual heritage of the New Deal and the nation's changing demographics, seen most clearly in the metropolis. Hirsch argues that "FWP officials can be described as both romantic nationalists and cultural pluralists."[25] Romantic nationalism, the idea that each nation had a distinctive soul legible in national culture, undergirded much of the thinking about the modern nation state. By the beginning of the twentieth century, many romantic nationalists settled on folk traditions as the key locus of national identity. Conservative variants of romantic nationalism sought to anchor American culture in unbroken European roots, such as attempts to find preserved English culture in Southern Appalachian dialects and ballads. However, the revaluation of culture initiated by thinkers like Franz Boas and W. E. B. Du Bois located the roots of American culture in its diversity and envisioned individuals flourishing in conditions fostered by, shaped by, and sustained by their communities. The work of Randolph Bourne, Horace Kallen, and Alain Locke in the 1920s redirected the search for American distinctiveness toward multiple sites and beyond the White working class. Challenges remained: as Gary Gerstle has pointed out, Progressive thinkers often disagreed on which groups contributed to national distinction and which ones threatened it.[26]

Cultural changes are as much a product of shifting social dynamics as they are of intellectual debates, however, and the interwar years saw the growth of urban intellectual social networks that facilitated pluralism. Many of the activists and intellectuals who developed New Deal programs had spent time in settlement houses or other urban reform causes, where despite attitudes of superiority and paternalism, they still came into regular sympathetic contact with a wide range of individuals from social groups. American expatriates in London, Paris, Havana, and Barcelona exported cosmopolitan sensibilities during the interwar years. The emergence of New York, Chicago, San Francisco, and Los Angeles as nodes of American modernism also heralded the growth of urban bohemian enclaves with concentrations of cultural intellectuals living among urban ethnic groups. Alsberg, like many other FWP employees, was a veteran of Greenwich Village bohemianism.[27] As Christine Stansell

---

24. Rodgers, *Atlantic Crossings*, offers a thorough account of the trans-Atlantic Progressive lines of influence that shaped the New Deal. See Blake, *Beloved Community*, for a discussion of the communitarian impulse among Progressives. See also Walzer, *What It Means To Be an American*, for further discussion of the community/modernity opposition.

25. Hirsh, *Portrait of America*, 4.

26. Gerstle, *American Crucible*, 9.

27. See DeMasi, *Henry G Alsberg*; Bold, *WPA Guides*, 23; and Mangione, *Dream and the Deal*, 54–55, for discussions of Alsberg's background.

documents, White bohemians often saw certain groups, Hungarians and African Americans in particular, through the romanticizing and objectifying lens of "vital contact," through which stultifying and repressive bourgeois habits could be relieved.[28] However, as in the settlement houses, cultural interchange also facilitated sympathetic understandings and brought visibility and, at times, also social and financial capital into urban working-class communities.

Writers were also emerging *from* urban communities fluent in multiple cultures. As a number of critics have noted, American literary modernism was built as much through networks of intellectuals who grew up in urban environments as the ones who moved to them.[29] Xenophobic policies halted the wave of immigration that fed the growth of the United States in the later nineteenth and early twentieth centuries, and the unintended result was the rise of a homegrown generation of intellectuals challenging Anglo-American cultural norms, including many second-generation immigrants and African Americans. The Great Migration from the South and the Caribbean had fueled the rise of robust Black urban communities in Northern and Midwestern cities. George Hutchinson links Harlem cultural networks to the New Deal's attempts to reconcile pluralism and the nation:

> Alliances and understandings formed during the Harlem Renaissance by chiefly cultural exchanges were critical to advances made during the 1930s—through inclusion in the Federal Writers' Project, the Federal Theatre Project, and the Federal Arts Project, for example—and a modicum of social inclusion that, though savagely short of equity, could scarcely have been imagined twenty years earlier.[30]

The interwar years, as Lawrence Jackson notes, also saw Black cultural networks take shape in Chicago and Washington, DC, also sites with prominent FWP presences.[31] These writers would shape FWP accounts of American cities with their firsthand knowledge of African American culture and urban social complexity, adding depth and substance to civic pluralism.

As local pluralist movements faltered in the 1920s due to the economic impacts of the crash, a new interest in the state and the nation began to overturn

---

28. See Stansell, *American Moderns*, 61–64, for a discussion of the bohemian idea of "vital contact," which suggested that stultifying bourgeois habits could be relieved through cultural interchange with immigrants.

29. For particularly strong accounts of the influence of second-generation immigrants on American modernism, see Klein, *Foreigners*, and Konzett, *Ethnic Modernisms*.

30. Hutchinson, *Harlem Renaissance in Black and White*, 13.

31. Jackson, *Indignant Generation*, 15–41.

ethnic localism and form the basis of a social democratic nationalism. By the 1930s, cultural Progressives were primed to argue for a more expansive notion of national community that reconciled romantic nationalism and pluralism.[32] Regionalists like Lewis Mumford, for example, sought a balance between cultural difference and unity in geographic regions that could serve as the basis for a complex national identity. New Deal civic pluralism, as expressed in the guidebooks, imagined a widened, if not quite all-encompassing, national community based in different social groups' contributions to culture and history. Promoting civic pluralism served several pragmatic functions for the New Deal. It offered a means of bridging the claims of local communities and social groups with the emerging nation. It also supported the expanded role of the state in distributing rights and goods by making it a broker of claims. Finally, it reflected the growing urban power base of the Democratic Party. Democratic machines had long depended on organizing and representing the claims and needs of urban social groups. By the 1930s, this pattern extended to urban African Americans in key cities like New York and St. Louis. The power of these groups provided a means of breaking the lock on the Democratic party platform and presidential nominations held by its Southern wing, leading to the rise of a new approach to governance.

Though compelling to many, this vision and its urban origins was quite controversial, and tensions over race were a fundamental part of New Deal politics. Seeking to appease the conservative Southern legislators who had long formed the most influential voting bloc in the Democratic Party, the early New Deal largely ignored African Americans. Early agricultural programs excluded Black tenant farmers, or even threatened their eviction. Work relief programs administered at the state and local level followed patterns of patronage and prejudice that excluded Black workers. Social insurance programs, one of the most important developments, excluded farming and service work, which formed the backbone of African American labor.

However, by 1935, as the FWP was getting under way, Eleanor Roosevelt and several cabinet members began to make inroads on implementing more inclusive policies. Harold Ickes at the Department of the Interior insisted on proportionate hiring and racial quotas designed to ensure inclusion of Black workers. The Washington-based race-relations advisors that Ickes and other cabinet members hired began to meet regularly and formed what many referred to as a Black Cabinet or Black Brain Trust, which coordinated atten-

---

32. See McCann, *Pinnacle of Feeling*, 67–99. McCann suggests that the 1920s cultural pluralism of Bourne and Kallen conflicted with both the earlier nationalistic impulses of Progressivism and the Boasian cultural relativism. The 1930s saw a reconciliation of pluralist and nationalist ideas under a broader framework of economic enfranchisement.

tion on African American communities and civil rights issues through advisory activity, policy-making, and press relations. Black advisors also played an important role in the FWP. Sterling Brown oversaw the projects' representation of African American social, historical, and cultural phenomena, and used his connections to gather information and talent.[33] As African Americans responded to this new opening, it became clear that Black voters might serve to shift the balance of power by forsaking historical ties to the Republican party and instead supporting coalitions of New Deal Democrats and Progressive Republicans. The 1936 election confirmed this, as Black voters turned out en masse to reelect Roosevelt and a number of pro–New Deal candidates, a shift that has shaped American politics since.

The New Deal's civic pluralist vision is most apparent in the FWP guides' attention to diverse social groups and spaces. Following the regime of federal immigration restrictions and a decade-long explosion of lynching incidents, and during the rise of fascism, the guidebooks offered extensive exploration of ethnic communities in terms that predominantly highlighted their contribution to national history and culture. The FWP served as a kind of recording machine for the nation, documenting the experiences of immigrants and former slaves and the emergence of new folk legends from city pavements. As Bold has shown, this approach often led to conflicts between the national and state FWP offices, particularly over the representation of African American culture and history in the South.[34]

Discussion of the folk in particular played an important role in constituting a national framework built through diverse contributions. Sonnet Retman explains:

> [Roosevelt's] New Deal seized upon the issue of the authentic folk to solve the problem of how to represent "the people," developing programs that set out to display the vernacular traditions of historically marginalized groups to tell a story of national fortitude and exceptionalism.[35]

By representing the folk as part of the national narrative, the FWP attempted to reconcile a range of social groups and their cultures with their vision of a modern nation. However, in its documentation of stories and traditions, the

---

33. Much of this history is drawn from Sitkoff, *New Deal for Blacks*, 44–76.

34. Bold, *WPA Guides*, 123–186.

35. Retman, *Real Folks*, 13. For the purposes of discussion, in this book, the term *vernacular culture* is used to designate the broad array of popular cultural phenomena including folk culture, and the terms *folk, folkways,* and *folk culture* to designate phenomena specified or conceived as such.

FWP was inconsistent, reflecting differing scholarly approaches, administrative imperatives, and generic conventions. FWP documents might celebrate folkways as living elements of group culture or resistance to injustices, but they also presented folkways as points of interest and authenticity for tourist consumption. Emergent urban vernacular elements sometimes featured, but not as regularly as established rural traditions or those brought from migrants' homelands, reflecting longstanding views of folkways as preindustrial cultural survivals.[36] Though intended to bolster a spirit of inclusion, representation offered no guarantee that the folk, as culture or people, would fit seamlessly into an image of a modernized nation. Folkways might just as easily mark points of difference, inequity, or injustice. Here, African American intellectuals had a decided edge, having long debated the value of folkways as leverage for civil and social inclusion and for cultural innovation. The FWP would provide an important role in aggregating and documenting African American vernacular culture, providing an opportunity for reworking understandings of its aesthetic and political utility.

FWP civic pluralism reached its fullest and most radical cultural expression in the projects of the FWP subunits devoted to ethnic history, folklore, and oral history, where vernacular histories and culture revealed the centrality of racial animosity in the nation's past and present. These subunits were especially important for African American writers, who not only participated in them but later repurposed the information and forms to explore questions of justice after their FWP tenure. As Sara Rutkowski has argued, their work formed the basis for a history from below, enabling a means of talking back to the welfare state.[37] *Dark Mirror* demonstrates that the vernacular cultural elements these units uncovered fueled a range of fictional and documentary countermodern literary projects, which by turns challenged and complemented state-directed modernization.

The FWP guides also highlighted the threat to a more inclusive modern nation posed by poor urban conditions, diagnosing socially and physically fractious metropolitan spaces as slums subject to state intervention. The emergence of the influential Chicago School sociological approach in the 1920s shaped most discussions of the city, including those in the guides. One of the Chicago School's most influential figures, Robert E. Park, had worked under Booker T. Washington, and its adherents included several African American sociologists, notable among them: Horace R. Cayton Jr., St. Clair Drake, and E. Franklin Frazier, who would help define understandings of the role of race

---

36. Retman, *Real Folks*, 121.
37. Rutkowski, *Literary Legacies of the Federal Writers' Project.*

in American cities in the years ahead. Chicago sociologists had influence in Washington and particularly close ties to the Illinois FWP unit. Pairing the Boasian approach participant ethnography with newer statistical and actuarial tools, they laid the groundwork for reformist social policies. Chicago sociologists rejected understandings of ethnic groups as inherently inferior and instead focused on how ecological conditions shaped culture and psychology. If pluralists and folklorists often romanticized ethnic culture, sociologists tended to see it as symptomatic. Social disorganization theory, advanced by Edwin Sutherland, built on the concept of urban ecology developed by Park and Burgess to suggest that poor neighborhoods failed to develop adequate social resources that would deter delinquency. In short, they were ecologically imbalanced. This view helped make inequity visible as the result of urban morphology and other social factors, and thus legitimated interventions to alleviate problematic urban conditions in education, health, recreation, and housing. However, in doing so, Chicago sociology tended to advocate assimilatory practices, reinforcing understandings of White middle-class culture as normative and working-class urban communities as inherently maladaptive and in need of redress.

For New Dealers, a crucial solution lay in state-directed modernization efforts. If civic pluralism provided a participatory creation narrative for the FWP, modernization in the form of planning, welfare, and infrastructure initiatives provided its expertly planned, assimilationist, utopian future. As actualized narrative, modernization reflected understandings of environmental causality that had shaped understandings of the city from Progressive urban reform movements through Chicago sociology. Modernization legitimates particular agents, actions, goals, and targets of action. It insists on a break from phenomena it assigns to the past as it reorients society for the future. New Deal modernization was achieved through a number of means: social insurance, work relief, coordinating labor/capital relations, bolstering families, and public works in electrification, transportation, education, and housing. Many of these ideas were based in Progressive urban and regional planning discourses, and the transformation of physical space would become one of the most potent means by which the welfare state would alter the American landscape from the 1930s through the 1960s.

As FWP guidebooks promoted modernization, they often undermined the pluralist and participatory elements of the New Deal project. Descriptions of urban life in the FWP guides placed ethnic culture, and by extension ethnic groups themselves, into temporizing social hierarchies, sorting elements that fit the prevailing winds of modernity from premodern holdouts. Often, the FWP reimagined spaces resistant to a benign pluralism through the lens of modernization, pointing to realized and planned public works projects, especially slum clearance and public housing. In doing so, the guides ended up consigning certain cultural and social phenomena to the past as they advocated the dramatic rebuilding of urban neighborhoods.

However, promising in their beginnings, many of the New Deal modernization efforts were undermined over time by poor design, bureaucratic apathy, cost-cutting, and neglect. To say they failed to bring about the harmonious society New Dealers envisioned is an understatement. In some cases, especially in housing, modernization programs exacerbated racial inequity. To be certain, White citizens, including many from ethnic groups whose racial status had been in question prior to World War II, experienced the benefits of the expanded welfare framework. They built wealth in the form of homeownership, employment, and education. Situated outside the growth of a permissive public sphere amidst plenitude fueled social and cultural freedoms, and among a set of anxieties about conformity, identity, alienation, and existential meaning that permeated postwar White literature in the US, African Americans were keenly aware of their distance from the New Deal promised land. Within a generation, public housing became both the presumed agent and visible marker of socioeconomic blight in political discourse. A "second ghetto," shaped by governmental intervention in working-class urban neighborhoods, rose in place of the prewar slums.[38] How did this happen? One influential story has been that social engineering projects inevitably entail unintended, often disastrous results. However, this story centers on the invisibility of problems in New Deal programs that were, especially to many African American intellectuals, quite visible. Hubris certainly played a part in the tragedy, but a better answer lies in the racially conflicted roots of New Deal power, which generated an equally conflicted approach to racial equity.

## Black Countermodern Intertexts of the New Deal

The writers featured in this book explored in their own work many of these problems and their roots, often by identifying the persistence of racializing discourses in the construction of modernity. For most of these writers, the problem, at its most basic level, lay in the same set of hierarchical valuations and narratives that created modern race thought alongside Western liberalism. African American writers would keep these fundamental contradictions in view as the welfare state developed. My book's focus on FWP intertexts

---

38. See Hirsch, *Making the Second Ghetto.*

explores the way Black authors anticipated the political, social, and conceptual difficulties the New Deal would face in overcoming racial inequity. Repurposing FWP forms, ideas, and information, they would highlight the systemic racism undergirding actions, beliefs, and values, warning of its corrupting effects. While some of these texts endorse the New Deal approach, a deepseated skepticism about the federal government's commitment and even its ability to address social, political, and economic inequality based in race manifests throughout this literature.

*Dark Mirror* also shows how these writers illuminated the strategies by which African Americans would seek to participate in and challenge liberalism in the years ahead. Lionel Kimble notes: "Even with New Dealers' unwillingness to address issues of race and racism head-on, African Americans still saw that the New Deal and World War II provided access to the common yet contested citizenship expressed by liberal democratic ideas."[39] The New Deal offered a crucial opportunity to rework liberalism and recast the national community in a more democratic mold. Kimble argues that by 1935, African Americans were responding actively to the New Deal, hybridizing Roosevelt's vision of a modern nation and their own, and "transform[ing] Rooseveltian liberalism into a new African American liberalism" that "became the catalyst for an emerging protest movement in the city and democratized the political, social, and economic landscape."[40] Black writers' FWP experience helped them formulate effective means of communicating the complexity of race and history. Drawing on sociological, documentary, and folk discourses, these authors set the terms of postwar African American literature—its focus on hard urban realities, its repurposing of vernacular modalities and development of new forms, and its insistence on maintaining the historical and social links hidden in welfare state consensus culture. Connecting histories and vernacular culture recovered through the FWP, they constructed countermodern literary visions, which preserved memories of oppression, struggle, and hope, and questioned the New Deal's assertion of national harmony by identifying alternate forms of political community.

The discussion of these intertexts reveals several emergent dynamics in wartime and postwar African American literature. First, the deterministic approach of the Chicago School and its influence on the FWP shaped a literary conversation about the nature of the Black urban neighborhood. Second, the tension between folk culture and modernity, shifts in understanding vernacular culture, and aggregation of cultural data that characterized FWP work

39. Kimble, *New Deal for Bronzeville*, 6.
40. Kimble, *New Deal for Bronzeville*, 6.

also reappear in these intertexts. Third, the emergence of another set of largely unexplored New Deal intertexts, the documentary social studies undertaken by former FWP writers, develops a conversation connecting cultural and political concerns. Fourth, in their narrative and documentary approaches, these texts rhetorically explore political possibilities for African Americans, highlighting both liberal and alternative paths to community, citizenship, and resistance. By adopting and contesting liberal discourses, these texts prepare the way for a robust engagement with twentieth-century liberalism, reaffirming the political salience of race, experience, and vernacular culture.

The conversation between the FWP and its African American intertexts engages the most persistent points of interpretive contention over these books, particularly those where political meaning rests on the representation of vernacular culture. In Hurston's retelling of Exodus in *Moses, Man of the Mountain,* is Moses an effective leader and nation-builder or a brutal dictator? What does Wright mean by using the words "folk history" in the subtitle to his documentary photobook *12 Million Black Voices* when the book suggests emergent political movements must reject older customs and concepts? Does Ann Petry's *The Street* present a social realist tale or subvert it with a framework of folk symbolism? How seriously should we read the idea of social responsibility and citizenship in the epilogue of Ellison's *Invisible Man*? In his exploration of how literature was constituted as part of the struggle against Jim Crow, Kenneth Warren identifies conflicting imperatives shaping African American literary production, particularly in the representation of Black vernacular culture.[41] *Dark Mirror* similarly explores the tensions in these books as attempts to represent and negotiate the paradoxes of the liberal vision of the nation advanced by the New Deal and to carve out a space for African Americans as part of a national vision. In consequence, while my book seeks to clarify these texts' engagement with the welfare state, it often exposes tensity as fundamental to their situation, reflecting authors' transitioning politics as well as the difficulties of navigating the territory of liberalism and race without yielding to reductive political or aesthetic perspectives.[42]

## Critical Conversations

*Dark Mirror* seeks to bridge several critical conversations: the cultural history of the FWP, the literary legacy of the New Deal cultural projects, interwar

---

41. Warren, *What Was African American Literature?*, 27.

42. Warren, *What Was African American Literature?*, 10–11, describes this as the tension between the instrumental and indexical imperatives of African American literature.

and postwar African American literary aesthetics, and literature's discursive engagement with the American welfare/warfare state. In general, the cultural implications of the liberal state as the ascendant state form in the US and many other countries require more intensive investigation. As Michael Szalay and Sara Rutkowski have pointed out, examining New Deal cultural projects offers a corrective to the communism-centered Cultural Front model that has shaped much of the literary scholarship of this era.[43] The story of literary communism's flourishing and eventual expulsion from the cultural scene, and its lingering legacies in aesthetics and writers' lives, is crucial to understanding cultural politics then and now. Work on the politics of African American literature in this era often centers communism.[44] Even Lawrence Jackson, whose *The Indignant Generation* offers an excellent summary of the importance of the FWP as an institution supporting Black writers, largely focuses on its role in concentrating writers from the Left. However, this focus on activities related to the American Communist Party (CPUSA) also mutes the diversity of approaches and political centers during the era. This critical gap reflects the terms of 1930s literary culture, as writers generally located their intellectual identities in the radical Left's orbit, or in trajectories toward or away from it. The Communist Party's Popular Front strategy, beginning in 1934, generated significant overlap between communist and liberal initiatives, as well. Moreover, as Szalay notes, the "newly forming welfare state apparatus did not jump out at contemporaries in anything like a full-blown totalized form," somewhat delaying a more direct intellectual reckoning until the 1950s.[45] Acknowledging that the FWP provided vital employment for writers and that it aggregated important cultural resources has becomes a critical commonplace, but the FWP was not a politically neutral talent incubator.

The magnitude of political support for New Deal liberalism among African Americans, far outstripping support for communism as it did among Americans generally, suggests a need for more exploration of the New Deal's cultural apparatus and its literary legacy. My book, then, seeks to show that the New Deal provided a complementary milieu, overlapping but not fully assimilable

---

43. Szalay, *New Deal Modernism*; Rutkowski, *Literary Legacies of the Federal Writers' Project*. Scholarship on the literary Left of the 1930s is extensive. Denning, *Cultural Front*, traces the continuities among cultural initiatives on the radical Left in the 1930s and their postwar legacies. More recently Alan Wald's trilogy *Exiles from a Future Time*, *Trinity of Passion*, and *American Night* has detailed even more connections through the complex lives of the authors associated with the Left. See also Foley, *Radical Representations*; Murphy, *Proletarian Moment*; Nelson, *Repression and Recovery*; Rabinowitz, *Labor and Desire*; Teres, *Renewing the Left*.

44. Notable work on the Black Left before World War II includes Dolinar, *Black Cultural Front*; Maxwell, *New Negro, Old Left*; Mullen, *Popular Fronts*; and Foley, *Spectres of 1919*.

45. Szalay, *New Deal Modernism*, 18.

to the communist-led Cultural Front, that helped generate the political contours and aesthetic features of wartime and postwar Black literature. As Szalay suggests, "Reclaiming the interventionist state as a site of cultural analysis might help us to negotiate between revolutionary politics and more seemingly prosaic debates over congressional funding and appropriation."[46] If the New Deal failed to offer an intellectual context as robust and fervent as the CPUSA, federal funding nevertheless concentrated writers on activities focused on concerns about the composition and development of Black communities and the nation for a lay audience. Writing for the *New Masses* or the *Daily Worker*, Richard Wright could focus on developing nuanced stances on culture for other communists, but moving beyond these organs meant reframing arguments for a liberal audience, and the FWP provided crucial practice. In their FWP work and subsequent intertexts, African American writers explored the possibility of a pluralized yet modernized liberal nation, interpreting the role of Black history and culture within it.

By looking closely at both the FWP's national vision and its literary legacy, *Dark Mirror* bridges another gap in scholarship between literary scholarship and cultural histories focusing on the New Deal. Szalay, Sean McCann, and Susan Edmunds have all explored the links between modernist literary aesthetics and the discursive landscape of the welfare state. As these critics have illustrated, literature's engagement with welfare state liberalism was often indirect, enacted though metaphor, allegory, and displacement as writers addressed issues of work, governance, citizenship, family, and home.[47] Likely a result of the FWP texts' relative invisibility *as* literary work, however, this body of literary criticism rarely explores the FWP texts themselves. Restoring the FWP to this conversation as a body of texts shaping social and literary dynamics is one my book's central aims. To do so, it builds on the work of cultural historians including Christine Bold, Jerrold Hirsch, Lauren Rebecca Sklaroff, and Catherine Stewart, who have explored the cultural and social ramifications of the New Deal cultural projects.[48] These scholars have established the importance of the FWP to New Deal nation-building, to understandings of American culture generally, and to African American history and culture in particular. My book is especially indebted to Bold and Stewart, who, in lieu of attention to the FWP guidebooks from literary scholars, have

---

46. Szalay, *New Deal Modernism*, 20.

47. Edmunds, *Grotesque Relations*; McCann, *Gumshoe America*; Szalay, *New Deal Modernism*.

48. Bold, *WPA Guides*; Hirsch, *Portrait of America*; Sklaroff, *Black Culture and the New Deal*; Stewart, *Long Past Slavery*. The prominence of cultural historians in studies of New Deal culture also suggests that literary history has followed a relatively narrow track.

examined the formal and thematic elements of the FWP texts, showing how they negotiated difficult social phenomena.

The concentrated exploration and preservation of African American vernacular material in the FWP nation-building project was a crucial contribution of the New Deal to writers' emerging aesthetic and critical consciousness. Leigh Anne Duck, Sonnet Retman, and Sara Rutkowski, alongside Hirsch, Sklaroff, and Stewart, offer important connections between Black modernist literary aesthetics, conceptions of the folk, and the New Deal cultural projects, and this book is indebted to their historical insights and interpretation.[49] In particular, Rutkowski's *Literary Legacies of the Federal Writers' Project* theorizes the links between Black writers' cultural work for the FWP, their subsequent literary output, and their aesthetic legacy.[50] My study complements hers by resituating interwar, wartime, and Cold War African American writing as a response to the New Deal's modernization aims as well as its perspective on history and culture. I agree with Rutkowski that a key legacy of the FWP is the material and impetus toward historical recovery that reshapes African American literature throughout the twentieth century, but my book identifies a more complicated engagement between folk aesthetics and political rhetoric, leading to a wide range of approaches to welfare state liberalism.

Tracking African American literary development against New Deal dynamics of social and institutional change, *Dark Mirror* also retraces some of the territory Kenneth Warren and Lawrence Jackson follow as they historicize Black literary aesthetics from the interwar period through the Cold War. My book does not aim to replicate the theoretical scope of Warren's intervention or the connective detail of Jackson's history. Instead, it provides a missing account of how state-sanctioned documentary work reshaped the thematics, form, and politics of African American literature from the interwar period through the Cold War. My focus on reading African American FWP intertexts draws attention to the way writers rhetorically mediated relationships between African American culture and national social change as American liberalism was in the process of reconstituting itself. In their focus on the city, the neighborhood, and the folk, these writers suggested how a modern liberal democratic nation might thrive in social inclusion or founder once again on its contradictions.

---

49. Duck, *Nation's Region*; Hirsch, *Portrait of America*; Retman, *Real Folks*; Sklaroff, *Black Culture and the New Deal*; Stewart, *Long Past Slavery*.

50. Rutkowski, *Literary Legacies of the Federal Writers' Project*.

## Chapter Outlines

*Dark Mirror* follows the FWP's attempt to create a modern national community from the discussion of urban spaces and people in New Deal guidebooks, through which the New Deal advanced its vision of modernity to the intertextual skirmishes revealing the promise and limitations of that vision. The first two chapters explore the FWP guidebooks, developing an account of how they negotiated the social and narrative problems of the metropolis by advancing an inclusive, Progressive rhetoric of community while promoting urban planning and modernist development as a means of achieving it. Valorizing New Deal programs while describing cities as culturally vital but also subject to reform, these guidebooks introduced readers to a national community and citizenry that they hoped to activate.

Chapter One explores the representation of urban ethnic cultures and communities in the FWP guidebooks and the image of civic pluralism they constructed. It illustrates both how the FWP texts presented social complexity and how they managed it, often by rewriting space and temporizing culture. The second chapter shows how the guidebooks played a crucial role in easing concerns about urban social woes by advancing a narrative of modernization that paired a sociological diagnostic of working-class neighborhoods with modernist planning. In particular, the guidebooks' valorization of New Deal public housing initiatives imagined state-oriented solutions to persistent urban problems. The chapter demonstrates how the guidebooks connect public housing projects to a broader futuristic vision for the nation, one that was undermined on several levels but particularly by its inability to adequately address racial antipathy and inequity.

The book then turns to focus on African American literary and documentary intertexts of the New Deal. Taken together, the last three chapters frame a larger conversation playing out from the late New Deal through the early Cold War years about the future of African Americans and African American literature. Highlighting the interplay of ideas about the folk and modernity across genres, they showcase rhetorical shifts that highlight important political and cultural realignments during the early years of the welfare state. Crucially, these works often reflect a deeply ambivalent and cautious approach to politics during these transitional years.

My third chapter introduces these dynamics through the works of two of the most well-known African American FWP writers of the late 1930s, Richard Wright and Zora Neale Huston. Often seen as dipoles, both writers had complex views on Black culture and politics that shaped open conflicts between them. However, both were experiencing political shifts during this period, and both drew on folk modalities to articulate critiques of the New Deal. Hurston's novel *Moses, Man of the Mountain* uses conjure work and signification to retell the biblical story of national formation in a way that calls into view the violence of nation-building. Also a story of national origins and development, Wright's photobook *12 Million Black Voices* is one of a number of documentary intertexts of the FWP. Wright's *12 Million Black Voices* generates a "folk history" that reflects the central tension in the New Deal between vernacular culture and modernization. While Wright's book offers a more hopeful vision of a national community, it also qualifies the story it seems to tell by using folk modalities to question the etiological and teleological certainties of modernization.

To further highlight the continuity between fiction and documentary intertexts, the fourth chapter provides an alternate view of FWP activity and its legacy in Black literature through the output of FWP subgroups focusing on Black history and social life in New York and Chicago, and on the documentary intertexts resulting from those projects during the 1940s. In particular, it focuses on Roi Ottley's *New World A-Coming* and Arna Bontemps and Jack Conroy's *They Seek a City*, which developed out of materials generated for social histories of Black life in New York City and Illinois, respectively. These books use anecdotal sketches to disrupt purely sociological approaches and highlight social complexity. They laud the promise of the progressive New Deal community vision while retaining a critical understanding of New Deal social policy. Negotiating the new state-oriented strategies of struggle in wartime, they call attention to complex political dynamics in African American communities as a warning against liberal failure.

My final chapter examines later critiques of the New Deal in novels by Ann Petry and Ralph Ellison as the nation moves into the Cold War, and the New Deal and wartime political coalitions fall apart. These years reveal the significant gap between aspirations and achievement in New Deal pluralism. These books build on earlier approaches to illuminate the interplay between political power and citizenship. Like Hurston's and Wright's novels, Petry's *The Street* famously offers a double reading. That duality functions both to confirm the sociological diagnostic of the slum and to highlight the cultural value it misses. In the end, the novel suggests the state is incapable of seeing past racial narratives to enable justice. Ellison's *Invisible Man* builds on the expansive approach to African American history and culture deployed in the FWP subgroups and documentary intertexts to reenvision history and liberal citizenship in a critical mode that resists modernization's self-blinding approach.

## Conclusion

Descriptive in form but prescriptive in outlook, the guidebooks promote a specific vision of the New Deal, one that does not reflect the complex and often ad hoc nature of New Deal programs but rather gives them a sense of unity as a national community project influenced by Progressive ideals. The guidebooks envision a new liberal nation based in shared contribution and forged by federal interventions. The political firestorms the FWP encountered spoke as much to its progressive reimagination of the nation's future along pluralist lines, as to its rumored status as a platform for communist subversion. Widely accessible and garnering considerable critical attention in both the literary and regular press, the FWP guides were crucial in the New Deal's self-promotion and national vision, and they fueled important debates about the reach and role of the state.

The conversation between this vision and the FWP's literary and documentary intertexts provides a preview of the forces that would shape both national and global spatial policy in the postwar era. These developments helped birth the terms on which African Americans would reformulate their claims on justice in the 20th century. African Americans were central in developing the conceptual tools by which urban populations were being understood. New Deal cultural programs offered a crucial opportunity to address questions of representation and inclusion that had long been central to both African American uplift work and to national self-imagining. The welfare state offered a new set of targets for organizing, such as housing, transportation, labor, education, social insurance, access to consumer goods, and civil rights. By the 1940s, African Americans and allies adapted a new set of state-oriented strategies effective in challenging Jim Crow: the ballot, the courts, laws, executive orders, and federal commissions. At the same time, racial nationalist strategies began to emerge, which more fundamentally challenged liberalism by calling into question its core presumptions.

When Richard Wright proclaims in *12 Million Black Voices,* "We are with the new tide. We stand at the crossroads. We watch each new procession. The hot wires carry urgent appeals. Print compels us," he imagines writers at the forefront of a specific vision of countermodernity.[51] Yet his image of a "dark mirror," signaling the tension between the community he hoped for and the vision of liberal and communist modernizers, proved as prophetic as the warning in his essay on Harlem for *New York Panorama.*[52] An account

---

51. Wright, *12 Million Black Voices,* 147.
52. Wright, *12 Million Black Voices,* 146.

of Black writers' involvement locates cultural politics at the heart of socio-economic transformation during the emergence of the modern welfare state, while also showing how the resources provided by the welfare state would fuel cultural politics in the difficult years ahead. African American writers exposed a more fundamental irony than unintended consequences undermining New Deal liberalism: the failure to match its rhetoric of liberal inclusiveness with a democratic approach to progress.

# CHAPTER 1

# New World Symphony

## New Deal Civic Pluralism in the FWP Guidebooks

"Here is the greatest city of the Jews," *The WPA Guide to New York City* declares, "the world's third Irish city. . . . The world's Negro metropolis is the most crowded of all."[1] In such bold, expansive terms, New Deal guidebooks reflect modern liberalism's concern with questions of social difference. They inform readers how people or commodities, even people *as* commodities, have become part of the national story. While the guidebooks take note of historical injustices, they rarely dwell on them, except where they serve the broader purpose of reinforcing a pluralist vision of the nation. Instead, the guides encompass diversity, locating it and translating it into a shared heritage undergirding a compelling vision of national community.

The commitment to a pluralistic and participatory vision of national community was arguably one of the most controversial elements of the guidebooks. One uproar occurred after the Massachusetts guide, published in 1937, devoted more lines to Nicola Sacco and Bartolomeo Vanzetti, Italian immigrant anarchists who were tried and executed for armed robbery and murder, than to the Boston Tea Party or Boston Massacre.[2] Widely viewed by liberal and left intellectuals as scapegoats tried for who they were rather than what they might have done, the Sacco and Vanzetti case had become one of the

---

1. FWP, *WPA Guide to New York City*, 51.
2. Mangione, *Dream and the Deal*, 217.

unifying causes for the Left in the 1920s. For FWP writers, the case seemed a natural touchstone of the recent past, but many politicians connected to it wanted that past buried. Although the Massachusetts guide remained in print, such conflicts arguably doomed the FWP in the long run. As Lauren Rebecca Sklaroff points out, it was no coincidence that Martin Dies and Clifton Woodrum, the Congressmen who headed the investigations that ended the political feasibility of the FWP, were both Southern Democrats. For these lawmakers, support for pluralism was un-American not just because it echoed communist and socialist platforms, but fundamentally because it threatened to disrupt their White supremacist vision of the nation.[3]

This chapter explores the FWP's promotion of New Deal civic pluralism through the form and content of its guidebooks to major cities in order to show how they mobilized civic pluralism while managing potentially disruptive elements of urban culture. It begins by illustrating the ways that urban guidebooks had long negotiated social diversity and structured relationships between the reader and the social subject material, and how FWP guidebooks departed from the social hierarchies embedded in the guidebook genre to embrace pluralism. It then highlights the way that FWP New York City guidebooks' organization narratively reorganizes the city to facilitate this vision. The New York guides' treatment of Jewish and African American culture and history also offers a window into the competing discourses shaping New Deal civic pluralism, and the balance of the chapter focuses on descriptions of these groups. Offering a powerful rebuttal to racist and nativist rhetoric, the guides introduce readers to the contributions of Black and Jewish Americans as part of a shared national history. However, the guides also utilize narrative modes that generate temporal and social distancing to contain potentially disruptive cultural and social elements.

## Writing Urban Social Complexity in Guidebooks

Published by both individuals and major newspapers, urban guidebooks of the late nineteenth century typically position middle-class readers in a moral and visual economy similar to that of the realist novel, with which these guide-

---

3. Sklaroff, *Black Culture and the New Deal*, 62–64, 76–77. Bold, *WPA Guides*, 94, suggests that the New Deal's congressional critics worried more than was necessary about the potential of the guides to advance a subversive vision influenced by communism since "as collective productions the guidebooks did something quite different. They promoted versions of the city which attempted to reassure readers about the stability of New York, the politics of its authors, and the values of the Federal Writers' Project."

books competed in defining urban social space.[4] Like William Dean Howells's 1889 novel *A Hazard of New Fortunes* or Stephen Crane's 1893 novella *Maggie: A Girl of the Streets,* guidebooks escort the reader through the city's web of class and ethnic relations, offering the reader a look at both the most beautiful and most degrading aspects of urban life, allowing the reader to view them from a safe distance. Some, written by men and women of old New York families, engage in the nostalgia for the antebellum mercantile city and its social order seen in novels by Henry James and Edith Wharton. Rupert Hughes's remarkable 1904 guidebook *The Real New York* is even written *as* a novel, narrating the experience of three first-time tourists—a clergyman, a businessman, and a young artist—led by three experienced guides through the city's ballrooms and its slums. It concludes with the artist abandoning her plans to study in Paris after being locked in the Statue of Liberty overnight. In a gesture of national solidarity and urban boosterism, she declares that New York has everything she could want and accepts the marriage proposal of the Knickerbocker playboy who has been her guide.

The tropes that organize these guidebooks generate a hierarchical, normative valuation of urban space, illuminating the city's social codes for the reader's benefit. The other tourists in *The Real New York* encounter more problematic moral and social landscapes than the ingenue. Guidebooks of the late nineteenth century often use terms that are visual, contrastive, and metaphorical: light and shadow, gaslight and candlelight, visible and hidden. Matthew Hale Smith, author of the 1869 guidebook *Sunshine and Shadow in New York* wrote, "Whoever writes of New York truly, will do so in lines of light and gloom."[5] Edward Winslow Martin describes the purpose of his 1868 guidebook *The Secrets of the Great City: A Work Descriptive of the Virtues and the Vices, the Mysteries, Miseries and Crimes of New York City* in these terms:

> It is designed to warn the thousands who visit the city against the dangers and pitfalls into which their curiosity or vice might lead them, and it is hoped that those who read the book will heed its warnings. The city is full of danger. The path of safety which is pointed out in these pages is the only one—a total avoidance of the vicinity of sin.[6]

---

4. For this study I have drawn on a sampling of guidebooks from New York's City Hall Library written between 1865 and 1935. These books include: Hughes, *Real New York*; Irwin, *Highlights of Manhattan*; *King's Handbook of New York City*; Shackleton, *Book of New York*; Smith, *Sunshine and Shadow in New York*; Martin, *Secrets of the Great City*.

5. Smith, *Sunshine and Shadow in New York,* 706.

6. Martin, *Secrets of the Great City,* 15–16.

Such guidebooks often establish their bona fides through a narrator who serves as a benevolent and authoritative guide to the city, offering vicarious eyewitness to experiences that might otherwise harm or corrupt the reader. *The Secrets of the Great City* does not avoid the "vicinity of sin" but instead plunges into it with titillating descriptions, which suggests that the real aim is the reader's pleasure (and purse) rather than their moral security. Martin later modifies his admonition to readers, suggesting that his guidebook aims to "satisfy a reasonable curiosity on the part of those who have never seen, and probably never will see New York, and to warn those who design visiting the city, of the dangers and temptations which await them here."[7] Forewarning here is both forearming and foreplaying.

Nineteenth-century guidebooks often make hierarchical distinctions among ethnic groups, praising some for their social pluck while scorning others. Eastern European Jews and Chinese immigrants often receive particularly disparaging treatment. Guidebook author Matthew Hale Smith writes of Jews as an alien infestation, insinuating that they had organized yeshivas as a fundamentalist defense against what he saw as rightfully normative Protestant teaching. He also suggests that Catholics had organized control over municipal government. Even Jacob Riis, whose book *How the Other Half Lives* drew on guidebook conventions even as it established a new documentary style to call for slum reform, reserves some especially vitriolic passages for the Chinese, who he suggests are "a constant and terrible menace to society."[8] Prior to the twentieth-century migration of African Americans and West Indians, however, Black citizens and communities are rarely given much notice in guidebooks to New York, a lacuna they share with many current guidebooks.

In contrast with their nineteenth-century predecessors, FWP guidebooks utilize an objective voice legitimated by federal authority and a hybrid form, reflecting different visions of the guidebooks that work together to create a widely encompassing view of urban space and society. The essays on important elements of social and cultural life, often researched heavily or written by experts, advance expert understandings of different elements of social, political, and economic life. Descriptions of specific places are the result of a desire to catalogue the complex forms and features of modern life. Finally, the extended tours of some of those places nod to the tourist audience. Like a cubist painting, these elements work together with a range of representational

---

7. Martin, *Secrets of the Great City*, 522.

8. Riis, *How the Other Half Lives*, 83. Ultimately, Riis suggests a solution in line with sentimental protest tradition: Chinese men should not be deported; instead, Chinese women should be encouraged to immigrate as a domesticating influence.

32 • CHAPTER 1

devices—including maps, photographs, illustration, brief narratives, and listings—to orient readers to the multilayered urban social environment.[9]

While nineteenth-century guidebooks present social difference as part of the landscape of urban problems, the FWP guidebooks embrace immigrants and their histories, and they focus on African Americans extensively. The essay sections of the guidebooks engage in the most overt blurring of interpretation and description, and provide a useful place to explore representation of social diversity and futurity. Many include essays focusing on the distinctive national makeup of the population of a city or state. Typically, the essays group people by national origin, rather than continental or regional ethnicity. The Illinois Guide uses the run of Halsted Street through the city to remind readers, "There is a German Chicago, and a Polish Chicago, and a Swedish, Italian, Jewish, Lithuanian, Czech, Greek, Negro, Chinese, and New England Puritan Chicago."[10] It frequently cites demographic percentages as well to foreground the city's landscape of migration. The Philadelphia guidebook's essay "The Imprint of Nations" notes:

> The varied characteristics of a majority of the nationalities of the world have blended with and balanced one another to form the personality of Philadelphia. Although many of them have settled in compact national communities established by compatriots who preceded them, yet the leaven of their customs and culture has permeated the life of the whole city.[11]

The passage simultaneously highlights poles of assimilation and ethnic enclaving, but, most importantly, it makes a claim about these groups' contribution to the city and, by extension, the nation. Frequently in the FWP guides, a separate essay addresses African Americans and other African diasporic groups such as Black Caribbeans or Ethiopian Falashas. In contrast, except in states where their visibility was particularly high, the guides often erase indigenous Americans as a contemporary presence by subsuming them temporally into essays on a state's history.

In *New York Panorama*, which serves as the essay section for the two New York City volumes, a chapter titled "New World Symphony" maps out the idea of a complex American culture to which immigrants have made numerous contributions. The chapter introduction points to the cultural diversity within

---

9. Bold, *WPA Guides*, 27, discusses the function of these sections, as does Griswold, *American Guides*, 135–145. See also Bold, 92–122, for detailed critical discussion of the photographs and artwork in the New York City guides.

10. FWP, *Illinois*, 191.

11. FWP, *Philadelphia*, 98.

Manhattan as early as 1646 in order to reassure the reader that pluralism is a historical norm rather than a uniquely present crisis. The authors suggest that what we have come to accept as American culture "is the direct contributions of persons of foreign stock."[12] The essay goes on to describe many of New York's ethnic groups, from Chinese to Estonians, concentrating on rituals, food, and the arts.

By acknowledging the fragmented and multicultural history of cities, the WPA guidebooks incorporate immigrants and African Americans into a more expansive, pluralist American identity. The focus on the histories and contribution of individual groups casts them as deserving of the New Deal's redistribution of social goods. The "New World Symphony" essay demonstrates this contributive framing capably, while it also unintentionally highlights cracks in the frame of inclusion. In the process of immigration and adjustment to the city, the essay suggests, "the immigrant gave far more than he received. His rich agrarian culture he traded for the poverty-stricken culture of industrial society."[13] Here, the essay romanticizes the supposed wholeness of the immigrant folkways, but then it turns to an assimilationist tone. While immigrants make positive contributions, the essay suggests they will ultimately have to adapt to ways of living in this country that predate their arrival. White ethnics, it notes approvingly, have become "socially invisible" through cultural adoption and intermarriage.[14] The essay confidently asserts that assimilation will occur over time, but makes exceptions for groups with strong religious traditions. It remains silent about incorporating non-White social groups. This silence is atypical; the FWP's representation of Black history was relatively robust, offering a plenitude of details writers later found useful. Here, the silence symptomatizes the problems the FWP had in representing social conflict and imagining a pluralist future when race was involved.

## Reshaping New York

Civic pluralism depends on the balance of difference and unity tilting toward the latter. One central concern of FWP administrators was how to depict the social, historical, and textual complexity of the multiethnic metropolis in a way that conveyed both unity and legibility. In *The WPA Guide to New York City*, FWP editors solved the problem of complexity in part by rescaling dis-

---

12. FWP, *New York Panorama*, 81.

13. FWP, *New York Panorama*, 82.

14. FWP, *New York Panorama*, 84.

courses of regionalism, which Progressives had used to conceptually reorganize the nation, to generate an organizational logic for the metropolis.

Archived arguments between the national FWP office and the New York City office over the construction of the guide show the process by which the urban landscape was harnessed to the New Deal community project. The organization of the New York guide was haphazard in the early years. Writers sent volumes of copy to the federal editors. Alsberg frequently chided the early New York City directors because of irregular production and confusion over completed materials.[15] The guidebooks' form eventually crystallized under the direction of Vincent McHugh, the New York City editor-in chief from 1936 to 1938 who reshaped both the layout of the guide and the methodology by which copy was produced.[16] Following a 1937 scheme that had been approved by George Cronyn, the national Associate Director in charge of editorial duties, the New York City office planned three guidebooks, the essay-based *New York Panorama* and separate guidebooks for Manhattan and the Outer Boroughs.[17] Still, the Washington office was frustrated with the difficulties of editing draft materials without knowing their place in the larger schema. As copy continued to pour in for review, the federal office became increasingly concerned that, despite reassurances from NYC, no solid organizational plan existed.

By July 1938, Alsberg had directed the NYC office to send him a comprehensive plan for the second guidebook, *The WPA Guide to New York City.*[18] The plan he was given divided Manhattan into a host of neighborhoods according to function, class, and dominant ethnic group. By adhering to the complex social geography of the city, the plan would have created an unparalleled understanding of urban social diversity. This was also its weakness; it offered little sense of unity. Washington quickly developed its own plan for the second guidebook, which divided Manhattan into a number of sections arranged based in "tourist convenience, that is, localities that are near each other" along the north-south axes of Fifth Avenue and Broadway.[19] Similar

---

15. Some of this copy was later used for a subscription filler service for newspapers and other FWP projects.

16. See Bold, *WPA Guides*, 96, 109. The NYC unit had several directors and acting directors: Walter K. Van Olinda, Orrick Johns, Travis Hoke, Donald Thompson, Vincent McHugh, Harry L. Shaw Jr., Harold Strauss, Carl Malmberg, and Frederick Clayton.

17. NARA RG69, Letter, George Cronyn to Travis Hoke, 4 March 1937, Central Office Records, Editorial Correspondence, Box 35.

18. NARA RG69, Letter, Ruth Crawford to Henry Alsberg, 20 June 1938, Central Office Records, Editorial Correspondence, Box 35.

19. NARA RG69, "Sectional Plan for Combining Locality Stories in Book II," 14 July 1938, Central Office Records, Editorial Correspondence, Box 35.

to most modern guidebooks, the plan minimized the city's social complexity, reconfiguring it as a consumable object with prescribed tourist routes. However, Mary Barrett and Stella Hanau, two of the editors in the Washington office, criticized several geographical impracticalities of the new plan.[20] The tourist would be asked to cover the island twice despite the relative proximity of the two avenues, which cross at Madison Square. It would be difficult for editors to figure out to which tour some locations should be assigned without being completely arbitrary. Instead, they suggested eliminating the Broadway/Fifth Avenue axes and replacing them with a simple division of the city into sections arranged from south to north, with narration within sections proceeding from west to east. The guiding logic of their plan was that it followed the historical development of the city northward and would simplify directions for tourists, "since both the sections and points of interest fall naturally into place."[21] The use of history as a guide to geographical organization proved influential in the final organization of the guide.

Ultimately, consensus emerged around a compromise that would render the city socially comprehensible, recognizing difference while emphasizing unity and coherence. Like the Barrett-Hanau plan, the compromise organized the city into a number of sections containing several neighborhoods. The sections were based on a combination of abstraction and existing social geography. Commonly understood divisions, such as Downtown, Midtown, and Uptown, and the East Side and West Side remained intact. Also, many neighborhoods retained their distinctiveness. Greenwich Village, in particular, was deemed too significant to combine with other downtown neighborhoods by writers whose own recent history had been shaped there.[22] At other points, however, the division becomes more creative. The "Middle West Side" section for example, was an area of mixed social functions and ethnic identities. Hell's Kitchen and Chelsea were both primarily waterfront Irish Catholic slums. The garment trade and other small trades, often providing employment and mobility for ethnic citizens, were nearby. Times Square was a burgeoning entertainment district. An established African American community lived on San Juan Hill and had been subject to lynching during the Draft Riots.[23]

---

20. NARA RG69, Memo, from Mary Barrett and Stella B. Hanau, 18 July 1938, Central Office Records, Editorial Correspondence, Box 35.

21. NARA RG69, Memo, from Mary Barrett and Stella B. Hanau, 18 July 1938.

22. NARA RG69, "Sectional Plan for Combining Locality Stories in Book II," 14 July 1938. The arbitrariness of this protection can be seen today in the common division of the area between Houston and 14th Street into three Villages: Greenwich, West, and East.

23. The 1930 US Census, like two previous ones, subdivided New York's boroughs into census tracts or "sanitary districts" in order to facilitate more precise statistics than the borough-level view of earlier censuses. Together, three tracts—M3A, M3B, and M4A—enclose and

36 · CHAPTER 1

Despite these social, functional, and historical divisions, the area shared a physical location on the West Side, in the grid above Greenwich Village's crosscutting diagonals, but below Central Park. The second guidebook's unification of this area emphasizes shared elements of transportation and certain public spaces, rather than specific social group histories, thereby increasing the sense of an organized city.

Sectional division of the city functioned similarly to the concept of the region as a subdivision of the nation. Reflected in many of its administrative divisions and programs, the region was important to New Deal thought. In his 1938 book *The Culture of Cities,* the influential critic Lewis Mumford argued that the region, as a geographic organizing concept, would be a space in which there was enough social diversity to prevent any single group from establishing community standards, but also where certain elements of shared history and geography would facilitate common interests.[24] For Mumford, the region is an area in which a tolerant and progressive community is made possible by the balance between diversity and commonality. Similarly, sectional organization allowed the *WPA Guidebook to New York City*'s authors to link wide swaths of urban space by bypassing fractious ethnic neighborhood divisions without erasing their presence altogether.

Occasionally, sectional boundaries became objects of contention, especially where they negotiated racialized geographies. Alsberg critiqued a copy of the guide that placed the southern boundary of Harlem at 94th Street on the West Side, suggesting that "unless the areas are given accurately, there will be complaints from the real estate people."[25] Other letters from Alsberg back up the need to be especially careful about delineating the boundaries of Black enclaves in the city. The fate of the planned third guidebook to the outer boroughs suggests that writers' preexisting sense of sociogeographic interest limited their ability to see important social developments. New York Editor-

---

exceed the area called the "Middle West Side" by the guidebooks. The census divides the population into "White" and "Negro," and then further specifies whether Whites are native born of native parentage, native born of foreign parentage, or foreign born. While the San Juan Hill neighborhood is observable in the high number of Black citizens in M3B, and all three districts have a higher number of first- and second-generation White immigrants than more established natives. Further useful ethnic divisions are not evident in the data.

24. See Mumford, *Culture of Cities,* 302–314, for a discussion of regionalism. See also Bold, *WPA Guides,* 31–32, on the importance of regionalism for the *American Guide* series as a means of managing difference while asserting a coherent national community. Bold, 32, notes: "In practice this [regional] vision amounted to unselfconscious paternalism and respect for difference of the right kind, joined with a typical New Deal zeal for planning." My next chapter takes up the implications of reconceptualizing space along regional lines for issues of governance and planning.

25. NARA RG69, Alsberg, "Critiques of Volume Two Galleys," Filed 6 March 1939, Central Office Records, Editorial Correspondence, Box 35.

in-Chief Lou Gody and Ruth Crawford, who worked with various state units before transferring to the Washington, DC, office, wrote to Alsberg in 1938 to complain that the writers and editors were frustrated with their subject material:

> Another weakness inherent in the present presentation is the overwriting that developed naturally from the effort to make much out of little. In many instances, we feel, that the writers were faced with the impossible task of giving character where character did not exist, and of creating points of interest where there were none worthy. Then, too, many of the neighborhoods were so much alike that the description became a stereotype.[26]

Ironically, New York's outer boroughs had been the focus of massive demographic and geographic shifts as the bridges and mass transit facilitated relatively affordable transportation to and from the urban core. While this change had produced a number of distinctive ethnic communities, these were apparently insufficiently distinct to the project's writers. Crawford and Gody wrote, "Unless one knows the location of Greenpoint, Tottenville, Flushing or Canarsie, he might as well be reading about Timbuctoo."[27] The editors at Random House agreed and suggested that the second and third volumes should be combined, with the majority of the copy devoted to Manhattan. Harry Shaw, director of the FWP New York City unit in 1938, objected that the interested citizens of the other four boroughs would sustain sales of a third guide, but he was not able to carry his point.[28] Eventually, these materials were incorporated in abbreviated form toward the end of the second volume. Although the *WPA Guide* still covers more territory than almost any other guidebook to New York, the disinterest in these neighborhoods suggests that the guidebooks often reflected social norms rather than challenging them.

## Jews and the Lower East Side

Within New York, different social groups also presented different representational challenges, and the *WPA Guide's* treatment of Jews and African Ameri-

---

26. NARA RG69, Letter, Ruth Crawford and Lou Gody to Henry Alsberg, 10 June 1938, Central Office Records, Editorial Correspondence, Box 35. Ruth Crawford information from George T. Blakey, *Creating a Hoosier Self-Portrait*, 58.

27. NARA RG69, Letter, Ruth Crawford and Lou Gody to Henry Alsberg, 10 June 1938, Central Office Records, Editorial Correspondence, Box 35.

28. NARA RG69, Letter, Harry Shaw to Henry Alsberg, 4 May 1938, Central Office Records, Editorial Correspondence, Box 35.

cans, particularly in the Lower East Side and Harlem, shows how the guides promote civic pluralism while also mitigating conflict. The FWP treatment of New York Jews foregrounds progressive elements of Jewish culture, while presenting traditional social and cultural elements in Jewish communities as anachronisms. By the 1930s, Eastern European Jews had become both the paradigmatic urban underclass and the immigrant model minority. Jews had made a significant mark on the culture of New York, and second-generation Jewish scholars who had studied with the Progressives were standard-bearers for many of the 1930s political movements, particularly on the Left. Jewish thinkers and politicians were well-represented in the New Deal coalition, and the "Jew Deal" became a common anti-Semitic slur against the New Deal. The stakes of representing Jews as positive contributors to the city and the nation were high.

Jews garner significant attention in in *New York Panorama*; an extended section in the "New World Symphony" essay is longer, at six pages, than the copy on any other group. The essay acknowledges the difficulties of labeling a multi-origin group with such diverse customs.[29] Despite these differences, Jews are treated as a coherent group making a collective contribution to American culture and politics. The essay traces the history of Jewish residence beginning in 1654 with the conflict in the Dutch New Amsterdam over a group of Sephardic refugees from Brazil. It describes the waves of nineteenth-century Jewish immigration from Germany and Eastern Europe. Focusing primarily on both the industrious pursuits of entrepreneurs and the strong labor and political organizing traditions, the essay paints a picture of a group whose members are active in both private and public life. While such activities were often cited to support anti-Semitic conspiracy theories, the guide highlights their importance to American social life. The end of the essay focuses with approval on the education and literary focus of Jewish urban culture. It takes pains to suggest that the education is "mostly of a non-religious kind" and that the many Jewish journals and newspapers "represent a wide range of social, political, economic, and cultural viewpoints."[30] The essay minimizes social differences between New York's Jews and society at large by emphasizing the secular and diverse aspects of the culture and by stressing a history of contribution.

Because of its focus on Jewish participation in commercial and political life, *New York Panorama* easily deploys normative ideas about how social problems could be relieved. The "New World Symphony" essay approv-

---

29. FWP, *New York Panorama*, 85, 125.

30. FWP, *New York Panorama*, 131.

ingly suggests that, despite religious resistance to assimilation—it makes no mention of external factors—Jews have frequently escaped ghetto problems through dispersal.[31] Citing labor organizing as important to creating opportunity, the essay states, "Higher wages and shorter hours made it possible for thousands of Jewish workers to move out of wretched tenements into brighter and cleaner homes in the healthier neighborhoods of the Bronx, Brooklyn, Queens, and Staten Island."[32] Through its loaded adjectives, this passage echoes slum reformers' belief that suburban dispersal would bolster individual opportunity, increase public welfare and health, and relieve urban congestion. Reformers also believed that suburbanization would break up the maintenance of old traditions and lingering connections to Europe. *New York Panorama* ultimately attempts to balance normative understandings of a healthy environment against its pluralist aims. It focuses on elements identified as contributive and adaptive and laments the loss of folk traditions in adaptation to modern life, even while suggesting that these losses are the inevitable cost of modernity.

If the first guidebook imagines New York's urban culture as a symphony, *The WPA Guide to New York City* asserts that Jews occupy many of the first chairs. With its focus on ghetto persistence on the Lower East Side, this volume displays less faith than *New York Panorama* in the inevitability of assimilation and downplays the unfolding exodus of Downtown Jews to other enclaves in the city and suburbs. Instead, descriptions of Jews remain split between the modernized and the yet-to-be-modernized. The "Lower East Side" section opens with a discussion of the role of the ghetto as a home for new immigrants, tracing the successive waves of immigrants that occupied tenements. While it explores the panoply of the ethnic groups on the Lower East Side, occupying discrete neighborhoods—Little Italy, the Jewish Quarter, the Bowery, Astor Place, and the area between Houston and 14th Street now known as the East Village—Jews still occupy a central role in the guidebook's account of the area. The second guidebook's discussion of the Jewish Quarter is more extensive than that of the other sections, and the discussion of the East Village is dominated by an account of Jewish theater.

*The WPA Guide to New York City* focuses on Jewish influence on American cultural and political life as well. Listing achievements in areas such as poetry, fiction, theater, and song, the guide is concerned to show that Jews have contributed in the arts and popular culture as well as in the businesses and trades with which the first volume associated them. Citing among other

---

31. FWP, *New York Panorama*, 84–85.

32. FWP, *New York Panorama*, 129.

intellectuals the proletarian novelist and editor Mike Gold; sculptors Jo Davidson and Jacob Epstein; and Abraham Cahan, whose stories and journalism helped to introduce the Lower East Side to other Americans; the guide focuses on Jewish literature, theater, and sculpture as evidence of the fruitful meeting of Old World culture and ghetto conditions. It also recognizes the influence of the ghetto on more popular arts such as comedy, song, and film. As evidence of the highly literate and intensely political nature of this culture, the second guidebook also focuses on the various political journals circulating in the community. It states, "The intellectuals among the immigrants brought with them their old-world avidity for culture, and their influence on the East Side provided thousands with their first contact with art and literature."[33] In an era of anti-Semitism and frequent Jewish exclusion from employment, the *WPA Guide*'s focus on contributions serves as a culturalist argument for inclusion.

While they trumpet modern, progressive elements of Jewish culture emerging on the Lower East Side, the second guidebook's authors had to deal with more intractable cultural elements. In the introduction, *The WPA Guide to New York City* suggests, "Here unconscious of all exoticism, thousands of persons celebrate the *bar mitzvah,* sit *shiva* for the dead."[34] The Jews described may be unconscious of exoticism, but the italics indicate FWP authors were aware. Certainly, the many Jewish writers and editors on the FWP, including Alsberg, would have been cognizant of the problems of an exoticizing perspective. However, the guides also reflect intragroup tensions here, taking the side of Jews whose cultural activities seem more aligned with the modern scene. Its measured temporal and aesthetic distancing of Yiddishkeit posits an interesting, but ultimately benign relationship between tradition and modern culture. This section on the Lower East Side's Jewish Quarter pictures it as aged and fading:

> Here tiny shops huddle between white-fronted chain stores and clothing establishments. Housewives carrying shopping bags walk to the dimly lighted food stores; shriveled old women sit on the steps before the tenements; an occasional elder in beard and *yarmulke* (skull cap) climbs the steps to a tiny synagogue maintained by some struggling congregation; a Jewish passerby may be solicited to come into the synagogue to make up *minyan* (quorum of ten) so that the service may start.[35]

---

33. FWP, *WPA Guide to New York City,* 112
34. FWP, *WPA Guide to New York City,* 51.
35. FWP, *WPA Guide to New York City,* 116.

The guidebook suggests that customs are "struggling" holdovers from the past rather than living elements of urban life. In doing so, it borrows from second-generation Jewish literature by writers like Anzia Yezierska, Henry Roth, and Daniel Fuchs to distinguish a fading Old World way of life from a modern urban culture, without acknowledging the ties between the former and the latter that these writers captured.

Instead, the *WPA Guide* presents these elements as unthreatening, part of a picturesque milieu offering cultural enhancement for the reader. The frequent use of definitions in the section offer the best illustration. The guide explains the meaning of several words, including: "*knishes* (boiled buckwheat groats or mashed potatoes, wrapped in a skin of dough and baked) . . . *schlepper* (pullers-in [for stores], a recognized profession on the Lower East Side)," and, humorously unnecessary for a contemporary reader: "*bagel* (doughnut-shaped rolls)."[36] Here, the guidebook suggests a richness of language that is an important cultural resource, a point prepared a few pages earlier where it notes the importance of urban immigrant expressiveness to American speech and humor.[37] *The WPA Guide to New York City* also smooths over intraethnic and interethnic conflict. It references political differences within the Jewish community but characterizes the differences as healthy debate in a democratic culture rather than divisiveness.[38] While noting that some of New York's most fearsome gangs were Jewish, the FWP suggests that these gangs are a past phenomenon.[39] The second guidebook also avoids discussion of other sources of tension such as intermarriage and competition for jobs.

With these potential internal and external conflicts diminished, *The WPA Guide to New York City* can deal with an issue dear to reformers: slum persistence. The "Lower East Side" section ends on a sociological note—a warning that is simultaneously a call for action: "But the tenements that have been home to so many generations will probably be home to many more. . . . Great slums die hard."[40] However, it also offers hope in the form of New Deal–sponsored redevelopment. The *Guide* cites approvingly the tenement buildings demolished for public works such as the Williamsburg and Manhattan bridges, the East River Drive, and an unusually large strip demolished for a park that lay bare for decades (now Sara Roosevelt Park). The passage also hails a new federal housing project in the works for the Lower East Side and states hopefully that "even the pushcarts," the subject of restrictive legislation

---

36. FWP, *WPA Guide to New York City*, 117.

37. FWP, *WPA Guide to New York City*, 112.

38. FWP, *WPA Guide to New York City*, 110.

39. FWP, *WPA Guide to New York City*, 110.

40. FWP, *WPA Guide to New York City*, 113.

42 · CHAPTER 1

due to their undesirability, "may yet be housed in respectable markets."[41] These future-oriented statements, discussed further in the next chapter, provided an important means of imagining the power of the New Deal to bring a planned national community into being.

## Black Americans and Harlem

The persistence of the color line in social and spatial inequity also threatened New Deal civic pluralism, undercutting even the long-term assimilationist scenarios. Christine Bold and Catherine Stewart have written about the conflicts generated by the imperative of representing African Americans.[42] Some state directors aided the federal office representing African Americans as part of state histories, while others, particularly in the South, actively fought it. The guidebooks often reflect representational conflict over African Americans in their very structure. The separate essay treatment of African Americans, on one hand, expresses the federal office's desire to make African American culture and its contributions to the nation visible to address gaps in representational and social equity. On the other hand, the separate treatment in FWP guidebooks of Black life in Southern cities, like Atlanta and New Orleans, also clearly reinforces racial segregation.[43] Churches, hotels, and other institutions serving African Americans come last in their respective sections in these guidebooks. The guides also anchor textual and social separation with White supremacist history. They repeat Lost Cause historiography by figuring African Americans as corrupt co-conspirators with exploitative carpetbaggers during Reconstruction. Given many Southern Whites' ambivalence about New Deal intervention, the guides' framing of the end of Reconstruction as the welcome removal of unnecessary federal authority reads as coded resistance to the New Deal programs if those programs also entail social equality.

At times, the tension between Jim Crow and civic pluralism in these guides yields peculiarly complicated accounts. This was especially true in their representation of Black vernacular culture. The New Orleans guide features the history of Congo Square as a gathering site for slaves and former slaves since it adds to the interest of the city, but the expulsion of Black social activities goes unremarked other than the guidebook mentioning the renaming of the square for Confederate general P. G. T. Beauregard in 1893.[44] The guidebook

---

41. FWP, *WPA Guide to New York City*, 113.
42. Bold, *WPA Guides*; Stewart, *Long Past Slavery*.
43. Georgia Writers' Project, *Atlanta*; FWP, *New Orleans City Guide*.
44. FWP, *New Orleans City Guide*, 18, 83.

rewrites historical conflict for the tourist's interest while erasing the modern racial politics of space. Another particularly odd section on "Folkways" places the reader in the position of a fictive White visitor guided by a Creole gentleman, who alternately disavows voodoo beliefs and adheres to voodoo practices and customs. The Creole guide takes the reader to the city's various sites to satisfy the reader's curiosity. Here, the nineteenth-century guidebook role of narrator-protector is revived, even while the second-person narration erases a layer of textual insulation. The tour recognizes voodoo as important to the cultural scene, part of the flavor of life in New Orleans. However, it suggests it is not to be taken too seriously; at one point the guide steals the money from a gris-gris offering in order that the two might lunch. The text then manages to have it both ways, at once recognizing the allure of Black folk culture and its importance to New Orleans culture, while simultaneously dismissing it with a knowing wink.[45] As this book will suggest, such tensions over representing resistant elements of culture, ongoing inequity, and pluralist futurity persist within the guidebooks, between the guidebooks and FWP social texts, and also between FWP texts and the documentary and literary intertexts produced by FWP writers.

Both *New York Panorama* and *The WPA Guide to New York City* devote entire sections to Black New Yorkers, representing a rich and varied urban culture. With New York's relatively robust African American staff, the New York City guides are more generous with their representation of Black urban communities than the New Orleans guide, and they center their discussions on Black experiences. While African Americans were the city's oldest minority group, the wartime Great Migration from the American South and the Caribbean fueled the population. With the growth of Harlem and Bedford-Stuyvesant as large African American districts, African Americans became central to questions of urban social justice in New York. While White businesses and wealthy patrons still controlled most commercial and financial activity in Black neighborhoods, African Americans founded a dense and complex political and cultural milieu.

*New York Panorama* devotes a section titled "Portrait of Harlem" to New York's African American history. Like "New World Symphony" had done for other ethnic groups, "Portrait of Harlem" focuses on Black history and social institutions, culminating in the development of Negro Harlem. Claude McKay, who was in charge of the Negro History unit from 1937 to 1938, drafted the essay. When McKay left, Richard Wright rewrote it with the help of photojournalist Arnold De Mille. Wright had transferred from the Illinois Writers'

---

45. FWP, *New Orleans City Guide*, 56–66.

Project in January 1938. He was recommended to Alsberg by James Weldon Johnson and Sterling Brown, who suggested Wright was the only person capable of handling the African American materials in the New York guides.[46] Along with its history of struggles to gain freedom and repeated race riots, "Portrait" notes the diverse national origins of groups that contribute to Harlem culture. The essay cites African American contributions to high cultural forms such as literature, painting, sculpture and dance, as well as popular entertainments such as sports, popular music, and film. This list serves to valorize Harlem's contributions to a national and urban culture. It also adds weight to the case for reform by highlighting the balance sheet between these contributions and the problems faced by Harlem residents.

The essay offers an insider's perspective on a number of issues, frequently exploring the kinds of social divisions that the material on Jews neglects. As it discusses African American employment and business ownership, it makes careful distinctions between opportunities for the Black middle class and those for the working class. It also contrasts the organizations of Black business leaders with Black workers' exclusion from many unions. Oddly, here it blames working-class Harlemites for showing "a lack of initiative" in business ventures rather than highlighting the economic and social obstacles they faced.[47] Where the essay on Jews often minimizes the religious elements of society, the essay on African Americans highlights religion as an organizing force: "Playing the central role in Harlem is not the cabaret or café, as is commonly supposed, but the church."[48] The focus on religion also works against popular depictions of licentious behavior in Harlem.

The discussion of racial injustice in "Portrait of Harlem" also serves rhetorically as a warning and a call for progressive federal action. The environment in Harlem, the essay suggests, threatens greater national political division. Citing the popular appeal of Marcus Garvey's Black nationalism, the essay expresses concern about "Harlem's peculiar susceptibility to social and political propaganda."[49] Warning of the dangers of continuing Black economic disenfranchisement, the essay notes that many African Americans had defected from a Tammany coalition for Communist and Socialist parties and connects the 1935 Harlem riots to the city's neglect of essential social services, particularly modern educational facilities for Harlem's residents. Though the essay is

---

46. NARA RG69, Letter, Donald Thompson to Henry Alsberg, 6 January 1938, Central Office Records, Administrative Correspondence, Box 30.

47. FWP, *New York Panorama*, 40.

48. FWP, *New York Panorama*, 40.

49. FWP, *New York Panorama*, 141.

not particularly militant in tone, the ending invokes "shadows of tragic premonition," as a warning against a failure to act.[50]

The second guidebook also devotes a large section to "Negro Harlem," while distinguishing it from Spanish and Italian Harlem. Project records from 1938 show that Richard Wright was the author of much of this material, again drawing on material from McKay's Negro History subunit.[51] The *WPA Guide* essay shows that Wright brought his experience with Chicago sociological perspectives with him. More explicitly bound to geography than Wright's essay in *New York Panorama*, it jettisons the first guidebook's expansive historical frame to concentrate on the recent history and contemporary social scene of Harlem.[52] It also provides an analytic of the racial ghetto, setting up an argument for state intervention.

Harlem was of course, by the 1930s, a known entity, and the Harlem essay borrows from earlier literary texts by addressing the problem of perspective head on. During the 1920s, Harlem had earned a reputation among Whites as an inhibition-free zone, a place where repression could be alleviated by engaging primal drives among people leading more authentic lives. Novels by both White and Black writers fueled this image, and McKay had run afoul of W. E. B. du Bois and other intellectuals with the depiction of African American culture in his 1928 novel *Home to Harlem*.[53] Many Black writers were at pains to contest primitivism or to highlight the racism undergirding it. Wright chose to reframe White experiences of Harlem as inauthentic. The Harlem essay directly undercuts the logic of primitivism, suggesting that "Jungle Alley," a place favored by Whites as a spot to witness and partake in the supposed libido-releasing energy of Harlem, had been carefully staged.[54] In his 1941 photobook *12 Million Black Voices,* Wright would contend that the playful activity Whites based their views on was, in fact, an expression not of freedom but of subjugation.[55] This rhetorical awareness of situation was crucial to much of the output of Black New Deal writers, both during and after their FWP tenure.

Like "Portrait of Harlem," the second guidebook's essay depicts a neighborhood that is divided, both socially and geographically, along class and religious lines. The essay, as Bold notes, also highlights the complexity of Harlem

---

50. FWP, *New York Panorama,* 151.

51. NARA RG69, Production Chart, 22 September 1938, Central Office Records, Editorial Correspondence, Box 35.

52. See Chapter Three for a discussion of Wright's relationship to Chicago Sociology.

53. Cooper, *Claude McKay.*

54. FWP, *WPA Guide to New York City,* 262.

55. Wright, *12 Million Black Voices,* 127.

social life, contrasting with more monolithic presentations of racial slums in Wright's *Native Son* and *12 Million Black Voices*.[56] Perhaps this reflects the influence of McKay's subunit, especially since Wright was a relative newcomer to New York. Citing exclusive areas like Striver's Row and Sugar Hill, the guide takes notice of geographic social differences. Like the *Panorama* essay, it locates religion as the center of Harlem social life, while highlighting distinctions between different groups so detailed as to include a description of an internal split among Falashas. Although African American novels of the period frequently explore internal discrimination based on class and skin color, the guidebook essay avoids discussing internal conflicts between different Black social and economic groups. In consequence, the essay maintains a complex racial unity among African Americans.

The Harlem essay places African Americans' social and political inequity front and center, while suggesting that the federal government has the responsibility and the means to address persistent problems. The essay recognizes the racial politics of consumption, pointing to organizing around patronage of businesses that refused to hire Black citizens. It cites protests over Harlem Hospital's overwhelmingly White staff as an example of the struggle to access jobs and services. The essay presents the 1935 riots over racial exclusion from jobs in retail on 125th Street as a harbinger of a future without intervention. While the essay does not directly offer a means of solving these problems, it ends with brief discussion of the Dunbar Houses and Harlem River Houses projects, prefiguring more extensive commentary on public housing in later sections. While decent and affordable housing was a central issue for urban Black Americans, the slippage from questions of employment inequity to physical reform of the urban environment here is a reminder of the New Deal's tendency to focus on the tools it had at the ready rather than on more structural issues.

## Conclusion

Although the New York City unit had a more diverse representation of social groups on its staff than most state units, the New York guidebooks were not exceptional in their approach to civic pluralism. Rather they reflect a Progressive consensus shared by Washington editors and many state directors.[57] The FWP guidebooks offer cultural terms through which social groups could be

---

56. Bold, *WPA Guides*, 113.

57. See Griswold, *American Guides*, 92–107, for discussion and tables tracking the FWP national and state directors' origins.

seen as full participants in the national community. With sections often written by members of the groups under discussion and edited by sympathetic figures at the federal office, they generally provide a complex portrayal of racial and ethnic groups, if one that minimizes conflicts with the New Deal vision of participatory community. Displacing conflict narratively and temporally, these descriptions undercut both more traditional and more radical understandings of culture. Yet, as the record of conflicts over representation of immigration and race attest, civic pluralism did not settle crucial debates about the shape of national community, especially since the color line was a foundational element of that community. The city's future, and the future of its ethnic groups, is instead imagined as the work of New Deal reforms.

Civic pluralism ultimately became one of the FWP's most consequential ideational frameworks. It would aid in the midcentury racial revaluation, in which many ethnic groups would find themselves more firmly placed in the category of Whiteness that secured their national inclusion. It also fueled the rise of identity politics for other groups as intellectuals found a reserve of documentation to reconstruct sociocultural identities and histories. These documents would also serve as inspiration for American subcultures and countercultures for much of the century. FWP documentation was no less useful to those groups for its failure to upend racial frameworks during the New Deal.

Civic pluralism, however, did not offer a plan of action. It did not have a way to address the problems of entrenched urban poverty, especially when problems were magnified through the racial slum. Instead, the focus on slum removal and public housing in the ending of the sections on Harlem and the Lower East Side in *The WPA Guide to New York City* suggest a way forward. The next chapter will discuss the way that civic pluralism and a sociological narrative of urban pathology were harnessed to urban and regional planning discourses to legitimate state-authored modernist development as an answer to entrenched urban inequities. It highlights the promise of these programs, the way they were written into the guidebooks, and the effects of the New Deal's problematic reliance on the racial discourses in housing programs.

CHAPTER 2

# This Wise Geolatry

## *Modernization and Urban Planning in the FWP Guidebooks*

One corollary of New Deal civic pluralism was that social groups that had contributed to the national community should share in its benefits. Modernization programs aimed at creating wider economic and social enfranchisement became an important part of the New Deal's effort to fulfill this promise and build a shared national community. The FWP guidebooks naturalize state-directed modernization, often slipping it into the fabric of spatial description, but at other times explicitly promoting it as a solution to social ills. The actual application of these programs across the color line was uneven, however. Some, like public housing, worked to include African Americans, although separate projects were built for Black families in predominantly Black neighborhoods, formalizing segregation and stamping it with federal approval. Others, such as the push for expanding single-family suburban homeownership, excluded Black citizens using both explicit and coded racial logics.[1] Conflicts among programs, political expediency, and bureaucratic rationalizing created further problems, so that eventually the New Deal's most ambitious reform efforts generated inequality in the years ahead.

This chapter explores the discourse of modernization in the FWP guidebooks, mapping the tension between the New Deal's commitments to civic plu-

---

1. See Gotham, "Racialization and the State"; Jackson, *Crabgrass Frontier,* 219–230; Rothstein, *Color of Law.*

ralism and to modernization. It highlights the influence of urban and regional planning and other reform movements that shaped the specific understanding of modernization promoted in the guidebooks. The FWP editors, like urban planners and sociologists, sought to make the unruly city legible and thus subject to diagnosis and intervention. They represented modernization of the built environment as a salient means of addressing urban problems. Like the previous chapter, this one focuses on the New York City FWP guides' open advocacy of progressive New Deal ideas but also draws from other FWP guidebooks to illuminate the breadth of this utopian vision. This analysis suggests that FWP guidebooks largely missed the ways that urban modernization might exacerbate racial inequality and failed to appreciate the pervasive nature of race as a force shaping values and decisions.[2]

Urban and regional planning provided the New Deal with a ready narrative of modernization—areas requiring intervention, models of causality, and modern methods of restitution overseen by experts. Paul Conkin notes that over 100 communities were planned under the aegis of New Deal programs. These projects' aims varied widely according to the competing ideas that inspired them but all shared the core tenet that government could, and *should,* engage in spatial planning activities in the interest of creating local communities that would contribute to citizens' inclusion in the national community.[3] New Deal agencies utilizing these methods to reform the physical landscape included the Tennessee Valley Authority (TVA), the Division of Subsistence Homesteads, the Resettlement Administration, the Civilian Conservation Corps, the Public Works Administration (PWA), and the Works Progress Administration.

New Dealers with an urban planning pedigree included the architect of the "Brains Trust" Raymond Moley; New York State Architect Robert D. Kohn; political scientist and National Planning Board (NPB, later National Resources Planning Board or NRPB) member Charles E. Merriam; NPB chair and director of the Regional Survey Plan of New York and Its Environs Frederic A. Delano; and Charles W. Eliot II, who served as the executive officer of the NRPB. These figures brought their experience in urban planning to New Deal programs as administrators, particularly through the NPB, and their continuing influence can be traced through the New Deal's spatial mod-

---

2. Portions of my analysis in this chapter appeared previously in Butts, "Writing Projects."

3. Conkin, *Tomorrow a New World,* 6–7. In addition to spatial reform, most of these programs had other, sometimes shifting, justifications, including work relief and government spending to stimulate the economy.

50 · CHAPTER 2

ernization programs in public housing, public works, slum reform, suburban resettlement, and rural electrification.[4]

The most prominent New Dealer affiliated with urban planning was Rexford Tugwell. One of the original Brain Trusters, and a key player in New Deal politics up until 1938, Tugwell had helped develop the City Planning Commission's Master Plan for New York City, which followed the precepts of Delano's Greater New York regional plan of 1929. The Greater New York plan was the most expansive attempt at cohesive urban and regional planning up to that time. Despite obstacles, like the plurality of governing bodies in the New York region, the regional plan attempted to weave the metro area into a coherent integrated entity, establishing directions for actions in housing, transportation networks, and use of environmental resources. While many of its proposals would never be adopted, Robert Moses derived his extensive parks and highways network from this plan and succeeded in transforming the metropolitan landscape.[5]

During the New Deal, Tugwell directed the Suburban Resettlement Administration, which developed the plans for the Greenbelt towns in Maryland, Ohio, and Wisconsin. Along with TVA and other hydroelectric regional plans, these were among the New Deal's most comprehensive attempts at planning environments and communities. Perhaps even more important than the Greenbelt towns was the narrative of modernization Tugwell's office advanced. Under his supervision, the Resettlement Administration sponsored several documentary films to rationalize and disseminate planning ideals, the most ambitious of which were *The River* and *The Plow That Broke the Plains* under the direction of Pare Lorentz. These films linked unplanned human activity to natural disasters like the Dust Bowl and flooding. They suggested that only wide-scale planning and development could avert such disasters in the future.

Tugwell's influence also secured the role of urban planning as a model for the early New Deal. As Alan Brinkley suggests,

> City planning and regional planning . . . served for a time as microcosmic models for a larger concept of a planned society. The federal government, through a combination of public investment, public welfare, and extensive

---

4. See Gelfand, *Nation of Cities*, 81–87, who notes that New Deal public works programs often drew administration from the field of urban planning as it provided experience in coordinating large projects. For discussion of these individuals' roles, see also Brinkley, *Liberalism and Its Discontents*, 56.

5. See Caro, *Power Broker*; Berman, *All That Is Solid Melts into Air*, for accounts of Robert Moses's use of the Regional Plan. See Schwartz, *New York Approach*, 67–88, for an account of the struggle between Tugwell and Moses over New York public housing projects.

regulation could become a major actor in the workings of the national economy, could direct its course, and shape its future.[6]

The influence of this model of governance diminished in the face of political pressure and the rise of Keynesian ideas about the government's role in providing social insurance and encouraging consumption. However, many of the New Deal's lasting effects—including the large, and largely White, postwar middle-class suburbs and economically depressed, racially segregated inner cities—resulted from its attempts to reform the urban environment.

In the nation's cities, the New Deal was everywhere. Building on the municipalization and good government movements, the federal government sought to deter corruption by undermining the authority over urban services held by politicians and political machines, removing essential services from the province of politics and placing them in the hands of expert federal administrators.[7] The New Deal set up health clinics, art classes, and educational programs. By putting people to work and training them in modern methods of building, nursing, shopping, and teaching, the New Deal aimed to ease the burden of the Depression and create a healthier and more capable workforce, as well as more discriminating consumers. Through public works, the New Deal sought to pull citizens together, prop up the ailing economy with jobs and work orders, and quite literally build a new society. In New York City alone, the WPA, among hundreds of other projects, built a wing of the City College library, new buildings for Bellevue hospital, a playground in Columbus Circle, and renovated the Statue of Liberty. Chicago saw New Deal planning and work relief activities in the building of Lake Shore Drive, the State Street subway, and the extension of Lincoln Park; the expansion of the runway at Midway Airport; animal specimen reconstruction at the Field Museum; as well as new schools, playgrounds, and pools. Drawing on modernist architectural principles, the housing reform legacy, and urban planning discourse, the PWA and, later, the Federal Housing Authority (FHA) bulldozed existing tenements and erected complexes of modern apartments designed for lower income families.[8] Public housing projects became centerpieces of urban reform in the New Deal narrative of benevolent state-led modernization.

---

6. Brinkley, *Liberalism and Its Discontents*, 56.

7. Abu-Lughod, *NY, Chi, LA*, 89.

8. See Jackson, *Crabgrass Frontier*, 226; Page, *Creative Destruction of Manhattan*, 102, for accounts of how laws authorizing federal money for housing projects required that these projects bulldoze many of the existing substandard lower-class tenements and homes.

The FWP provided the New Deal with a forum to highlight the importance of these projects for urban society, making them comprehensible to citizens. The guides offer narrative coherence to what was in reality a patchwork of incompletely realized programs. In general, the didactic presentation of cause and effect in Resettlement Administration films is less apparent in the FWP guides. To be sure, the guides feature work pursued by the various New Deal programs. Frequently absent, though, is an explicit narrative framework explaining the meaning of projects in the larger scheme of averting disaster and building community that the films advanced. The paucity of explicit commentary does not entail absence of meaning, however. Rather, it is a feature of the genre. Christine Bold suggests that the guidebooks are full of "futuristic predictions, masquerading as documented facts, which distance the city from current conditions and function as an instrument of WPA survival."[9] The conflation of description and prescription, then, is important to the guidebooks' operation as New Deal propaganda. If the guidebooks describe immigrants and African Americans as participants in American history, they supply the warrant for an inclusionary approach to modernization. If the guidebooks point to the existence of a housing project, playground, or bridge and call attention to the program that built it, the implication is that the item is a public good and evidence of the state's benevolence. Moreover, the guides operated alongside other New Deal texts. Speeches, essays, and pamphlets promoted New Deal achievements as part of a broad public relations effort, echoing the guidebook descriptions while providing context and interpretation. The news media could also be relied upon to track these programs for specific audiences, and the Black press also highlighted New Deal achievements in areas of particular concern for African Americans.[10]

A few FWP guidebooks, however, are notable for the extent to which they do provide a framework for understanding New Deal modernization, particularly those located in a robust intellectual milieu or high concentration of government works. New York then, as now, offered a commentary-rich public sphere, and its centrality to planning and architectural discussions meant that the guidebooks would need to address the specifics of government efforts directly. A similar concentration of commentary occurs in the Tennessee guide, where the TVA radically reshaped the landscape on a regional scale, both utilizing and challenging the federalist framework of governance. The Tennessee guide recasts resistance by people who might lose their way of

---

9. Bold, *WPA Guides*, 107.
10. Sitkoff, *New Deal for Blacks*, 53.

life, their homes, even entire towns as backwardness, emphasizing the future benefits that would accrue to citizens.

Similarly, the New York City FWP guides offer both a logic for understanding the city and models for its reformation. *New York Panorama* rejects "those who consider that it is impossible to find any unity in the chaotic pattern of New York; or that, romantically enough, the emergence of unity would cancel its major charm."[11] Instead it asserts that the principle of healthful urban unity is latent in urban citizens themselves, despite "the uneconomic and antisocial nature of many of the city's living ways":

> The potential unity necessary to such a reorientation already exists in the New Yorker's own concept of his city. In this shared consciousness—generated by a look, a grin, an anecdote as cabalistic to outsiders as the shop talk of mathematicians—the complex of the metropolis finds its organizing principle, deeper than civic pride and more basic than the domination of mass or power. To the degree that this principle, this wise geolatry, can be instrumented by the forms and processes appropriate to it, New York will emerge in greatness from the paradox of its confusions.[12]

The idea of a "wise geolatry," literally worship of the earth, suggests a just organizing principle based in the observable workings of the city. These principles are what the FWP guidebooks attempt to clarify and promote. Somewhat ironically, the invocation of "potential unity" resembles Jane Jacobs's famous defense of the city's hidden order, the unrecognized vitality of the unplanned street, in *The Death and Life of Great American Cities*. Both suggest a need to reread urban space for its working principles. However, for the FWP, the key word is "potential," as its emphasis is on a "reorientation" and the "forms and processes" that could be "instrumented" to make the city work for its citizens.[13]

The FWP guidebooks take on the task of making the city's workings visible, creating legibility in the interest of expanding state power. In *Seeing Like a State*, James C. Scott argues that the first task of state-directed intervention has been making complexity legible through abstraction, classification, and establishment of metrics. These actions become the means of legitimating intervention through reorganizing populations and spaces to enable more effective governance. FWP descriptions make cities comprehensible in a way that is germane to New Deal aims, while simultaneously making the case that those

---

11. FWP, *New York Panorama*, 19.

12. FWP, *New York Panorama*, 19.

13. FWP, *New York Panorama*, 19.

aims will have beneficial outcomes. The previous chapter traced the way that *The WPA Guide to New York City*'s sectional organization of the city is analogous to Lewis Mumford's regionalism in its logic. As the *media via* between the extremes of local, insular communities and large, fragmented, abstract spatial divides, regionalism secured a role for the federal government in organizing and coordinating activities. In advocating regionalism, Mumford was making an argument for the extension of planning ideals for the purposes of active governance.[14] The FWP guides similarly promote planning and modernization ideas as the means of achieving a national community.

## New Deal Modernism

The guidebooks' focus on coordinated planning is particularly evident in *The WPA Guide to New York City*'s discussion of the newly built Rockefeller Center. Accounts of New York's 1930s architecture might reasonably focus on the Empire State Building or the smaller but flashier Chrysler Building as paradigmatic expressions of heroic skyscraper modernism. However, in the FWP guide, the Rockefeller Center outshines its midtown neighbors in both length of discussion and tone of praise. Even though Rockefeller Center was not a New Deal project, the guides' attention helps to establish aesthetic and narrative features that echo in their discussions of public housing and the future of American cities.

Michael Szalay has argued that the New Deal's modernism was based in a transvaluation of aesthetics away from the artifact as the object of value toward the idea of value in work and process.[15] This is one key component of a New Deal aesthetic, but there is no shortage of New Deal artifacts from which one might infer a different understanding. Even a cursory glance at the architecture and visual art produced under Federal One's auspices suggests remarkable similarities in their style, subject, and function. Stylized figural sculptures decorated new playgrounds and public housing. Murals celebrating the past adorned WPA-built post offices and town halls. This is the other New Deal modernism, an aesthetics shaped by cultural memory, coordination, and complex interconnection. Each element functions in tandem with other elements to reinforce a sense of community and achievement. Together they also serve as a promise of the future benefits of state-directed modernization.

---

14. See Mumford, *Culture of Cities*, 302–314.

15. Szalay, *New Deal Modernism*, 5

Rockefeller Center exemplified this aesthetic—a coordinated and thorough reworking of the old chaotic city into a complex new unity.[16]

A detour through the Illinois guidebook provides a useful summary of the lineage of New Deal urban design leading to its valorization of Rockefeller Center. The architecture essay in the Illinois guide stakes out a modernist line in its discussion of building design, exulting Louis Sullivan and Frank Lloyd Wright as functionalists and attacking the tendency to disguise skyscrapers in eclectic historical ornament. It also heralds a desirable increase in the scale of design, from individual buildings to integrated urban and regional planning, focusing on Daniel Burnham's plan for the 1893 World's Columbian Exposition and the Chicago regional plan Delano commissioned as important steps in establishing a coherent, modern city. Finally, the essay showcases the unification of modernist functionalism in architectural design and integrated planning evident in the 1933 Chicago World's Fair, ending with Daniel Burnham's famous exhortation to "make no little plans."[17]

Rockefeller Center offered a ready demonstration of how the Chicago model could change New York and other cities. The tour of the Rockefeller Center in *The WPA Guide to New York City* introduces the reader to a model of modernist design. Three blocks wide, Rockefeller Center contains twelve vaulting rectangular buildings clustered around the RCA Building skyscraper and Rockefeller Plaza. The *Guide* hails it as capturing the essence of the city:

> In its architecture Rockefeller Center stands as distinctively for New York as the Louvre stands for Paris. Composed of the essential elements of New York skyscrapers—steel framing and curtain walls, encasing elevators and offices—the group relies for exterior decoration almost exclusively on the pattern of its windows, piers, spandrels, and wall surfaces. Its beauty derives from a significant play of forms, and light and shadow. Its character—abrupt, stark, jagged and powerful—arises fundamentally from the spacing of the buildings, from their direct functionalism, their mass, their silhouette, and their grayish-tan color; not . . . from ornamental roofs, reminiscent styles, or elaborate setbacks.[18]

A paean to modernist form, the celebration of simplification and functionalism, as well as the masculine descriptors, are all characteristic of architectural modernism.

---

16. Bold, *WPA Guides*, 102, argues that the view from the Rockefeller Center served as "the most insistent trope" of *New York Panorama*. Both of the FWP New York guidebooks figure the Rockefeller Center centrally.

17. FWP, *Illinois*, 108–109.

18. FWP, *WPA Guide to New York City*, 334.

56 · CHAPTER 2

However, Rockefeller Center's distinctiveness lies not in any single element but rather what *The WPA Guide to New York City* calls the coordinated "play of forms," the balance of complexity and unity.[19] The *WPA Guide* focused praise on the overall planning of the site, rather than on any single building. One of the most notable achievements is that "the three blocks were freshly considered as a unit."[20] The architects of the Rockefeller Center took inspiration from European theorists such as Walter Gropius and Le Corbusier who favored the creation of aggregated superblocks to allow for more creative and open large-scale structures. Although Rockefeller Center works with the existing street grid rather than superblocks, its massing around a central plaza creates a complex within the city.

In the FWP assessment, the Rockefeller Center's architects tackled the problem of developing and aesthetically integrating a large multifunctional site, a democratic and corporate balance evident in its mixing of office space, retail, and entertainment functions as well as its blend of high and popular culture. Rockefeller Center offered several open public spaces, as well as a number of private entertainment spaces. Both Radio City Music Hall and the broadcasting facilities in the RKO building were home to popular forms of entertainment. The design encouraged the occupants' sense of participation in something larger than themselves. Sculptures and paintings celebrating progress and the unity of labor and art were prevalent throughout the complex, and the guidebook finds much to admire in the integration of art and urban activity. Ultimately, the *WPA Guide*'s depiction of Rockefeller Center celebrates the way that a new, more beautiful, progressive, and humane urban order is thoroughly planned and then carved out of the old. If Rockefeller could harness such organizational power, couldn't the United States do the same for its citizens?

## Development as Justice: Writing Projects

Throughout the discussion of Rockefeller Center in *The WPA Guide to New York City*, the attentive reader hears echoes of slum reform discourse. The *Guide* notes, for example, that the site is arranged well, so that all buildings are "easily penetrated by sunlight and fresh air."[21] If Rockefeller Center offers a lesson on modernization, the guides suggest, housing would be the natural place to implement similar reforms. The section on architecture in

---

19. FWP, *WPA Guide to New York City*, 334.
20. FWP, *WPA Guide to New York City*, 334.
21. FWP, *WPA Guide to New York City*, 335.

the Illinois guidebook reinforces the link between modern design and slum reform by calling for the PWA to create more open, planned districts in rundown neighborhoods, establishing a direct line of influence from the vision of ordered community in the 1893 World's Columbian Exposition to public housing.

New Deal public housing programs, the first large-scale federal attempts to create housing for citizens, tied together a range of slum reform, urban planning, and modernist architectural ideas that had informed the New Deal.[22] Where Hoovervilles had been a visible expression of governmental failure, public housing offered a manifestation of the New Deal's commitment to providing for citizens regardless of race. As settlement houses had established beachheads for Progressive reformers in the late nineteenth and early twentieth centuries, public housing extended governmental authority at various levels through working class neighborhoods. Under the aegis of the PWA, WPA, and the United States Housing Authority, these programs posed a solution to substandard housing by erecting modern replacement units replete with adequate plumbing, electricity, and access to light and air. In addition, the housing projects destroyed substandard housing stock, ensuring that no one would be forced or would choose to use these structures as housing.

The earliest New Deal housing projects drew heavily on European modernist urban planning and architectural theory. Richard Plunz has shown how these ideas, promoted in the United States in the writings of Philip Johnson and Henry Russell Hitchcock Jr. and the architecture of William Lescaze and Richmond Shreve, influenced New Deal housing project design.[23] Architects following Bauhaus *Zeilenbau* ideas suggested that buildings could be arranged in such a way as to allow for minimal coverage on a block, facilitating maximal sunlight and free space, while retaining profitable density. While no WPA projects followed the linear forms of *Zeilenbau* architecture exactly, the influence is apparent in the simple building forms and arrangement of these projects. For example, the Williamsburg Houses, built in a predominantly Jewish

---

22. The only significant federal precedent is the creation of housing for veterans of World War I. The literature on public housing is extensive. See Armstrong, "Public Housing"; Conkin, *Tomorrow a New World*; Gelfand, *Nation of Cities*; Goetz, *New Deal Ruins*; Wright, *Building the Dream*, for strong overviews of the history. For studies of public housing in specific sites, see also the following: Boston: Vale, *From the Puritans to the Projects*; Chicago: Hirsch, *Making the Second Ghetto*; Kimble, *New Deal for Bronzeville*; Cincinnati: Fairbanks, *Making Better Citizens*; Cleveland: Wye, "New Deal and the Negro Community"; New York City: Plunz, *History of Housing in New York City*; Schwartz, *New York Approach*. See also Bauer, *Modern Housing*; Wood, *Housing of the Unskilled Wage Earner*, for influential interwar discussions of public housing.

23. Plunz, *History of Housing in New York City*, 181–182.

and Italian section of northern Brooklyn, remain striking today both because of their repetitive clean lines and their angled departure from the surrounding rows of street-facing tenements. In contrast with later projects inspired by Le Corbusier's Radiant City featuring identical tall towers, the early New Deal projects utilized low-rise building exclusively. When the towers were attacked as incubators of crime in later decades, the low massing of the earlier public housing projects has helped them maintain favorable standing in many architectural accounts.[24]

FWP guidebooks link modernist design to community development. If environmental conditions posed an impediment to realizing community, more humane housing, along with spaces for play and public gathering, should foster community spirit. Quoting an unnamed review of the Williamsburg Houses, FWP editors state:

> In every really important general matter of land usage—in air, in light, in a sense of green and growing things as a concomitant of living; in the creation of an atmosphere of humanity and decency, a place where children would be glad to grow up; in the development of a community that brings with it a new vision of democracy and of progress, . . . [this development has] qualities that no money can buy.[25]

The passage and its surrounding text imaginatively link public housing to community-making and suggest that the result will benefit the national polity. In the process of making the city intelligible, then, the *WPA Guide* introduces readers to the methods by which modern government might reshape the nation to fit its progressive vision.

Public housing addressed a clear need for African Americans, and New Deal promises provided useful rhetorical leverage in arguments over access to housing. Exclusionary real estate practices, including redlining and property covenants, and community organizing against African Americans crowded Black citizens into neighborhoods where they payed higher rents for substandard housing. Black citizens organized resistance to these limitations in several ways. In Chicago, Carl Hansberry, owner of an accounting firm and father of playwright Lorraine Hansberry, repeatedly challenged racial covenants in court, eventually winning a case before the Supreme Court in 1940. During

---

24. See White and Willensky, *AIA Guide to New York City,* for current discussions of First Houses, Harlem River Houses, Williamsburg Houses, and Queensbridge Houses.

25. FWP, *WPA Guide to New York City,* 459. I have not discovered the source of this quote. It is possible that it was an internal quote from Roderick Seidenberg, who served as the FWP's architectural advisor.

the 1930s, communists led anti-eviction and rent strike actions, generating organizational tactics that would prove useful to other groups such as the Consolidated Tenants Association, the Tenants' League, and coalitions like Harlem's Coordinating Committee for Unemployment.

Public housing offered an important opportunity to address housing needs and commit the government to recognizing its obligations. African American community activists worked with allies to ensure allocation of public housing resources and related jobs to majority Black communities. Kimble asserts, "As during the Depression era, the coalition of African Americans and their allies continued to argue that access to clean, affordable, and safe housing was one of the central tenets of citizenship established by the Roosevelt administration."[26] These coalitions set the conditions and the continuing demand that Roosevelt's commitment in his 1937 inaugural address to using the powers of the federal government to address the problems of the "one third of a nation ill-housed, ill-clad, ill-nourished" would extend to Black citizens.[27] At the Federal Public Housing Authority, Robert C. Weaver, the architect of Roosevelt's public housing policies and one of the Black Cabinet members, worked to place African American housing needs at the forefront of New Deal initiatives.

A 1937 promotional bulletin titled "WPA and the Negro" put together by Director of Racial Relations James Ross, highlights WPA achievements benefiting urban African Americans, such as sewing units, the Emma Ransom House YWCA, and a YWCA Trade School. It also reproduces a 1936 speech by Carita V. Roane about the PWA's Harlem River Houses project:

> Slum dwellers will leave ill-ventilated and unsanitary buildings and move into sunny apartments with playgrounds for children. . . . It is impossible to estimate the effect that these apartments will have upon the morale of the occupants. . . . In this community there will be, I should guess, a thousand children, and from this group we ought to have a thousand law-abiding citizens who will be an asset to the community.[28]

In brief, federal intervention would build equity, community, and citizenship for African Americans. This federal imperative guides the inclusion in *The WPA Guide to New York City* of a somewhat unconventional tour of the Harlem River Houses alongside those of more familiar Gotham landmarks such

---

26. Kimble, *New Deal for Bronzeville*, 53.

27. Franklin D. Roosevelt, Inaugural Address, 20 January 1937.

28. Ellison Papers, "WPA and the Negro," Promotional Bulletin, Box 19, Folder 7. See also Gallagher, *Black Women and Politics in New York City*, 50–51, on Roane's work with the Harlem Office of the New York State Labor Department.

as the Brooklyn Bridge, the Metropolitan Museum of Art, and Rockefeller Center.

Harlem River Houses—designed by a team of architects including John Louis Wilson Jr., the first Black graduate of Columbia University's architecture school—were the second of the New Deal's housing projects in New York City, and the first to be built from the ground up by work relief laborers.[29] Along with the newer Williamsburg houses and the planned Queensbridge Houses, *The WPA Guide to New York City* holds the Harlem River Houses up as models of urban housing, with implications for all socioeconomic groups. The description compares these apartments favorably with Park Avenue's upper-class residences, praising their modern amenities, among them "electric refrigeration and lighting; steam heat, ample closet space, steel casement windows, and a tiled bath."[30] The apartments, the guidebook's reader is led to understand, are the expression of a New Deal government that provides, and provides well, for its hardest-hit citizens no matter their race. It claims the project "is significant not only as a step toward solving the problem of the 'ill-housed one-third,' but also toward the raising of housing standards of high-income housing groups" and cites a new private development in the Bronx as an example of the WPA's influence.[31]

In addition to the material benefits, the FWP guide also details the elements of design that would contribute to community. The site's aesthetically pleasing arrangement brings order and beauty into the daily lives of the inhabitants, and the guide dwells on the virtues of the arrangement at length. Public art is distributed throughout the site. It provides a number of spaces specifically designed for community support, including a playground, a nursery, a laundry, a health clinic, and social rooms. The creation of a residents' association, responsible for activities in these spaces, would provide a participatory venue for residents to decide the character of their community. The guidebook sums up the effect of these elements in the following passage:

> Transcending the physical aspects of the development are the social, and one item in the first year's record spoke eloquently: not a single case of delinquency or crime or social disorder was reported for Harlem River Houses.

---

29. An earlier project in the East Village, First Houses, had involved conversion of a row of tenements by destroying every third building and combining the remaining two to allow more penetration of light and air. Kimble, *New Deal for Bronzeville,* 32, notes that public housing projects for black citizens came with promises of employment not only for black laborers but also higher paid work for architects and engineers.

30. FWP, *WPA Guide to New York City,* 394.

31. FWP, *WPA Guide to New York City,* 392.

Apartments and courts were maintained with scrupulous care by young and old. A compact, progressive community had emerged, and its very success made the plight of the less fortunate residents of Harlem seem by contrast more bitter than ever.[32]

Though the assessment after a single year is premature, it stands in the guidebook as confirmation of New Deal modernization. The emphasis on the progressive character of the new community and the implied warning about the failure to follow through with more projects make a case for the continuation of New Deal modernization projects.

At the same time, the FWP guides often neglect to address visible problems in its public housing programs. Racial segregation was written into these programs from the beginning, and city councils often made certain to site projects in undesirable areas, away from centralized neighborhood resources.[33] In his history of public housing policy, *New Deal Ruins,* Edward Goetz notes that the distribution of segregated public housing, extended "chronic shortages of decent housing for African Americans in most cities."[34] Federal rules prevented public housing from changing the racial composition of existing neighborhoods, exacerbating the problem of overcrowding. Screening of applications meant that only qualified African Americans could apply reinforcing the liberal welfare's state reliance on an earlier era's insistence on focusing aid on the deserving poor. Notoriously, the FHA's reliance on race-driven underwriting tools in restructuring of the home mortgage market and exclusive real estate covenants dramatically increased housing options for White citizens while African Americans continued to experience significant market pressure and exclusion.

## Democracity

While Rockefeller Center served the New York guides as an inspiration for New Deal spatial modernization, and New Deal public housing demonstrated the communitarian benefits of reform, the 1939 World's Fair provided a utopian vision of a planned future. Both New York guidebooks close with an account of the upcoming fair, and they advance the planning elements of the New Deal and its implications. But the fair's contradictions, to borrow Warren Susman's framework of analysis, also provide an interesting point from which

---

32. FWP, *WPA Guide to New York City,* 392.
33. Goetz, *New Deal Ruins,* 31.
34. FWP, *WPA Guide to New York City,* 36.

62 • CHAPTER 2

to reconsider the myopic elements of the New Deal's communitarian vision.[35] The guidebooks promote the rationalizing, legible elements of the fair's state-sponsored exhibits, but fail to grapple with the implications of either the corporate-sponsored exhibits, which promoted a different, consumerist vision of the future from which African Americans would often be excluded, or the background racial tensions that exposed the limits of modernization.

*The WPA Guide to New York City* emphasizes the official rhetoric of the 1939 World's Fair, highlighting elements heralding democracy, order, and technological progress. These elements in turn reinforced the inclusive national community promoted throughout both New York City guidebooks. The *WPA Guide* description clearly identifies the fair's origins in urban modernization. The fair's site reclaimed undesirable land, a giant nineteenth-century ash heap on the banks of the Flushing River. The arrangement of the fair recalled the earlier City Beautiful movement, placing premiums on visibility and coordinated arrangements, like the District of Columbia's National Mall, the restoration of which had also been underway since 1902. However, like the 1933 Chicago Fair, the 1939 World's Fair employed a distinctly modernist architectural vocabulary throughout the site, with designers and architects who were drawn from a modernist pantheon, including Norman Bel Geddes, Donald Deskey, Phillip L. Goodwin, Wallace K. Harrison, William Lescaze, Raymond Loewy, and Edward Durrell Stone. The fair also exhibited sculptures and murals by prominent modern artists including James Earle Fraser, Leo Friedlander, Paul Manship, Hildreth Meiere, and Augusta Savage. From the fair's central Theme Plaza, the Constitution Mall ran east to the Lagoon of Nations, and avenues along perpendicular and diagonal axes branched out to various functional zones, another legacy of modernist urban planning.

The central Theme Plaza reflected the modernist communitarian vision for the city sketched by the guidebooks. Under the direction of Theme Committee chair Robert Kohn—who had cofounded the Regional Planning Association of America with Lewis Mumford, and later worked as the PWA housing division director—the Theme Plaza became a showplace of coordinated urban reform. The centerpiece of the 1939 Fair consisted of three sculptures by Wallace K. Harrison and André Fouilhoux, former collaborators in the building of Rockefeller Center. These streamlined and reflective sculptures—the Perisphere, the Trylon, and the Helicline—embodied the ideology of New Deal modernism. Simplified, abstract, interactive forms, their design evoked the essence of functional machines: ramps, wedges, wheels, ball bearings. The

---

35. See Susman, *Culture as History,* 211–229, for his discussion of the fair. See also Harrison, *Dawn of a New Day*; Gelernter, *1939*.

700-foot high Trylon thrust upward dynamically, suggesting progress and flight. Beside it, the Perisphere surrounded by the spiral ascending Helicline evoked a globe that could be mastered with the right tools. The three sculptures were also functional, coordinating the activity of tourists. The Trylon held escalators to an exhibit in the Perisphere, and the Helicline's curved ramp provided egress. These sculptures suggested a triumphant cosmopolitan view, an aesthetic harmony of function and form rendered ironic by the approach of another world war.[36]

The fair's theme exhibit in the Perisphere, titled "Democracity," showcased a diorama of idealized progressive landscapes in the countryside and the city. *The WPA Guide to New York City* notes that spectators were positioned above the diorama as if they could see "from Olympian heights to pierce the fogs of ignorance, habit and prejudice that envelop everyday thinking, and gaze down on the ideal community that man could build today were he to make full use of his tools, his resources, and his knowledge."[37] In this position, the tourists saw the world as planners did. They looked down upon a city organized for industrial and commercial enterprise surrounded by Greenbelt towns where residents would raise families. The exhibit simulated the shift from day to night, as a pageant ensued in which, the *WPA Guide* suggests, "A thousand-voiced chorus is heard. Ten columns of figures—the various types of people necessary to such a city—march across the sky. They converge above the city and form a circle of heroic figures as the song reaches a crescendo."[38] The pageant ended with a figural dawning of a new day as the lights were turned on again.[39] Descending the Helicline as they left the exhibit, visitors found the exhibit's planning ideals reinforced by the panoramic view of the fair's layout. These ideals were also bolstered by exhibits like "The Road of Tomorrow" and "The Town of Tomorrow," which showcased modern highways and housing. *The City*, the American Institute of Planner's documentary paean to Greenbelt planning, aesthetically indebted to the FSA hydropower films, also debuted at the fair.

While the FWP guides stress the progressive civic vision in the theme exhibits, the fair's showcase of corporate goods suggested that planning might be harnessed to more directly capitalist ends. Corporate exhibits encouraged a more immediate engagement with the future in imagined landscapes of consumption. The most popular exhibit at the fair was not "Democracity," but

---

36. Multiple historians of the fair have commented on the irony that the three sculptures were eventually sold for scrap to further the war effort.

37. Quoted in FWP, *WPA Guide to New York City*, 632, original source unknown.

38. FWP, *WPA Guide to New York City*, 633.

39. Gelernter, *1939*, 67.

rather General Motors's "Futurama."[40] The *WPA Guide* devotes little space to this exhibit, mistakenly suggesting that it echoes the main theme exhibit when it actually offers a different vision of the future.[41] While the spectators' position in the "Democracity" exhibit placed them outside and above the World of Tomorrow, planners contemplating a more humane spatial order in Futurama launched spectators on a motorized ride through a dioramic landscape of superhighways. Ford, Consolidated Edison, du Pont, the Carrier Corporation, RCA, and American Telephone & Telegraph similarly offered exhibits that showcased a future imagined along the lines of what Lizabeth Cohen has called the "consumer's republic," with its emphasis on private life and available mass commodities.[42] Social critic Walter Lippman worried that these exhibits essentially predicated the future of the growth of corporate enterprise while they suggested that the government should foot the bill for the required infrastructure.[43] Like *The City,* these exhibits encouraged a mobile, suburban future, but they supported Levittown's mass aggregation as readily as Greenbelt's careful site planning, and they did not address suburbanization's racial exclusions.

Racial conflicts building around the fair called into question whether either of its visions of democracy, the Progressive version or the consumerist version, could adequately address deeply embedded racial inequities. Like New Deal civic pluralism, the fair drew on the contributions of different ethnic groups. It showcased the work of several African American artists, including Augusta Savage, Bill "Bojangles" Robinson, and William Grant Still, who composed the theme song for "Democracity." A "Negro Week" in 1940 highlighted Black contributions to the arts and popular culture. The fair effectively replicated the New Deal's inclusive focus on African American culture. Yet the democratic vision of the fair did not extend behind the scenes. The NAACP and the Harlem Community Cultural Conference attacked discriminatory hiring practices that all but excluded Black citizens from employment at the fair.[44] The fair's poor hiring record on race suggested that its democratic rhetoric might disguise exclusion of African Americans from the material basics needed to participate in its envisioned futures. Despite the FWP guidebooks' frequent references to racial injustice embodied in everyday spatial practices, they miss the racial implications of the fair's vision of the future.

---

40. Susman, *Culture as History,* 218.

41. FWP, *WPA Guide to New York City,* 639.

42. Cohen, *Consumer's Republic.*

43. Susman, *Culture as History,* 225.

44. See Gelernter, *1939,* 356–358, for a discussion of the fair's representation and employment of African Americans.

## Conclusion

The FWP guidebooks' treatment of urban space and history offers a record of the expectations of the New Deal and the elements that were thought to be shaping a new modern community. The guidebooks highlight the dynamic tension between progressive multiculturalism and progressive urban reform in the New Deal. They profess admiration of urban ethnic life, particularly its cultural forms, but they also support efforts to change its material conditions according to normative ideals of healthy space. The FWP guides attack essentialist notions of the connection between ethnic groups and unsanitary or socially deleterious conditions but, at the same time, fail to take into consideration the way that values held by ethnic groups might influence the kind of community they would like to see. By simultaneously assuming a universal American audience and attempting to define their future, the guides presuppose their readers shared the values of federal administrators. Despite the participatory rhetoric and some notable instances of advising, New Deal experts ultimately retained the power to envision and shape the vision of community and its spatial manifestation.

The political and social institutions built by the New Deal improved the lives of many people both during and after the Depression. The model housing projects built by the WPA and PWA attempted to solve the adequate housing shortage and remain some of the most habitable public housing to date. Work relief projects not only gave people work and sustained industrial production but also created a number of public institutions and improved the urban infrastructure. Educational and work programs gave New Yorkers a chance to learn modern ideas in health, construction, home economics, and the arts. A social security net was built that remained in place for sixty years, providing citizens with a measure, however small, of insurance from financial hardship. Finally, the FWP guidebooks themselves are truly impressive works of urban representation.

However, the irony that modern readers cannot help but feel when reading the FWP guides' exuberant discussion of public housing is that it became a concrete symbol of structural inequity and the failure of welfare-state governance. Noting Lewis Mumford's lofty praise for the Harlem River Houses, the editors of the *American Institute of Architecture Guide to New York City* wryly remark, "perhaps he was being too exuberant."[45] As the urban housing program expanded, administrators sought efficiency in ways that streamlined construction at the expense of quality. Crime rates grew in neighborhoods

---

45. White and Willensky, *AIA Guide to New York City*, 512.

where public housing was built, and new theories suggested that the modernist design of towers in a park actually facilitated crime. New Deal and post–New Deal housing policies that largely excluded African Americans helped create a large middle-class out of White urban ethnic groups and encouraged them to leave the city for the suburbs to pursue the dream-nightmare of the consumer's republic. The resulting evisceration of the middle- and upper-class tax base left New York and other cities with massive social responsibilities to their remaining citizens and little means of supporting those burdens.

The broader modernist planning aims that FWP present as catalysts of a new community also fared poorly. They earned a scorching rebuttal from Jane Jacobs, who charged that housing reforms had actually destroyed the fabric of urban communities by confusing visual order with functionality. Citing tenant complaints over the useless lawn of a housing project in East Harlem, she stated: "There is a quality even meaner than outright ugliness or disorder, and this meaner quality is the dishonest mask of pretended order, achieved by ignoring or suppressing the real order that is struggling to exist and be served."[46] After World War II, the New Deal's most ambitious modernization efforts became politically untenable. However, while projects coordinated on the scale of TVA were no longer possible, housing, infrastructure, and military programs continued to dramatically transform the landscape and shape access to opportunity. Moreover, large-scale modernist development, harnessed to postwar recovery in Europe, and international investment in decolonizing areas in Africa, the Middle East, and Southern Asia became one of the signature tools of American Cold War power.[47] These too, were critiqued as heavy-handed and insufficiently attuned to local dynamics. In their FWP work, African American writers explored historical and cultural elements they would later deploy to generate countermodern narratives, questioning both the premises and certitudes of New Deal modernization. The rest of this book highlights the richness of their response through the FWP's fictional and documentary intertexts.

---

46. Jacobs, *Death and Life of Great American Cities*, 15.

47. Gilman, *Mandarins of the Future*, 37–39. See also Manzo, "Modernist Discourse and the Crisis of Development Theory" for discussion of international development in the postwar period. Reynolds, *Apostles of Modernity*, discusses postwar American writers' engagement with the development narrative.

CHAPTER 3

# Other Than What We Seem

## *The Folk Histories of Hurston and Wright*

As FWP employees, African American writers advanced sociological discourses that redefined Black urban neighborhoods as places subject to state-directed modernization while they worked to recover African American historical, social, and cultural dynamics. The guiding concepts and representational strategies deployed by the FWP contributed to problematic blind spots. As my first two chapters demonstrate, the guidebooks pass judgment on what elements belong to the national past, present, and likely future. They often assume social cohesion will prevail over social tension, downplaying ample evidence to the contrary. In highlighting material elements of culture, history, and space, they ignore important psychosocial dynamics of race that would compromise the New Deal vision. Finally, their approach to folk culture tends to locate folkways as anachronisms inherited from a preindustrial past. While the FWP guidebooks highlight folk contributions to national culture and the pictorial elements of folk culture, folkways are, like Black urban neighborhoods, subject to modernization's erasure.

As Jerrold Hirsch has shown, the FWP approach to African American folk culture was shaped by a broader conflict among cultural intellectuals about how to understand folkways.[1] John Lomax, who initially directed the FWP's

---

1. See Hirsch, "Cultural Pluralism and Applied Folklore: The New Deal Precedent," 46–67; *Portrait of America,* 17–40.

focus on folk culture, viewed folkways as residual cultural elements functioning as a negative critique of the rationalizing processes of modern industrial society. Though the FWP guidebooks affirm Lomax's view of folk's temporal location, in their depiction of harmonious pluralism and benevolent centralized modernization, they generally neutralize the more critical elements. Folk culture is not critical of modernity; it is simply outdated. However, an emerging view—led by Benjamin Botkin, Sterling Brown, and Morton Royse, the FWP's consultant for ethnic and social studies—shifted this approach in later years. After Lomax's departure, these administrators began to focus on the developing elements of vernacular culture, particularly in urban environments. Their idea of ongoing vernacular adaptation generated an understanding of folk memory not only as premodern resistance but as a continuously creative force engaging with the present and the future.

While FWP projects could document folklore and detail the historical developments contributing to the New Deal vision of a nation, they do not offer a means of reworking representation through the vernacular terms they uncovered. Their lens separates the folk as an object of study from its active role mediating modern culture. African American culture, however, was full of precedents in which vernacular modes—signifying, irony, parody, coding, and allegory—challenged historical representation by reshaping narratives and exposing unspoken social dynamics. Nineteenth-century spirituals rewrote biblical visions such as Ezekiel's wheel into narratives of racial justice. The stories of High John de Conquer and Brer Rabbit offered coded knowledge essential to survival under slavery and Jim Crow. Charles Chesnutt repurposed and invented folk stories to highlight the way they allegorized Jim Crow power relations, contesting both the "lost cause" vision of Southern apologists and Northerners' claims to a moral high ground in questions of race.

These modalities are on display in FWP reporting on Black culture as well, although their inclusion does not overturn the broader framework of objective representation. The ambitious projects Brown outlined—oral histories of ex-slaves, studies of folklore, and geographically delineated social histories of African Americans—would reclaim African American history and culture, and highlight its value in the present. Catherine Stewart has pointed out that the informants that FWP reporters and oral historians used frequently coded their versions of history to speak about power indirectly and protect themselves from exposure and retribution. Alternate versions of history appear in folk stories recorded for Royse by Ralph Ellison in Harlem, and in Florida, Zora Neale Hurston both captured and promoted a range of evolving folk expressions.

African American FWP writers continued to explore alternate possibilities of history and modernity mediated by Black vernacular culture in their own work as well. As Sara Rutkowski has shown, women in particular drew on FWP historical materials to generate novels that retold history from below.[2] Black writers also utilized folk modes of narrative and other vernacular elements to reconnect the past and the present in ways that interrogated the New Deal vision. These authors differed in their approach to the complex problems of the racialized city, reflecting diverse aims and understandings of culture and justice. In some cases, they reinforced the slum pathology model and ideas of modernization that marginalized folk culture. Others saw new possibilities in the city and in folk culture. They also varied in their assessment of New Deal liberalism. Some writers rejected New Deal liberalism's claims of equity and envisioned alternatives, while others saw the liberal project as highly promising yet incomplete. However, nearly all offered a cautious assessment of the future, a dramatic departure from upbeat New Deal rhetoric, as they highlighted racism as a pervasive, corrupting force that might derail progress or hijack the process of modernization.

This chapter begins the book's exploration of the countermodern vision of African American FWP intertexts by looking at the function of Black vernacular modes in a novel by Zora Neale Hurston and a photodocumentary book by Richard Wright. Though admittedly an odd pairing, both generically and because of their authors' antipathies, these texts offer folk engagements with the welfare state, offering criticisms of its expanding sovereignty and its racially compromised politics. Hurston and Wright famously disagreed on folk culture and the role of politics in literature, and they conducted these disagreements through critiques of each other's writing. These disagreements have shaped a view of Hurston as folk writer and Wright as social realist, even while both, in their own ways, shared commitments to documenting social problems, to exploring and utilizing vernacular culture, to modernization, and to a critical view of liberalism.[3] Both writers also used their FWP experience to explore community representation, and both found ways to critique the emergent welfare state as their FWP tenure came to an end. Hurston's *Moses, Man of the Mountain* (1939) allegorizes the violence attendant on national formation and modernization, introducing uncertainty into the Exodus story and

---

2. Rutkowski, *Literary Legacies of the Federal Writes' Project.*

3. Wright and Hurston traded critical assessments of each other's work in Wright's review of *Their Eyes Were Watching God* and Hurston's of *Uncle Tom's Children.* See Hurston, "Stories of Conflict," *Saturday Review of Literature,* 2 April 1938; Wright "Between Laughter and Tears," *New Masses,* 5 October 1937. Discussions of the antipathy between Wright and Hurston are commonplace to the point that they have structured an understanding of a sociological-vernacular divide in African American literature since the 1930s. While few critics see them as aligning in their views, many critics now see them as sharing several concerns, including Southern folk culture and modernity. See for example, Duck, "Go there tuh know there"; Maxwell, *New Negro, Old Left*; and Nicholls, *Conjuring the Folk.*

disrupting the New Deal's attempt to project order and continuity by warning that expanded state power might yield harmful outcomes. Wright's 1941 documentary book *12 Million Black Voices* stages a conflict between sociological discourse and an allegorical folk history. This conflict generates a hopeful, yet also cautionary vision of a modern future based in working class radicalization, questioning whether the racialized state is equipped to generate equity. Significantly, the ambiguities that critics have noted shape both books yield deeply ambivalent political assessments, which echo through African American writing of this era.

## Moses, Modern Man of the Mountain

Hurston began her work for the New Deal in New York. For six months in 1935 and 1936, she worked with the FTP's Negro Theatre Project led by John Houseman and wrote an unproduced adaptation of Aristophanes's *Lysistrata* set in a Black town in Florida. During this time, Hurston also wrote *Mules and Men,* which covered her work on hoodoo and folk tales in the South during the 1920s. Upon receiving a Guggenheim fellowship, Hurston left the FTP in April 1936 to study voodoo in Jamaica and Haiti, where she wrote her most famous novel, *Their Eyes Were Watching God.* By that time, Hurston appears to have been done with Harlem, and when she returned, she moved quickly back to her childhood home in Eatonville, Florida.

In Florida, the FWP unit was starving for talented writers eligible for relief. FWP editors there offered Hurston consulting work on the manuscript for *The Florida Negro.* As her Guggenheim funding began to run out, the offer became more tempting, and Hurston joined the FWP in April of 1938, working under state director Carita Dogget Corse, a popular historian of Florida, and Stetson Kennedy, who directed the Florida unit's materials on folklore and African Americans. As the most prominent writer on the Florida project, Hurston was underpaid and knew it. On a visit to the National Folk Festival in Washington, she backchanneled to Henry Alsberg to see if she could be appointed the director of *The Florida Negro.* Alsberg recommended Hurston's appointment, but Corse, following Jim Crow social norms, would not put Hurston in charge of White writers.[4] As a compromise, Hurston was allowed to work mostly from home, checking in from time to time. There, she could

---

4. Retman, *Real Folks,* 127, notes that while the Florida state guidebook challenges Jim Crow by depicting African American oppression, like other FWP guides to Southern states, it maintains racial segregation in its topical organization.

spend time developing folk material, including her 1938 account of her Caribbean travels *Tell My Horse,* and also focus on her planned Moses novel.[5]

In "Zora Neale Hurston and the Federal Folk," David Kadlec suggests that Hurston's relationship to New Deal documentary culture was fraught because the act of documentation seemed antithetical to her notion of what folk culture was:

> As [Hurston] stated over and over, "Negro folklore" was vibrant not because it was authentic or indigenous to any people or place but because it was "still in the making." It was not something to be documented but something to be done. . . . The documentation of people and places signified for Hurston only if the act of documentation itself became a kind of cultural activity.[6]

Hurston's view of the folk put her at odds with both communist proponents of social realism looking for evidence of political resistance and "the federal folk who, in administering a New Deal for American tourists, portrayed America's emerging culture as a dewy thing to 'behold.'"[7] Hurston's understanding of folk culture differed even from Botkin's ideas insofar as it saw folk activity not only as ongoing creation but also as a communal performance constitutive of community.

Nevertheless, Hurston grasped the possibilities in the FWP's vast recording apparatus as an opportunity to promote folk culture. She sent the unit materials that they incorporated for local color into the main Florida guide. She also provided several pieces for the unpublished *Florida Negro* manuscript, including one on a 1920 race riot in Ocoee, one on the influence of Black church life on culture, and "Go Gator and Muddy the Water," which developed an account of folklore and folksong. Her essays also included the polemic "Art and Such," which struck back at the dismissals, including Wright's, of *Their Eyes Were Watching God* as insufficiently sociological and political.[8] Hurston dismissed race leaders whose focus on those vernacular elements seen as most

---

5. I have taken much of the account of Hurston's New York City and FWP experiences from Boyd, *Wrapped in Rainbows.* Other sources include: Pamela Bordelon's biographical essay in Hurston, *Go Gator and Muddy the Water*; Kadlec, "Zora Neale Hurston and the Federal Folk"; Retman, *Real Folks*, 115–188; Stewart, *Long Past Slavery*; Wall, "Zora Neale Hurston's Essays."

6. Kadlec, "Zora Neale Hurston and the Federal Folk," 483.

7. Kadlec, "Zora Neale Hurston and the Federal Folk," 483.

8. Wall, "Zora Neale Hurston's Essays," notes that this essay was left out when the materials were published as *The Florida Negro, A Federal Writer's Project Legacy.* The essay was published in Gates, *Reading Black, Reading Feminist,* 21–26, and Hurston, *Go Gator and Muddy the Water,* 139–145.

valuable to a story of noble contribution and uplift, in her view, denied the messy, democratic community origins of the folk and, in effect, Black humanity. She coordinated FWP demonstrations of folk material, and in early 1939, Benjamin Botkin asked her to reprise her earlier work with Alan Lomax by taking charge of equipment for recording Florida folklore and folksongs. She worked with the anthropologist and folklorist Herbert Halpert, serving as a participant facilitator—much as she had done earlier as in her ethnographic work in Eatonville, New Orleans, and the Caribbean—in recording sessions with various groups of Black Jacksonville citizens.

Though the FWP kept her working on topics relevant to her interests, Hurston was no fan of the New Deal. She remained a Republican even while many African Americans switched party allegiances after 1936 and, though she was supportive of modernization efforts, she was deeply critical of federal centralization. This stance was most starkly evident in her later years. In a 1951 *Saturday Evening Post* article, she argues:

> Throughout the New Deal era, the relief program was the biggest weapon ever placed in the hands of those who sought power and votes . . . under relief, dependent upon the Government for their daily bread, men gradually relaxed their watchfulness and submitted to the will of the "Little White Father," more or less. Once they had weakened that far, it was easy to go on and on voting for more relief and leaving Government affairs in the hands of a few. The change from a republic to a dictatorship was imperceptibly pushed ahead.[9]

Though Hurston was not so opposed to governmental intervention in the 1930s, the roots of Hurston's antipathy to centralization likely had two origins: in her strong belief that African American communities could and should develop their own institutions, and also in experiences where the problem of who mattered as part of the nation-state was acutely evident. Hurston had witnessed federal neglect of Black migrant workers whose itinerancy resisted mechanisms of locating and cataloguing during the Florida hurricane in 1927, which was echoed in the Labor Day hurricane of 1935, and inspired the famous flood scene in *Their Eyes Were Watching God*.

The problem of who mattered to the nation-state was also acutely evident in a range of nationalist and populist movements of the interwar years which sought to use expansive executive power to reimagine national identity. The rise of German fascism with its emphasis on *herrenvolk* and open

---

9. Hurston, "Negro Voter Sizes up Taft," 29.

endorsement of violence was, of course, present in the mind of many Americans in the 1930s, but much of Hurston's activity during this decade located her in places in the Southern US and Caribbean where powerful executives sought to secure power, often by reforming communities in both reality and in the imagination. Huey Long's consolidation of political power as governor of Louisiana, built through patronage and graft in public works, coincided with Hurston's investigation into New Orleans hoodoo work. In her Guggenheim-sponsored fieldwork in Haiti in 1937, Hurston also observed postcolonial nation-building firsthand. Although she left prior to the 1938 formation of the journal *Les Griots,* which served as an intellectual venue for the *Noirisme* movement advocating a Haitian national identity based on African heritage and voodoo, François Duvalier's ideas and those of Jean Price-Mars were already circulating widely. Hurston was aware of them and witnessed how these ideas fueled executive power consolidation under President Sténio Vincent. Leigh Anne Duck shows that *Tell My Horse* offers ambivalent assessments of the Griot movement and includes a number of passages approving US intervention that undercut seemingly positive assessments of Haitian cultural nationalism.[10]

Political ambivalence and narrative ambiguity are crucial to the account of nation-building in *Moses, Man of the Mountain* as well. Indeed, this novel has long produced broadly divergent critical understandings of its titular figure.[11] On one level, the novel seems to approve of a strongman approach: the determined will to build a nation embodied in the powerful right hand of Moses. However, it uses folk modalities and themes to introduce uncertainty in its source material and highlight the narrative component of nation-building. While Hurston's story of national formation does not reference the New Deal as directly as some other FWP intertexts, like other signifying works, it condenses and encodes a multidirectional critique. Hurston's novel foregrounds elements of the Mosaic tale that question the presumed just ends of nation-building, highlighting a will to power in Moses's executive vision, the fundamental cruelty of many of his actions, and the co-optation and removal of key voices of dissent from his national project.

On its surface *Moses, Man of the Mountain* retells the biblical Exodus story, but the tension between the story being retold and the vernacular mode of its

---

10. Duck, "Rebirth of a Nation," 133.

11. See, for example, Edwards, "Moses, Monster of the Mountain," and Lackey, "Moses, Man of Oppression," who both see Moses as a figure Hurston marks out as an agent of gender and state oppression, as opposed to Thompson, "National Socialism and Blood-Sacrifice in Zora Neale Hurston's *Moses, Man of the Mountain,*" who reads Moses as an indicator of Hurston's attraction to the efficacy of a generalized fascism.

74 · CHAPTER 3

telling facilitates signifying. Biblical certainties crumble in Hurston's retelling. Miriam falls asleep and loses track of the basket bearing her brother, condemned to die by the Pharaoh, down the Nile. She never learns the actual outcome of her brother's passage. Instead, she becomes entranced by the Pharaoh's daughter bathing by the river. When the princess's aides suggest that Miriam might be there to harm her, the princess replies, "Governments are not overthrown by little girls."[12] Yet Miriam sets in motion the overthrow of the Egyptian government when she fabulates the princess's recovery of a casket of bathing materials into her brother's rescue to cover her own lapse. This rumor legitimates Moses's place among the Hebrews, but in unsettling Moses's origins in the biblical account as the child of enslaved Hebrews Amran and Jochebed, the novel rewrites his position as uncertain. Moses's natural authority is always in question, and he must constantly perform acts reassuring his followers of his power.

As John Lowe demonstrates in *Jump at the Sun,* signifying acts and conjure work abound in Hurston's Moses novel, disrupting etiologies and facilitating a multidirectional social critique. As vernacular modes place an emphasis on the generative power of narrative, they reveal the dependence of modernization on storytelling. The novel reveals that the Egyptian leaders' power is sustained by magicians whose primary art is using illusion to convince the people of the gods' power and, thus, the authority of the rulers. Under the stableman storyteller Mentu and then Moses's Midianite father-in-law Jethro, Moses undertakes to study and best the magicians at their illusions, and in so doing becomes a first-rate hoodoo man, an adeptness he uses to build his own power. Other causal uncertainties follow, reflecting Hurston's own experience with hoodoo and voodoo practice. Moses's first crossing of the Red Sea takes place at a low tide event, suggesting his prior knowledge of the climactic scene when the Hebrews cross the parted waters and the Egyptian army is drowned. While many events seem to be caused by acts of magic in the book, the novel's problematizing of the line between the natural and the supernatural is crucial to its ability to keep the story from settling into a single causal explanation and allowing it instead to tell many tales, including political ones.

The unsettling extends to the very core of patriarchal biblical authority. Moses comes to embrace Jethro's God, but develops power largely in communion with "Nature" and its symbols. He knows for example, that the people see the presence of God in a cloud on Mount Horeb, and that he can use the smoke from incense to evoke that presence:

---

12. Hurston, *Moses,* 28.

So when Moses lifted his hand the smoke of the incense ceased to be smoke. It became the Presence. If it was not the actual Presence, then it enclosed and clothed the Presence. Finally the smoke itself was deified. It was not understood so it became divine.[13]

Jethro grasps this complex erasure of the lines among power, presence, and symbol when he suggests that Moses "done found them secret words that's the keys to God that we all been looking for."[14] It also illustrates the idea of folk meaning being created in the Griot interplay between Moses and the audience.

Later, the novel suggests Jethro tricks Moses into taking up the task of leading the Hebrews into a new land with a new object of worship. Eager to establish a new nation, Jethro runs into complacency; Moses has no wish to be a leader and instead prefers the sweet life studying nature as a local conjure man with a wealthy patron. However, like other figures in African American folk tradition, he is subject to moments of self-delusion. Jethro states, "Maybe there is still something about snakes that [Moses] can learn. The backside of that mountain may get too hot to hold him yet."[15] The details of this aside render suspect the signals of God's intention for Moses, a talking burning bush and snake that turns into a staff, as Jethro's conjure work. The scene also erases the line between hoodoo and Abrahamic monotheism, exposing the latter as a kind of beard for the former. Like many other events in the book focusing on authority, it denaturalizes power, revealing its transactional, unstable, narrative-based dimensions.

If governments can be overthrown by stories, they can be built on them as well. Hurston's novel highlights rewriting extensively, not only in its tweaks to the Book of Exodus, but in Moses's own national project. The novel's linkage between storytelling and power is crucial to its story of modernization. To bring his charges in line as a nation, Moses knows he must replace one cultural story with another. Sean McCann, who also sees the novel as an exploration of executive and state power speaking to US and global politics, argues that the novel enacts a fable in which Moses replaces cultural localism with a modern streamlined religion.[16] Moses, as a patriarchal executive authority, becomes the agent of national reformation and modernization, and he goes about his task methodically. He enlists power-seeking locals, frees the Hebrews, substitutes a new culture for their old one, defeats the Pharaoh's military, and sets up a state structure under his own control. When the Hebrews wandering in the desert

---

13. Hurston, *Moses*, 116.

14. Hurston, *Moses*, 117.

15. Hurston, *Moses*, 124.

16. McCann, *Pinnacle of Feeling*, 81.

become too demanding, Moses makes them wait forty years before entering Canaan, ensuring that the older generation beholden to Egyptian norms is eclipsed by one that has only known his power.

In an unpublished 1945 essay, Hurston called Moses a "dictator" who formed a "police state."[17] Lowe cautions that we should not read that commentary as definitive, or even entirely condemnatory, but at the very least, it argues against reading Hurston's Moses or other executive modernizers as unproblematic, heroic figures. One of the key questions this problematic version of Moses raises is what Hurston thought of concentrated executive power. Hurston was deeply concerned with the relationship among culture, democracy, modernization, and nation-building during the 1930s, and her discussion of US and Caribbean politics usefully reveal her growing political ambivalence. Hurston had embraced a nationalist perspective throughout much of the 1930s, embracing the centralized state as an agent of necessary modernization, even while remaining skeptical of its leaders.[18] Hurston grew up with the example of Joe Clarke, the influential Eatonville mayor who served as a model for the powerful Joe Starks in *Their Eyes Were Watching God. Tell My Horse* cites the modernization programs led by Rafael Trujillo in the Dominican Republic as a model for Haitian modernization. Hurston's praise has been used as evidence of her support for state centralization and charismatic leadership. Mark Christian Thompson goes so far as to contend that Hurston embraces a generic fascist theory of politics, which would suggest that her Moses is a figure of necessary power and violence in building a cohesive and effective political community.[19] Hurston had hopes that Haiti's leaders would borrow Trujillo's determination to curtail what Hurston saw as ineffective politics and colonial subservience to guide their nation into the future. However, Duck notes that Hurston's depiction of Trujillo is far from heroic and is muted still further by sympathetically noting the threat he posed to Haitians.[20] At most, Hurston seems to have had an ambivalent perspective on centralized authority.

At the root of Hurston's ambivalence was the tension she felt between the need for effective political leadership and the threat of an imposed social and cultural order. This ambivalence carries over into Hurston's examination of the Griot movement in *Tell My Horse*. Duck shows that Hurston qualifies what

---

17. Lowe, *Jump at the Sun*, 232. The essay's draft title was "The Elusive Goal: Brotherhood of Mankind." Lackey, "Moses, Man of Oppression," 577, mentions a similar assertion in a letter to Carl Van Vechten.

18. McCann, *Pinnacle of Feeling*, 82; Duck "Rebirth of a Nation," 130.

19. Thompson, "National Socialism and Blood-Sacrifice," 395.

20. Duck, "Rebirth of a Nation," 140.

sometimes looks like admiration for the Griots is actually qualified at several points and does not extend her praise to the *Noiriste* focus on cultural nationalism. Though Hurston favors a modern Haiti, she rejects a politics based in racial heritage. Instead, Duck asserts, Hurston advances civic nationalism, "representing the nation as a group united in its demand for democratic rights but potentially diverse in its cultural affiliations."[21] In this regard, her views accorded well with the New Deal's civic pluralism, and her participation in the FWP and recognition of the overlap between its cultural activities and her own are significant.

While Hurston's political sentiments occasionally leaned favorably toward centralized modernization in postcolonial contexts, they tilted more firmly toward identification with those modernization efforts left behind in the US. Hurston's views on US politics, as Duck shows, were shifting in response to disappointment in Roosevelt's policies at home and abroad:

> During the 1940s . . . Hurston became skeptical of US civic nationalism. . . . She began to speak of [democracy] as a governmental form that had yet to be realized. Her writing from this period reflects an increased conviction that the US government's racist practice—in both domestic and foreign policy—derived not only from the prejudices of the majority but also from the state's commitment to capitalism.[22]

Hurston's growing negative assessment of the centralized state, Duck further argues, reflects a skepticism already perceptible in her focus on individualism and resistance to political communities in her novels of the late 1930s.[23] While civic pluralism cast a relatively wide net of inclusion, the modern centralized future the New Deal promoted generally did not include the people and cultural elements Hurston wrote about, and Hurston understood the New Deal was compromised by its dependence on the White supremacist views of the Southern Democrats.

Rewriting history in the service of continuity with an imagined future was a key element of New Deal nation-building, but its tendency to smooth over social conflict troubled Hurston. McCann suggests Hurston rejects the

---

21. Hurston, *Moses*, 130.

22. Hurston, *Moses*, 131. Duck suggests that Hurston, like many other African Americans, initially expressed support for US intervention in Haiti in the 1930s to ensure a stable democracy, but she came to view the Roosevelt administration's support of Vincent and then Élie Lescot as politically cynical.

23. Hurston, *Moses*, 143.

78 · CHAPTER 3

New Deal's "vision of empathy as an instrument of social democracy."[24] *Moses, Man of the Mountain* insists on highlighting forms of resistance and violence in nation-building. The violence preserved in working-class folk expression appealed to Hurston because it rejected liberal empathy's softening of race, class, and gender inequities. New Deal paternalism threatened to erase the realities of group existence in favor of an unmediated relationship between the state and individuals.[25] McCann's insight cautions against a reading of violence in the novel as inherently negative. Hurston's novel highlights a wide range of personal and group antipathies that undercut and test Moses's political leadership. Yet, this view of resistance reveals a more insidious violence lurking in his national project and its erasure of competing claims.

As the story of Aaron's comeuppance suggests, the novel is ambivalent about accepting the violence Moses inflicts as collateral for unification. A leader of the Hebrews prior to Moses's arrival, Aaron, who Moses sees as a "short, squatty man who wanted things" aligns himself with Moses to maintain his own power.[26] On the sly, he remains one of Moses's most vocal critics, and he uses any opportunity that arises to benefit himself. Aaron is a problematic figure, to say the least, likely revealing Hurston's ire toward many Black intellectual and political elites. Aaron's pompous self-dealing and maneuvering often undercut Moses's national ambitions. When, after years of wandering the wilderness, he confronts Moses about his reward for service, Moses takes him to the top of Mount Hor, strips him of his priestly robes, reveals that he was never called by God, tells him his sons were killed in the name of national purification, and then knifes him. Moses covers up the murder and commands the people to build a memorial tomb to a leader who "was denied many pleasures for your sake," sardonically converting Aaron's political rivalry into national martyrdom.[27] This is a comeuppance story, a staple of folk stories. However, Moses's vengeance is disproportionate, even malicious, further revealing, as John Lowe suggests, the novel's focus on interested and corruptible powers deviling the state and perverting its legal guarantees.[28]

The broader political disengagement of the masses serves the novel as both a problem Moses must overcome in his national quest and a reminder of a rightful suspicion of unchecked power. Throughout the novel, the Hebrews crankily resist Moses's exertions on their behalf in favor of maintaining what status they have. Were the Egyptians not so bent on worsening their living

---

24. McCann, *Pinnacle of Feeling*, 89.
25. McCann, *Pinnacle of Feeling*, 95.
26. Hurston, *Moses*, 131.
27. Hurston, *Moses*, 276.
28. Lowe, *Jump at the Sun*, 227.

and working conditions, the Hebrews might well abandon Moses. They complain incessantly about the trials Moses leads them through, occasionally stage revolts, and seek out the familiar comforts of the Egyptian pantheon. This is an implicit rebuke to intellectuals who mistook the activity of small groups for majoritarian sentiment, but also to the New Deal's vision of engaged citizens working toward the same ends. The masses' dissent speaks to a suspicion of unchecked power and political uncertainty in African American voting patterns noted by African American political commentators from former FWP writer Henry Lee Moon in the 1940s to pundit Charles Blow in 2016.[29] Erica Edwards connects the people's suspicion in the novel with a sense of awareness that Moses might be as much murderer as hero.[30]

Hurston focuses on the violence of nation-building in Moses's treatment, showing that only through the denial of older beliefs and steady, repressive application of power is Moses able to forge a new nation. Moses repeatedly inflicts suffering on the Egyptians—fair game as retribution for the Hebrews' enslavement, of course, but when Moses has the opportunity to end the curses, he continues to make certain that the Egyptians will remember their suffering. The military that Moses builds and trains during the march is similarly uncompromising with enemies. The use of violent power against enemies is matched by internal application as well. One of the most jarring moments in the text occurs in the resolution of the famous golden calf episode. Angered at the deviance of the people who have chosen to return to worshipping Egyptian gods while he was on Mount Sinai, Moses sets aside the legal principles he has just acquired and commands a slaughter:

> You all know what a foul thing has happened in Israel today. . . . If this is to be a great nation, it must be purged of all evil-doers. . . . Spare not a soul who is guilty. . . . For hours there was fleeing and screaming and hiding and bloody swords. Then there was quiet again in the camp.[31]

Here, the rewriting reminds readers of the violence in the biblical account, which estimates a death toll of 3,000. As McCann notes, it is Moses's power rather than the law that holds the Hebrews together, reflecting African American experiences of liberalism in which the law has often served as an instrument that could be utilized, reinterpreted, or set aside by authorities to maintain White supremacy.[32]

---

29. Moon, *Balance of Power*; Blow, "Bernie Sanders and the Black Vote."
30. Edwards, "Moses, Monster of the Mountain," 1091.
31. Hurston, *Moses*, 239.
32. McCann, *Pinnacle of Feeling*, 94.

80 · CHAPTER 3

*Their Eyes Were Watching God,* Lowe reminds us, presents a world of women as Janie Crawford negotiates controlling men and community leaders like Logan Killicks and Joe Starks.[33] *Moses, Man of the Mountain*'s comparatively male social sphere complements Hurston's preceding novel by placing its focus squarely on the development of patriarchal power and its effects on women. Moses's vision is based on obligation in the father-son relationship with Jethro, writ larger in their relationship to God. The Mosaic pattern of individual male heroism, Erica Edwards notes, is fairly common in narratives of Black leadership, and she argues that the novel illuminates the gendered dimensions of leadership stories.[34] *Moses* specifically highlights the way that it's titular figure circumvents women's power, sometimes through violence. Jethro encourages his daughter Zipporah's power over Moses up to the point that Moses is securely married into his household, but then he undercuts her by reminding Moses of his "mission" for God. The novel satirizes Zipporah's desires to be recognized as a princess in the Egyptian mold, but her claims that Moses increasingly marginalizes her in favor of maintaining his vision are largely borne out.

Miriam's case is even more troubling. Hurston shows concern with the ways that women might be channeled into roles and institutions that diminish and coopt their power. Prior to Moses's arrival, Miriam has built a powerful reputation and political base as a conjure woman. Moses's consolidation of power is directly at her expense, and, like her brother, she has to ally herself with Moses to maintain her influence. When later she argues with Moses over their power sharing arrangement, she contracts leprosy. One of the novel's most poignant scenes depicts the level of loss she has sustained when she begs Moses to be allowed to die. Moses implausibly denies responsibility for her suffering. After her death, he rewrites her image as a "patriot" of the new nation, rather than one who suffered under his rule.[35]

In the end, Moses has successfully rewritten his story and created a modern nation with a unified culture. However, he has done it at the expense of most of the people who were enlisted in the exodus. Moses's advice to his successor Joshua on statecraft captures his changing views:

> You can't have a state of individuals. Everybody can't just be allowed to do as they please. I love liberty and I love freedom so I started off giving everybody a loose rein. But I soon found out that it wouldn't do. A great state is

---

33. Lowe, *Jump at the Sun,* 226.
34. Edwards, "Moses, Monster of the Mountain," 1089.
35. Hurston, *Moses,* 265.

a well-blended mash of something of all of the people and all of none of the people.[36]

Taken straight, the passage figures all the sacrifice as necessary in the interest of state power and national cohesion. However, little in Hurston's novel, and especially its folk telling, suggests that a straight reading holds, and the passage speaks to the corruption of power in the service of political efficacy. Hurston was deeply aware that state-directed modernization might well effectively exclude specific groups and cultural elements from the national community. More problematically, by rewriting their history and relationship to the state, it might erase the memory of the violence through which the modern, centralized nation was constructed. The etiological uncertainties of conjure and signification call into question Moses's executive power while keeping a focus on its violent exercise.

The ambivalence about centralized authority and national community in *Moses* prefigures Hurston's own political trajectory. Hurston's sense of the limits of American liberalism's capacity to transcend its embedded racism increased over time, leading to conservative positions out of sync with a younger generation embracing state-oriented solutions during the postwar era. In a 1955 letter to the *Orlando Sentinel* criticizing the *Brown* v. *Board of Education* decision, Hurston argued the federal government was effectively out of its depth in its attempt to compel integration in social structures with deep roots in race and worried that the emphasis on state-directed integration might distract from and undercut the attempts of Black communities to generate their own solutions.[37] Although Hurston in the 1930s was more open to the possibilities of the centralized state than she was later in life, *Moses, Man of the Mountain* refuses the New Deal's vision of pluralistic cultural contribution or its faith in technocratic development. In its place, she offers an ambivalent folk allegory of modernization and nation-building that blurs the line between heroism and tragedy.

## Richard Wright's Folk History

Hurston's novel of nation-building utilizes vernacular uncertainty and allegory as a way of disrupting myth. Similarly, Wright's *12 Million Black Voices: A Folk History* challenges the New Deal narrative of cohesive community by

---

36. Hurston, *Moses*, 278.

37. Hurston, "Court Order Can't Make Races Mix," *Orlando Sentinel*, 11 August 1955. Boyd, *Wrapped in Rainbows*, 423–425, discusses Hurston's letter and the reaction to it.

82 · CHAPTER 3

reimagining national historical myths through Black social geography. Wright was the most famous figure to emerge from the FWP milieu. His position as a FWP employee in Chicago and New York, as a Black writer, and as an active member of communist literary circles, situated him critically in the era's discussions of race, governance, and the city. This chapter rereads Wright's 1941 photobook as a FWP intertext to highlight the way that it balances conflicting understandings of Black vernacular culture and modernity to generate a deeply cautious account of the future. *12 Million Black Voices* participates in redefining Black neighborhoods as slums, describing a symptom pattern that reinforces calls for broad-reaching intervention. The government is not the imagined agent of redemption though; instead, Wright offers the possibility of cross-racial alliances among modernized class-conscious workers as a more promising and democratic telos. Simultaneously, the book deploys a folk modality that complicates the historical and sociological discourses it advances and defers any conclusive political agenda. Wright destabilizes both New Deal and communist visions of the future as he reveals the complex ways that race operates to produce patterns of inequity.[38]

Wright's emergence as a writer was tied up with the tensions he experienced in his personal and political life. Having spent his youth as the grandson of freed slaves in Mississippi, Arkansas, and Tennessee, Wright, like so many others of his generation, was a Southern migrant to Northern cities. After moving to Chicago from Memphis in 1927, Wright worked for the US Postal Service. He began to move through circles affiliated with the CPUSA in the early 1930s and, in 1933, joined a John Reed Club, which fostered the work of young Left writers. Wright began publishing poetry in journals promoting proletarian literature and edited the journal *Left Front.* Influenced by Chicago sociology and placing economic strategies of uplift ahead of the cultural ones favored by the 1920s Harlem intellectuals, many Black writers in Chicago became involved in Leftist cultural institutions during the 1930s. Seeking to address issues of race and labor, the National Negro Congress, held in Chicago in 1936, was supported by the CPUSA. Wright had been disappointed when the CPUSA's 1934 shift to its Popular Front strategy ended support for the John Reed Clubs and *Left Front,* and he used the energy from the National Negro Congress held in Chicago in 1936 to organize the South Side Writers Group. This group consisted of several African American intellectuals who shared

---

38. Some of the analysis of Wright has also been published in Butts, "New World A-Coming." Other elements are forthcoming in a chapter in *African American Literature in Transition, 1930–1940* titled "New Deal Discourses."

commitments to Leftist ideas—including Arna Bontemps, Frank Marshall Davis, Fenton Johnson, and Margaret Walker, among others.[39]

Like many of the South Side writers, Wright, who had lost his job with the postal service, went on relief during the New Deal and found a position in 1935 at the Illinois state unit of the FWP, which was housed in Chicago. The Illinois FWP benefited from the concentration of sociological activity through the University of Chicago and the city's centrality to planning discourse. Wright had already developed relationships with University of Chicago professor Louis Wirth and his graduate student Horace Cayton that fueled his understanding of the complex racial and psychosocial dynamics of space.[40] At his FWP job in Chicago, Wright worked on the American Guide series volume *Illinois: A Descriptive and Historical Guide,* published in 1939, and an unpublished study called *The Negro in Illinois.* This nexus of the organized Leftist Black cultural scene and sociology shaped the class- and race-conscious analyses of Chicago in the Illinois guidebook as well as its explicit orientation toward spatial reform. Through these projects, Wright gained essential practice in writing about the racialized urban environment.

In May 1937, Wright moved to New York, hoping that a transfer from the Illinois FWP unit to the New York City unit would come through.[41] Unfortunately for Wright, it took a half a year for him to establish eligibility as a New York resident. However, in January 1938, with the recommendation of Sterling Brown to Henry Alsberg, Wright joined the New York City unit and began working on the two guidebooks and the Negro History subunit.[42] His work there included rewriting the material Claude McKay had begun on Harlem for the first guidebook and also writing much of the account of Harlem for the second guidebook. That Wright was a relative newcomer made this all the more remarkable, and Wright left a Chicago stamp on these materials, linking emerging social dynamics in Harlem to broader patterns across the nation.

In New York, Wright continued his activities on the literary Left, writing for the *Daily Worker.* Though he disliked the work because of the hours required and the political infighting, Wright's reporting for the *Daily Worker*

---

39. See Dolinar, *Black Cultural Front*; Jackson, *Indignant Generation*, 55–62; Mullen, *Popular Fronts*, for discussion of Black writers and Leftist organizations in Chicago.

40. See my fourth chapter for further discussion of FWP, *The Negro in Illinois: The WPA Papers*, which was compiled and edited from draft materials by Brian Dolinar.

41. Rowley, *Richard Wright*, 123. Rowley's book, the FWP archival holdings at the NARA, and the Wright Papers at the Beinecke Library are the primary sources of my account of Wright's time in Chicago and New York. See also Cappetti, "Sociology of an Existence" and *Writing Chicago* for discussions of the relationship between Chicago School sociology and Wright's representation of space and history.

42. NARA RG69, Donald Thompson to Henry G. Alsberg, 6 June 1938, Box 30.

on issues in Harlem during his FWP hiatus expanded his knowledge of the city. Early in his New York tenure, Wright also helped launch the Left-leaning literary journal *New Challenge* with Rebecca West and Marian Minus. He also wrote several articles for *New Masses,* giving him a voice in one of the most well-known Left literary journals.

For Wright, like many others, working for the federal government while holding communist views could be difficult. The mid-1930s communist policy shift to the Popular Front had aligned some of the aims of communists and liberals, particularly in their commitments to antifascism and, to some degree, antiracism. The New Deal cultural apparatus was a useful but unstable entity. As the head of the communist-affiliated New York Writers' Alliance, Wright advocated expansion of FWP support for writers while criticizing administrators and policies seen as unfriendly to the Left. Communism's economic and social principles conflicted with liberalism's commitment to individuals and property rights. However, Wright's reservations about the Communist Party were growing. His intellectualism and his views on art and culture at times put him at odds with the CPUSA's cultural and political leadership, and he was only a few years away from a very public break with communism when he left the FWP.[43] Yet he continued to share a belief that the government was too compromised by the politics of racial division to serve as an effective agent of racial equity.

Within the dual FWP/Popular Front context, Wright flourished as a writer. In Chicago, he published "Big Boy Leaves Home" in the anthology *The New Caravan* in 1936. His biographical piece "The Ethics of Living Jim Crow" appeared in 1937 in a collection of FWP work titled *American Stuff: An Anthology of Prose and Verse* released by Viking Press. In 1938, he published his first major book, the story collection *Uncle Tom's Children,* and one of the stories in the collection, "Bright and Morning Star," featured in a special *New Masses* issue devoted to the work of FWP employees that May, the existence of which signals the complex relationship between the literary Left and the FWP. Publicity around *Uncle Tom's Children* catapulted Wright to the forefront of emerging writers and helped secure him a much-sought-after place as one of the few FWP employees assigned time for creative writing.[44] This assignment

---

43. Wright announced his break with communism in the essay "I Tried To Be a Communist." He told the press that by 1940, he had split with the CPUSA, though biographers highlight the break occurring in 1942. See Rowley, *Richard Wright,* 292–295, for an account of the essay and the reaction to it.

44. Mangione, *Dream and the Deal,* 245, notes that the writers in this semi-secret group, who were mostly previously published authors, also included: Maxwell Bodenheim, Edward Dahlberg, Sol Funaroff, Harry Kemp, Willard Maas, Claude McKay, Harry Roskolenko, and Charlotte Wilder.

and a Guggenheim fellowship set Wright up for his most powerful literary achievement, his 1940 novel *Native Son*. Arguably the most influential novel written on the federal government's dime, *Native Son* offered a stunning refutation of the idea that FWP work stifled creativity even while it highlighted governmental maintenance of White supremacy.

Bernard Bell identified *Native Son* as the most influential example of Black naturalism, one of the most prolific postwar African American literary genres.[45] Novelists in this vein—including William Attaway, Chester Himes, John O. Killens, and Ann Petry—explored the influence of environment on agency and psychology in tight prose, but they also examined the effect of racial ideology as a primary shaper of the spatial and social environment. Depictions of characters navigating inescapable moral and ethical dilemmas provided a powerful means of condemning the systems and beliefs that produced such conditions. Black naturalism often reinforced the slum diagnosis offered by Chicago sociology and reinforced in New Deal texts, but it rarely offered viable agents of reform.

However, the most direct New Deal intertext in Wright's oeuvre is not *Native Son* but rather *12 Million Black Voices*, the documentary photobook he published the following year, at a time when his political commitments were changing. *12 Million Black Voices* paired Wright's narration with photographs taken by Farm Security Administration (FSA) photographers and selected with the help of Edwin Rosskam, who had worked under Roy Stryker as an FSA design specialist. Wright's photobook essentially widened the conceptual frame of *Native Son* to encompass a broader American history and geography. The photographic method of presentation, the jumps in narrative, and the narrative voice in *12 Million Black Voices* all resemble New Deal-era cinematic and photographic documentaries such as Pare Lorentz's FSA films and Time, Inc.'s *The March of Time* television series.[46] With the exception of the narrator's voice, these characteristics are also quite similar to the methods utilized by the FWP in its guidebooks. FWP influence is also evident in the spatial focus of

---

45. Bell, *Afro-American Novel and Its Tradition*, 150–187. See also Wright, "How 'Bigger' Was Born," offered first as a lecture, then published as a supplement to *Native Son*, and finally appended as an introduction to the novel, for a discussion of methods. Wald, *Trinity of Passion*, 126, critiques this label suggesting that, despite many of these books' pessimistic plotlines and conclusions, "the outlook of such Left writers cannot be reasoned out in terms of the passivity in relation to the power of environment or the denial of human agency that the term 'naturalism' connotes."

46. See Allred, *American Modernism and Depression Documentary*, 133–166; Moore, "Voice in *12 Million Black Voices*;" Smith, "They Sing the Song of Slavery"; Woller "First-Person Plural" for discussions of the relationship between Wright's photobook and other New Deal–era documentary texts.

86 · CHAPTER 3

the text, its formal hybridity, its attention to folk culture, and its sociological concern with urban living conditions.

The FWP guidebooks seek to make places visible and coherent, and thus amenable to reform. Wright's documentary project operates similarly, as a guide to African American life offering a symptomology, a diagnosis, and a prescription. The book's plot is progressive and linear, traveling from past to present to future, South to North, agrarian tenant farm to urban-industrial slum, confusion to class consciousness. Early in the first section, "Our Strange Birth," the narrator offers a comment on the book's purpose and its method. In discussing the use of nineteenth-century Christian teachings to establish a racialized social order, the narrator highlights the roots of the problem, asking, "How did this paradoxical amalgam of love and cruelty come to be?"[47] The narrator explains its origins in material relations:

> A division of labor among men, splitting them up into groups and classes enables whole segments of populations to be so influenced by their material surroundings that they see but a little phase of the complex process of their lives and the whole is obscured from them, thereby affording them the unfortunate opportunity to move and work at cross-purposes with one another, even though in their hearts they may feel that they are engaged in a crusade of common hope.[48]

The problem of the paradox, then, is an epistemological one, rooted in an incomplete understanding of totality. The book's abstraction of Southern agrarian and urban industrial experiences seeks to remedy this gap, providing a picture that connects the two. Wright suggests that if the whole can be made visible, then perhaps racial problems can be addressed.

In his discussion of the folk culture of the agrarian South, Wright explores several key questions about vernacular culture: How did African American folk culture arise? What cultural elements if any survived from Africa? What purpose does folk culture serve? Could it fit into a modern urban industrial world? For Wright, African American folk culture must be understood in its relationship to historical shifts in the material conditions of power. The experience of the South, Wright contends, was particularly important because it was where African Americans learned a new culture to adapt first to slavery and then to Jim Crow. One particular cruelty of slavery, the narrator asserts, was that African Americans were stripped of their culture in the shock of the

---

47. Wright, *12 Million Black Voices*, 24.
48. Wright, *12 Million Black Voices*, 24.

Middle Passage and the contingencies of their lives as slaves. Wright rejects the idea of African survivals, one of the major debates among folklorists in this period. Instead, the narrator suggests that folk culture is primarily based in borrowings and innovations within an American context.

Wright contends that the primary function of folkways in the South is communicating understandings of injustice while keeping hope alive. The narrator discusses how a sermon becomes a lesson on injustice and hope, and how song and dance allow for a freedom of expression and individuality that is restricted from the public sphere. Folk culture provides a coded means of engaging with power, allowing African Americans to form a tight-knit community in the presence of White supremacy and absence of material goods. Wright states, "We are unable to establish our family groups upon a basis of property ownership," which leads to "delicate families . . . held together by love, sympathy, pity, and the goading knowledge that we must work together to make a crop."[49] Wright sees in this situation the possibility of a community bond denied to people who accept the competitive terms of capitalism: "That is why we black folk laugh and sing when we are alone together. There is nothing—no ownership or lust for power—that stands between us and our kin."[50] Wright's view echoes that of John Lomax and other folklorists who saw folk culture as a resistance to liberal individualism, one that preserved the memory of precapitalist social relations and thus the possibility of an alternative to the present.[51] These elements of culture maintained a vision of community based on shared experience and culture rather than property and self-interest.

The turn to industrial capitalism and its accompanying organizing form in the metropolis necessitates new cultural modes of engagement, even while older ones persist. Wright seeks to illuminate the material basis for these changes and their implications for political action. By titling the third section "Death on the City Pavements," Wright immediately undercuts the more exuberant understandings of urban modernity found in works like Alain Locke's essay "The New Negro." Building on modernist themes of metropolitan alienation and epistemological confusion, Wright suggests that for African Americans who join the Great Migration, the first cost is exacted in their sense of relations to other people. The narrator notes the confusion of sitting next to White people on the bus: "The impulses to laugh or cry clash in us; we bite our lips and stare out the window."[52] The text also emphasizes the common

---

49. Wright, *12 Million Black Voices*, 60.

50. Wright, *12 Million Black Voices*, 60–61.

51. See Hirsch, *Portrait of America*, 29–31, for a discussion of competing views of vernacular culture held by New Deal administrators.

52. Wright, *12 Million Black Voices*, 100.

modernist lament about city relationships: "We cannot see or know a *man* because of the thousands upon thousands of *men.*"[53] It continues, identifying the directness of capitalist objectification:

> It seems as though we are now living inside a machine; days and events move with a hard reasoning of their own. We live amid swarms of people, yet there is a vast distance between people, a distance that words cannot bridge. . . . In the South life was different; men spoke to you, cursed you, yelled at you, or killed you. The world moved by signs we knew. But here in the North cold forces hit you and push you. It is a world of *things.*[54]

These passages highlight the extent of the book's dialogue with theories of urban anomie. They also suggest that African American migrants arrive in the city culturally ill-equipped for the struggle to establish themselves. Wright's book seeks to guide the reader to an understanding of this gap and its underlying urban material and social conditions.

For Wright, Black urban vernacular culture is primarily composed of residual elements from the South and thereby serves primarily as a social expression of alienation. Wright's portrayal of urban religion focuses heavily on its compensatory value, its service to the needs of people whose options for meaningful community are limited from outside. Wright suggests that the real reason the church remains important in Black urban social life is that "going to church on Sunday is like placing one's ear to another's chest to hear the unquenchable murmurs of the human heart."[55] The churches provide a place of "wholeness and humanity" that allow people to gather hope and strength against the "Bosses of the Buildings."[56] He also notes the secondary functions of churches, which often provided recreation and social activities as well as worship. Wright claims that women, in particular, adhere to the tradition of church-going "for emotional security and the release of their personalities" and often serve as the bearers of folk culture.[57]

Folk culture still has functional value, insofar as it allows the oppressed to express themselves, but the mode of expression is out of joint with their lives. The narrator states:

---

53. Wright, *12 Million Black Voices*, 100.
54. Wright, *12 Million Black Voices*, 100.
55. Wright, *12 Million Black Voices*, 131.
56. Wright, *12 Million Black Voices*, 131.
57. Wright, *12 Million Black Voices*, 131.

THE FOLK HISTORIES OF HURSTON AND WRIGHT • 89

> Day after day we labor in the gigantic factories and mills of Western civilization, but we have never been allowed to become an organic part of this civilization; we have yet to share its ultimate hopes and expectations. . . . Instead, after working all day in one civilization, we go home to our Black Belts and live, within the orbit of the surviving remnants of the culture of the South, our naïve, casual, verbal, fluid folk life.[58]

Wright tracks other uses as well. Against people who argued that the elevated investment of Black citizens in performance arts is a natural aptitude, Wright contends that "play" is an essential feature of all oppressed peoples whose means of direct confrontation are limited.[59] He suggests that vernacular cultural elements may contribute to cross-cultural community as well. The broad appeal of jazz and the blues, he speculated, may well be that "so many of those who live in cities feel deep down just as we feel."[60] Wright shows that expression and communication remain important, even as he moves to question the political efficacy of folkways under urban conditions.

Wright's depiction of urban living conditions, largely in alignment with the FWP and Chicago School analysis, further illustrates distance from the agrarian folk culture. To make sense of continuing social inequality in the North, Wright explores the role of urban ecology shaped by race and capitalism. He begins by highlighting the role of race as a primary fallacy in value assessment, by noting White people's entrenched belief that "our presence in their neighborhoods lowers the value of their property," and continuing in wonder: "We do not understand why this should be so."[61] Wright suggests that instead of the presence of Black residents, it is actually Whites' reaction that causes the decline in property values. However, rather than laying the blame entirely on White flight, he focuses on the more fundamental profit motive guiding the Bosses of the Buildings, who make use of redlining to raise rent prices while reconfiguring single-family brownstones into more profitable multi-family units. While Wright curiously did not make this connection directly, the racial logic of value he identified also guided lending practices for housing and businesses in New Deal programs that expanded spatial segregation.

Like the New Dealers, Wright was particularly concerned about substandard housing. Wright's critique focuses on the kitchenette, which was created by subdividing existing housing units. He describes the kitchenette as, "our

---

58. Wright, *12 Million Black Voices*, 127.
59. Wright, *12 Million Black Voices*, 127.
60. Wright, *12 Million Black Voices*, 128.
61. Wright, *12 Million Black Voices*, 103.

prison, our death sentence without a trial, the new form of mob violence that assaults not only the lone individual but all of us."[62] Paula Rabinowitz notes the procedural language through which the text repeatedly exposes not an individual crime, like the True Crime stories on which it was modeled, but a social one motivated by profit and White supremacy.[63] The narrator explains the birth of the kitchenette:

> What they do is this: they take, say, a seven-room apartment, which rents for $50 a month to whites, and cut it up into seven small apartments, of one room each; they install one small gas stove and one small sink in each room. The Bosses of the Buildings rent these kitchenettes to us at the rate of, say, $6 per week. Hence, the same apartment for which white people—who can get jobs anywhere and who receive higher wages than we—pay $50 a month is rented to us for $50 a week.[64]

Clearly referencing Wright's own depiction of Bigger Thomas, the narrator further suggests that kitchenettes "inject pressure and tension into our individual personalities."[65] Pictures in the text of Black families crowded together in cramped, messy quarters echo the text and reinforce links with New Deal photographs of tenant farmers.

In making visible the effects of urban life on Black children, Wright echoes Progressive reformers' focus on the family and children as object and justification of reform. Through the voice of the parents, Wright suggests that the schism between the modern life of the city and folk culture is particularly problematic. The plate facing Wright's discussion of children contains a photograph of a young boy in a herringbone jacket leaning against a doorway. The boy is in a pose that would later be referred to as "hip." One arm is lifted with fingers curled, perhaps in contemplation or preparing for action. His other hand rests on a cocked hip. He surveys the street with steady eyes. The caption reads, "Strange moods fill our children."[66] Wright notes the hope of the parents in these children, who "feel the world hard enough to yearn to wrestle with it."[67] The parents worry that urban pressures claim the children before they are able to fight back. The boy in the photo, the text seems to suggest, could channel his sense of dispossession either into struggle or self-

---

62. Wright, *12 Million Black Voices*, 106.
63. Rabinowitz, *American Pulp*, 99–100.
64. Wright, *12 Million Black Voices*, 104.
65. Wright, *12 Million Black Voices*, 109.
66. Wright, *12 Million Black Voices*, 137.
67. Wright, *12 Million Black Voices*, 135.

destruction. This split, this uncertainty about the future, as I will argue later, echoes throughout the text as it develops its political outlook.

While the New Deal's sociological analytic of space reverberates through Wright's discussion, his book evinces skepticism of the government's willingness or ability to address injustice. When *12 Million Black Voices* says what "black folk want" is "what others have, the right to share in the upward march of American life," it sounds remarkably like a call from a liberal organization like the National Association for the Advancement of Colored People (NAACP), arguing that New Deal social benefits should extend to African Americans.[68] Immediately, however, this demand is met in the text's imagined dialogue with refusal by the Bosses of the Buildings and Lords of the Land. Wright condemns the Republican Party for assuming an unpaid historical debt binds African Americans to the party rather than its pursuit of policies addressing racial inequity. Wright also refuses to see African American voters' ability to serve as a "balance of power" in urban districts as hopeful. Instead, Wright invokes the "gangster-politicians" who, "once our vote has established them in the power of office, grant a free hand to the Bosses of the Buildings to proceed with a policy of dishonesty against *all* the citizens of the city."[69] Wright also notes that the soldiers who returned from World War I, proud of their service to the country, still face lynching at home: "Our black boys do not die for liberty in Flanders. They die in Texas and Georgia. Atlanta is our Marne. Brownsville, Texas is our Château-Thierry."[70]

*12 Million Black Voices* most often undercuts the New Deal through omission. However, the narrator offers more direct criticisms as well, referencing the contradictions of the Democratic Party's reliance on its Southern wing and the effects of the federalist implementation of programs:

> We hear men talk vaguely of a government in far-away Washington, a government that stands above the people and desires the welfare of all. We do not know this government; but the men it hires to execute its laws are the Lords of the Land whom we have known all our lives.[71]

The presence of New Deal documentary photography throughout the text, much of which had been used to legitimate federal intervention, ironically points out the absence of a redemptive vision of New Deal programs. Though

---

68. Wright, *12 Million Black Voices*, 146.
69. Wright, *12 Million Black Voices*, 121.
70. Wright, *12 Million Black Voices*, 88–89.
71. Wright, *12 Million Black Voices*, 48.

little in Wright's analysis departs from the focus on urban ecology in the FWP guidebooks, the book refuses federal intervention as a solution.

Instead, hope appears in the book's depiction of working-class alliances. The discussions of Harlem that Wright had authored in the FWP guidebooks pointed to communism and Black nationalism as symptoms of deleterious slum conditions, suggesting that African Americans might pursue these political visions if liberalism continued to fail them. In the New Deal guidebooks, this is a rhetorical warning, a call for governmental action. *12 Million Black Voices* concurs with this symptomology but shifts the political outlook by portraying the development of radical political consciousness as a positive development. Toward the end of the text, in a chapter titled "Men in the Making," the narrator claims that "the seasons of the plantation no longer dictate the lives of many of us; hundreds of thousands of us are moving into the sphere of conscious history."[72] With this passage, Wright suggests the ways that urban industrial conditions remake the conditions of African American political power.

Wright describes how the Bosses of the Buildings capitalize on animosity between White and Black workers, but he holds out the possibility of bridging this divide. Wright argues that racial restrictions on jobs and exclusion from trade unions encourage African American workers to break strikes. Job restrictions, he suggests, also lead to Black urban dwellers becoming beholden to "gangster-politicians" who provide services and jobs for votes.[73] The paradox, Wright notes, is that this allows the Bosses of the Buildings to create further division by suggesting to White workers that African Americans receive undue benefits from political corruption. Although the title of the chapter, and much of the discussion of labor, focuses on men, *12 Million Black Voices* also figures women essentially as workers. Captions under paired photographs suggest the link between urban space and labor as women move "from the . . . kitchenette to the white folk's kitchen."[74] Addressing the concerns of reformers about family roles, Wright notes the prevalence of women needing to work outside the home. Despite these obstacles, Wright suggests that the result of African American workers encountering White industrial workers and realizing their common situation is the development of a consciousness transcending the agrarian, race-based understandings provided by vernacular folk culture. He approvingly cites instances where Black industrial workers— whom he continues to narratively figure as men, although the section includes

---

72. Wright, *12 Million Black Voices*, 147.
73. Wright, *12 Million Black Voices*, 121.
74. Wright, *12 Million Black Voices*, 133.

THE FOLK HISTORIES OF HURSTON AND WRIGHT · 93

a photograph of women protesting lynching in front of the White House—come to stand "shoulder to shoulder" with White workers.[75]

In place of New Deal civic pluralism, then, Wright's text develops a Popular Front appeal to worker alliances, deploying familiar Marxist binaries—rural/urban, prehistory/history, unconscious/conscious. He suggests:

> In this way we encountered for the first time in our lives the full effect of those forces that tended to reshape our folk consciousness, and a few of us stepped forth and accepted within the confines of our own personalities the death of our old folk lives, an acceptance of a death that enabled us to cross class and racial lines, a death that made us free.[76]

Rejecting the "naïve, peasant rage" that Wright suggests drove the Harlem riot of 1935, the book instead makes a case for "disciplined, class-conscious groups," citing organizing around the Scottsboro case, underwritten largely by communist activism, as an example.[77] Wright's approach in *12 Million Black Voices* suggests a rereading of the New York guidebooks as more critical than they might otherwise appear. Indeed, when Alain Locke criticized the propagandistic elements of the *New York Panorama* essay on Harlem in a review in *Opportunity*, he was more likely referring to the material leading to its pessimistic conclusion, the "shades of tragic premonition," which undercut hope for a state-led racial justice.[78]

Wright's invocation of "the death of our old folk lives" as a condition of political efficacy poses the same problem the FWP encountered in its early conceptions of folk culture. It highlights the complicated status of folk culture in the book and a tension in Wright's work generally. The FWP sought to highlight folk culture as part of the contributory framework to civic pluralism, while often suggesting folkways were anachronisms that modernization would dispel. As Carla Cappetti has demonstrated, Wright simultaneously recognized the value of African American folkways but advanced a conception of progress that undercut their value.[79] Throughout *12 Million Black Voices*, a sociopolitical telos that posits agrarian folkways as useful but outmoded challenges the subtitular idea of a folk history. As byproducts of Southern Black agrarian life, folkways are ill-fitted to the modern industrial city, and their abandonment is linked with the emergence of class consciousness as a

---

75. Wright, *12 Million Black Voices*, 144.
76. Wright, *12 Million Black Voices*, 144.
77. Wright, *12 Million Black Voices*, 145.
78. Rowley, *Richard Wright*, 543, note 82.
79. Cappetti, "Sociology of an Existence," 25–43.

94 · CHAPTER 3

prerequisite for effective political action. Emergent ideological and cultural frameworks, Wright suggests, will be needed to challenge modern exploitation and develop an effective politics.

The tension in Wright's photobook points to a vexing question of how politically conscious writers should approach Black vernacular culture. Wright's 1937 essay "Blueprint for Negro Writing" condenses his ideas on the relationship between vernacular culture, modernity, and writing, and provides a partial guide to understanding his idea of a folk history. Written for *New Challenge,* the quarterly Wright edited with Dorothy West and Marian Minus, and at the peak of Wright's involvement with New York's communist literary scene, the essay marks out a view that largely aligns with *12 Million Black Voices*'s narrative framing of the folk. It rejects what Wright saw as a dominant trend in Black literature to write for a White critical audience in favor of writing to develop a revolutionary African American class consciousness. Like Langston Hughes's influential 1926 polemic "The Negro Artist and the Racial Mountain," Wright's essay sets up a dialectical understanding of folk, in which Black writers need to draw on essential folk material but also to transcend them. Both authors suggested engaging with Black vernacular expression was central to challenging White-normative aesthetics and developing new modes of literature. However, Wright's essay more closely aligns folk expression with agrarian life than Hughes's had, positing it as anachronistic in an increasingly industrialized and urbanized environment, but also inherently oppositional insofar as it developed as a response to slavery and Jim Crow, and thus useful to a complex critical understanding of racism and capitalism.

For Wright, in the absence of a shared experiential culture built around urban industrial modernity, African American folkways and religious observances remain crucial as a national experiential language. Wright had been deeply attracted to communist leader Harry Haywood's Black Belt Nation thesis, which held that African Americans would need to set terms for their own self-determination to generate a revolutionary consciousness. In "Blueprint," Wright is relatively critical of the church, which he sees as too accommodating even when it offers a means of maintaining dignity in hope. However, he points to a range of characters and ideas focused on survival and resistance in Black folk tales and song. Black writers, Wright argues, should tap into their yearning for freedom, their expression of both individual and collective will in the face of limitations on their agency. "Negro writers," he argues, "must accept the nationalist implications of their lives, not in order to encourage them but to change and transcend them."[80] He goes on to state:

---

80. Wright, *12 Million Black Voices,* 199.

> In order to depict Negro life in all its manifold and intricate relationships, a deep, informed, and complex consciousness is necessary; a consciousness which draws from its strength upon the fluid lore of a great people, and molds the lore with the concepts that move and direct the forces of history today.[81]

Folk expression, then, is of "revolutionary significance" as a kind of negative utopian critique and a shared national mode of expression.[82] In Wright's view it serves to put expressive substance and complexity on the "skeleton of society" Marxist social abstractions provided, preventing writers from rendering overly simplistic depictions of Black life.[83] Wright stresses that both critical and forward-looking literature would be necessary, preemptively deflecting an emphasis on clarity of political direction some communist reviewers would use to criticize the ending of *Native Son*.

In Wright's work, vernacular culture appears not only in depictions of religious belief and folk practice but also in the allegorical exploration of the effects of power. "The Ethics of Living Jim Crow" provides an analysis of power through autobiography, its gaps and title serving as indicators that Wright's personal history contains broader implications for understanding Black experiences. His own rereading of *Native Son* in the 1940 lecture and essay "How Bigger Was Born" similarly illustrates the way that allegory rewrites historical meaning. While the essay purports to explicate the origins of Wright's most famous character through Wright's own background and those of other individuals he knew, it actually performs more complex work, revealing *Native Son* as an allegorical response with multiple layers of historical meaning. Instead of presenting the tragedy of an individual, Wright argues, *Native Son* draws Bigger as a composite of several individuals Wright had known who had been denied conditions supporting a sense of self-value. It traces the emergence of a proto-fascist consciousness out of the racial slum's state of nowhere-being in the slum. These usages work, as "Blueprint" suggests, to offer a more developed social analysis, and in doing so, they establish a dialectical relationship that opens theoretical assertions to revision.

Folk modalities of allegory and coding also remain structurally active throughout *12 Million Black Voices*, demonstrating their power to highlight complex social dynamics and emergent political communities. They highlight African Americans' experiences with systemic racism. They maintain connections between past suffering and present inequity, presenting an opposi-

---

81. Wright, *12 Million Black Voices*, 200.
82. Wright, *12 Million Black Voices*, 199.
83. Wright, *12 Million Black Voices*, 200.

tional, countermodern understanding of history. Wright's didactic language on the Lords of the Land and Bosses of the Buildings, the eruption of dialogue in each geographical section highlighting African Americans talking back to these representatives of capitalism, and especially the abstraction of African American experiences in the South and North all point to an allegorical mapping of power. As Wright had suggested in "Blueprint," the folk offers a revealing power, one that illustrates the lived experience of racism and capitalism. Going beyond adding complex detail to a theoretical skeleton, these elements suggest that the techniques of realism cannot fully capture the experience of a people. Wright shows that working through the folk leads to a more fully realized understanding of Black life, although, as my next chapter shows, Wright left out many elements and social dynamics that did not accord with his narrative.

The book's utilization of the folk extends beyond representing social totality. It also actively shapes its negotiation of potential political communities. From its opening statement, "Each day when you see us black folk upon the dusty land of the farms or upon the hard pavement of the city streets, you usually take us for granted and think you know us, but our history is far stranger than you suspect, and we are not what we seem," *12 Million Black Voices* highlights this distinction.[84] As many critics have suggested, the text draws a line between an assumed White reader and the author and subjects of the text. The reader is told that the subjects, represented by photographs of wearied agrarian and urban Black men, are other than what they appear.[85] Wright's text reinforces this schism:

> Our outward guise still carries the old familiar aspect which three hundred years of oppression in America have given us, but beneath the garb of the black laborer, the black cook, and the black elevator operator lies an uneasily tied knot of pain and hope whose snarled strands converge from many points of time and space.[86]

The passage intentionally defamiliarizes African Americans, suggesting that they are simultaneously individuals and products of a complex history and geography rather than immediately legible objects. The narrator goes on to suggest that the hidden "knot" derives from the founding ironies of a nation built on liberalism and slavery, and crucially, the primary problem of legibility lies not with those being read about, but with the reader. This early warning

---

84. Wright, *12 Million Black Voices*, 10.
85. Wright, *12 Million Black Voices*, 10.
86. Wright, *12 Million Black Voices*, 11.

heralds the book's coded framework, its folk elements operating to restructure an understanding of national history and its vectors. The representation of this history through folk modes provides a means of making the complex knot that Wright invokes early in the narrative both visible and legible.

Where the introduction presents African American life as a tangled knot, the ending of 12 *Million Black Voices* cements the centrality of Black experience, both introducing and withholding the possibility of national community in the image of a mirror. "We black folk, our history and our present being, are a mirror of all the manifold experiences of America," Wright claims, invoking both the ways African American experience reveals American trauma and the possibility of an identification that could heal the narrative and real-world schisms between the author and the audience.[87] Indeed, the next line seems to erase the divisions between subject and reader that characterized the earlier sections of the text. Directly addressing the reader, the narrator states: "Look at us and know us and you will know yourselves, for *we* are *you*, looking back at you from the dark mirror of our lives."[88] Though it draws on an image that could be read as unifying on a national level, this is not the New Deal's civic pluralism. Wright's earliest notes show 12 *Million Black Voices* was initially conceived as a history of the nation based in "a guiding Marxist concept of the National Question" but written in "non-Marxist phraseology."[89] As Robin Lucy argues, Wright's conclusion suggests that "the Black folk, and specifically, the vestiges of Black nationalism rooted in southern experience will be assimilated in this process of *national* emancipation."[90] Wright uses Popular Front national rhetoric to advance a vision of community rooted in mutual recognition and purposive struggle.

However, Wright's emphasis on the distinction between appearance and meaning throughout the text also serves as an important caution to readers, qualifying the book's prophetic voice and asserting contingency. Instead of offering an image of immediate identification, the dark mirror image, Jeff Allred argues, establishes a dialectic of identity in which the reader and the narrator/subjects must work to find their common aims, while deferring the actuality of this identification until racial inequalities are addressed.[91] Archival drafting records reveal that the ambiguous image was inserted relatively late in the drafting process of 12 *Million Black Voices* and evolved from a "black

---

87. Wright, 12 *Million Black Voices*, 146.

88. Wright, 12 *Million Black Voices*, 146.

89. Wright Papers, "Notes," Box 63, Folder 734.

90. Lucy, "Flying Home," 264.

91. See also Allred, *American Modernism and Depression Documentary*, 165–166, for discussion of this passage.

curtain" to a "mirror" between the early and intermediate drafts, hovering between images of division and identification before Wright settled on "dark mirror."[92] These origins and particularly the shift to re-emphasize darkness suggest that this image preserves a crucial element of separation. For Whites to look into the dark mirror is to confront historical injustice directly and their own role in it. The dark mirror warns of investments in racial division that run deep, inform ideas of progress, and shape political community. For Wright, a new national community built on class consciousness organizing across racial lines remains desirable, but, as in his Harlem essays for the FWP, the potential for tragedy haunts the present.

Wright knew that the failure to address racial inequity could also derail the communist vision of political community, and his growing ambivalence about the CPUSA bled into his manuscript. The year 1941 was one of significant political transition for Wright. He would split with the CPUSA the next year over concerns that the party sidelined its racial justice efforts after its sudden reversal to full-throated support for the war after the Nazis invaded the Soviet Union in 1941.[93] Wright had run into difficulties with the CPUSA earlier, from the closing of the John Reed Clubs to distrust of his leadership in Harlem communist circles, and biographers suggest these factors also shaped a growing disillusionment by the early 1940s. Literary success gave Wright an authoritative, national voice. However, many communist critics disliked *Native Son*'s portrayal of communist characters as naïve and even harmful in matters of race, and also its pessimistic ending in which Bigger Thomas's communist lawyer fails to convince any of his audiences—the jury, the Chicago media, Bigger, even many readers—of the correctness of his analysis. As he was writing his folk history, Wright staked out more independence. Loaded images of a "red hot iron" and "strange white men" talking of revolution presented as catalysts for action in early drafts of *12 Million Black Voices* are missing from later drafts, indicating a pullback from a more direct invocation of communist agency.[94] Wright's political movement was visible to some readers. When Arna Bontemps and John T. Frederick discussed the photobook for a radio program in November 1941, Frederick noted, "The writing is very largely free of the element of special political direction which Mr. Wright's preceding book *Native Son* led me to expect."[95]

The unresolved tension between *12 Million Black Voices*'s political narrative and its folk history asserts the stickiness of race in utopian politics,

---

92. Wright Papers, Box 62, Folders 728–731.

93. Rowley, *Richard Wright*, 261; Rampersad, *Ralph Ellison*, 161.

94. Wright Papers, "Early Draft," Box 62, Folder 728.

95. Wright Papers, "Of Men and Books," *Northwestern University on the Air* 1, no. 8, 18 November 1941, Box 63, Folder 742.

whether liberal or communist. It offers hope for a new national community, while simultaneously destabilizing the certitudes of both Popular Front and New Deal visions of the future. Like the ending of *Native Son*, *12 Million Black Voices* floats the possibility of identification across racial lines toward the hope of a class-conscious modernized national community, but the photobook suggests that, if warnings went unheeded, race would prove the rocks on which that community would again founder. Any attempt to reorganize society, Wright suggests, would have to grapple with the way that racial meaning was encoded in culture, in space, in history itself. In a move characteristic of many other Black writers of this era, Wright expresses a profound caution and ambivalence about political teleology. Wright anticipates the critique of the "cult of reason," the tendency toward positivist political analysis, and the development of "contingent thinking" that Alan Wald identifies as common to modernist literary and intellectual projects after World War II.[96]

## Conclusion

Though Hurston and Wright disagreed about politics and culture, they both found folk modalities useful as a way of making thorny political problems legible as they dissented from New Deal liberal narratives of national community. *12 Million Black Voices* and *Moses, Man of the Mountain* rework national myths to generate analyses of power that highlight complex personal and racial interests. The tensions in these texts between appearance and meaning, between the tale and the mode of its telling lead to ambivalent and contingent assessments of national community.

Other New Deal intertexts in both documentary and fiction would also confront the problem of how to represent African American culture and geography as they imagined possible political futures and pointed to the ways that race haunts the ongoing construction of modernity. *12 Million Black Voices* was just one of several documentary intertexts of the FWP. Indeed, the 1940s saw a bumper crop of guides to Black America. As my next chapter shows, these projects not only reused typical New Deal forms but also directly redeployed unpublished FWP materials on African American history and culture to advance understandings of liberalism as an incomplete project rather than a fundamentally compromised one. Many of these projects reached an accommodation with welfare state liberalism that Wright and Hurston could not embrace. But they also offered prescient warnings about the consequences of liberalism's failure to address its racial underpinnings.

---

96. Wald, *American Night*, 84–85.

CHAPTER 4

# They Seek a City

*The Future of African America in
FWP Social Histories and Intertexts*

In the politically unstable atmosphere of the late New Deal, the FWP sub-units that Sterling Brown and Morton Royse tasked with producing social and historical studies of ethnic and racial groups emerged as some of the most interesting FWP projects. These projects linked the politics of cultural and historical representation to visions of modernity in their representation of social groups. Like the guidebooks, they develop understandings of time, space, and culture that align the social groups they study with the modern nation. In this regard, they all accept and advance civic pluralism. However, these texts also challenge the basis, trajectory, and certainty of New Deal modernization by asserting alternative communal and political futures. Consider the quixotic vision of New York City's Yiddish Writers Group (YWG) FWP subunit, which managed to publish two books in Yiddish, a language that FWP national editors could not effectively edit.[1] In place of the FWP's narrative of modernization through development, the YWG books assert the spiritual persistence of Yiddishkeit through *landsmanschaften,* or hometown organizations, and family circles, organizations that were soon to be eclipsed by linguistic, cultural, and demographic shifts. This departure highlights the need to understand

---

1. FWP, *Yiddish Families and Family Circles in New York; Yiddish Landmanschaften of New York.* The two books were later abridged and combined for an English language manuscript, which was cancelled but later edited by Hannah Kliger and published as FWP, *Jewish Hometown Associations and Family Circles in New York.*

the documentary texts by FWP subunits as more than merely reflections of broader FWP priorities, but as documentary interventions in their own right, entering into emerging sociopolitical circumstances.

FWP subunits provided opportunities for African Americans to rewrite their own local and national stories, while highlighting rifts between liberalism's promise and its record of racial inequity. In addition to advising on production of the FWP state guidebooks, Sterling Brown envisioned several studies, mostly unpublished, in key areas focusing on African American life.[2] These studies explore several key concerns: How could the complexity of Black culture best be communicated? What elements of culture have been rendered visible or invisible, privileged or deprivileged in the framework of national community? What would be the status and role of vernacular culture in a modern society? What effects would modernization have on Black communities? They also raise a corollary question: could the welfare state counter the embedded elements of racism in liberalism's own history, or was it too compromised, even dependent on them, to offer effective resolutions? Their concerns about culture, national community, and modernity put these projects squarely in conversation with African American literature in wartime and the postwar era.

The FWP subunits left behind valuable unpublished research and draft materials, from which a number of writers generated their own documentary studies of Black America.[3] These documentary intertexts typically figure in scholarship as historical footnotes, dated by their situation between the New Deal and the Civil Rights era, and neither academic enough to be considered alongside texts like *American Dilemma* or *Black Metropolis* nor literary enough to stand with books like *Native Son* or *Their Eyes Were Watching God.*

---

2. See Sklaroff, *Black Culture and the New Deal*, 81–121, for a discussion of Brown's role and his plans for FWP work on African Americans. During the existence of the FWP and its state affiliates the Illinois FWP unit's *Cavalcade of the American Negro*, *The Negro in Virginia*, and *Drums and Shadows* were the only book-length studies published, although Sklaroff, 107, also notes that the *New Orleans City Guide* was also seen as an effective representation of Black culture there. The manuscripts that have since been published include: *The Florida Negro*, *The Negro in Illinois*, *The Negro in New York*, and *The WPA History of the Negro in Pittsburgh*.

3. These intertexts include Bontemps and Conroy, *They Seek a City*; McKay, *Harlem: Negro Metropolis*; Ottley, *New World A-Coming*; Moon, *Balance of Power*; Wright, *12 Million Black Voices*. With an understanding of intertext that focuses on the conversation about Black America rather than authorial affiliation with the FWP and postdated publication, other texts might also be included. For example, Cayton and Drake, *Black Metropolis*, began as a WPA project, though not an FWP one. Hurston's *Mules and Men* predates her FWP tenure. While neither Ann Petry nor Gwendolyn Brooks were FWP employees, their essays for *Holiday* magazine about Harlem and Bronzeville, respectively, cover similar territory to the intertexts here. Petry's essay is discussed in the next chapter. Similarly, the White writer Bucklin Moon's *Primer for White Folks* and, of course, Gunnar Myrdal's *American Dilemma* might also be included.

102 · CHAPTER 4

Of these, only Wright's *12 Million Black Voices* has received much attention as a literary text, largely because of Wright's prominence and the formal complexity detailed in the last chapter. However, these intertexts participate in the dynamics of postwar African American literature and should be understood as a fundamental part of it. In particular, they offer interpretations of African American folk and working-class vernacular phenomena and connect these to inclusive political visions, participating in a dynamic Kenneth Warren sees as central to the larger African American literary project of this era.[4] These texts also participate in the postwar revaluation of African American urban space, often advancing the sociological account of urban pathology that informed the New Deal, though the origins of these texts often mean that they highlight a social and political diversity missed in the psychological dramas of urban realist novels. They also signify a sustained African American presence in the documentary aesthetic engaged with other forms of literary modernism.[5] Building on these elements, these texts create countermodern visions for the reading public, leveraging crucial critiques of the welfare state even while many largely accepted its terms.

This chapter traces the trajectories of two of these subunits, one in New York City and another in Chicago, focusing on the ways that the FWP manuscripts and their wartime intertexts engage with the New Deal. Though neither *The Negro in New York* nor *The Negro in Illinois* was published during the New Deal, both manuscripts advance Black cultural vitality, persistence, and connection. Both also offer an insightful understanding of slum dynamics without wholly subscribing to the New Deal modernization narrative. Additionally, they place an emphasis on employment and civil rights that sets them apart from the FWP guidebooks' planning and development panacea. The most direct documentary descendants of these FWP subunits were Roi Ottley's 1943 survey of African American life, *New World A-Coming*, and Arna Bontemps and Jack Conroy's 1945 study of Black migration, *They Seek a City,* which reworked the New York and Illinois manuscripts, respectively. These two intertexts largely reflect the framing of civic pluralism and the potentially beneficial power of the robust state. In doing so, they accept the terms of New Deal liberalism to a much greater extent than either Wright or Hurston. These intertexts rhetorically position the New Deal as an incomplete project and warn of emergent nationalist undercurrents, suggesting that the government

---

4. Warren, *What Was African American Literature?*, 19–27.

5. The idea of the documentary aesthetic was elaborated in Stott's *Documentary Expression and Thirties America*. Other significant studies of Depression and wartime documentary culture include Allred, *American Modernism and Depression Documentary*; Foley, *Telling the Truth*; Rabinowitz, *They Must Be Represented*.

must step up its approach to racial equity in the wartime context or face the collapse of liberalism.[6]

## *The Negro In New York*

Writers for New York's FWP Negro History Unit investigated the history, institutions, and culture of Black New York. These writers included Ralph Ellison, Claude McKay, Henry Lee Moon, Roi Ottley, Ted Poston, Joel A. Rogers, Ellen Tarry, Dorothy West, and Richard Wright, among others.[7] Their work shaped the guidebooks, as earlier chapters have shown, but their primary aim was developing a sociohistorical study originally titled *Life Ain't Been No Crystal Stair: An Informal History of Negroes in New York,* but it eventually assumed the more authoritative title *The Negro in New York: An Informal Social History, 1626–1940.* The unit's work began under Claude McKay's stewardship and during that time developed a wealth of research and draft materials.[8] McKay and Lewis Bryan reported on theater. Ralph Ellison collected quotes on antislavery movements. The song and folklore collector Lawrence Gellert collected material on folk idioms and Haiti. McKay was offered a position with the Creative Writers subgroup in early 1938, allowing him to work on his own material, which included his own 1940 study *Harlem: Negro Metropolis* and the recently published novel *Amiable with Big Teeth.*

Wright was considered for the directorship. He had handled the revision of material for the guidebooks capably, but a November 1938 memo from NYC FWP director Harold Strauss to Alsberg suggests that Wright was unable to handle the "pictorial aspects of Harlem."[9] The FWP archives do not reveal

---

6. Elements of this analysis of Ottley have also been published in Butts, "New World A-Coming." My argument also draws from discussions of *New World A-Coming* and *They Seek A City,* which will appear in Butts, "New Deal Discourses." That chapter also focuses on Henry Lee Moon's *Balance of Power.*

7. Other names that appear in the Schomburg archives of the FWP Negro History Unit include: Alyse Abrams, Wilfred R. Bain, Everett Beanne, Waring Cuney, Wesley Curtwright, Norie Frazier, Sydney H. French, Arthur J. Gary, Sadie Hall, Odette Harper, Lawrence Gellert, Abram Hill, Oakley Johnson, Richard J. Latimer, Mary McFadden, S. Michelson, Vivian Norris, Richard Bruce Nugent, Carl Offord, Harold Robinson, Claire Spitz, Lila Valde/Vaida, Simon Williamson, Ted Yates, and Wilbur Young.

8. The initial title appears in drafts in the FWP Negro Group Papers at Yale. Other collections of these draft materials and administrative records survive in New York City's Municipal Archives, the New York Public Library's Schomburg Center, the Richard Wright Papers at Yale University, and the National Archives in College Park, MD, as well as in archival holdings of some of the FWP authors.

9. NARA RG69, Letter, Harold Strauss to Henry Alsberg, 25 November 1938. Reports and Misc. Record Pertaining to Negro Studies, 1936–1940, Box 1, Incoming Letters.

104 · CHAPTER 4

why, but it is possible that Wright's relative newcomer status or his tendency to focus on politically telling cultural elements and events put him at odds with a project that had developed a wealth of material that would not easily fit a sociological narrative. Wright had likely also signaled that he preferred to work on his own material, and his literary successes bolstered his decision. Moon, another capable writer, and future editor of the NAACP's *Crisis* informally took on the job of managing the unit for a time, but he was eyeing a move to work with Robert Weaver in Washington where he thought he could help more directly in ensuring New Deal housing resources went to African Americans.[10] Eventually, another journalist, a canny New Yorker named Vincent Lushington "Roi" Ottley, took the position and guided the manuscript draft into publishable form.

Ottley is perhaps the least-known author featured in this book among literary scholars. However, he had a long and distinguished career in journalism. Born in Harlem to Grenadan immigrants, Ottley first attended Saint Bonaventure's College and then studied journalism at the University of Michigan. He worked for the *Amsterdam News* in the 1930s, alongside Moon and Poston, who would become famous as an investigative reporter during the Civil Rights era. Ottley's journalistic experience helped him secure a position with the FWP in New York City in 1937 after retaliation for their role in a 1935–1936 strike at the *Amsterdam News* threw the considerable talents of the three journalists onto the relief rolls. Many of the archival manuscripts for the project list their names as either reporters or editors. During and after World War II, Ottley worked as a war correspondent for the *Pittsburgh Courier,* another major African American newspaper, and the Left-liberal daily *PM.* Later, he joined the staff at the *Chicago Tribune.*[11] He only published one novel, *White Marble Lady* (1965), which focused on an interracial relationship. However, he made his mark with nonfiction books focusing on African diaspora society and culture in the US and Europe, including *New World A-Coming* in 1943, *Black Odyssey: The Story of the Negro in America* in 1948, and *No Green Pastures* in 1951.

Ottley's tenure as director saw significant changes to the manuscript. In 1938, the material completed under McKay's watch was sent to the national office with a split recommendation. Charles Cumberbatch, a project editor

---

10. A sequence of letters in the Moon Papers between Henry Lee Moon and Sterling Brown from September 1937 to January 1938 suggests that both Moon and Wright were being considered as editors for the NYC subgroup, but Brown wanted Moon to work with him in the FWP national office, and Alsberg wanted Wright for a job heading the local Washington, DC, FWP unit.

11. See Ottley, *Roi Ottley's World War II,* for coverage of Ottley's wartime reportage.

who edited many of the early materials, saw it as complete, with needing only a rewriting of the materials into a whole, and indicated that Richard Wright should be hired for that purpose. NYC Project Supervisor Stephen Naft thought the project "still very far from completion" and, despite a fairly impressive roster, argued for the need for more capable writers, suggesting that Ottley was the only writer who was "more than an average newspaperman."[12] From 1938 to 1940, the manuscript was heavily revised, bringing the various draft materials into alignment and shifting the structure from one that resembled the essays sections that headed the American Guides to a more historical overview.

This FWP subunit was beset with the same tensions between communist factions and between communists and noncommunists that shaped the New York City office politics generally.[13] Former FWP writer Baxter P. Leach floated rumors that the impact of the 1938 transition from the anticommunist McKay to Ottley would be a rewriting of the material with a "revolutionary slant."[14] While the book does take note of various kinds of radical politics shaping Black life and culture, it does not bear Leach's charge out. Nor do the drafts suggest a move toward a communist rewriting of history. In fact, Ottley's tendency to shift with the prevailing political winds often left other writers suspicious of him. Ottley ran a course from interest in communism during the 1930s to progressive liberal positions during and after World War II and eventually toward conservatism during the Cold War. Ralph Ellison saw him as opportunistic and politically unsophisticated, suggesting in a letter to Richard Wight in 1945 that he was surprised to find Ottley "show[ing] signs of an awakening awareness that there was a world beyond the bar, the bed, and the table."[15] This assessment is somewhat unfair. Ottley had established himself as a political commentator with *New World A-Coming* and in his war correspondence, but Ellison's charge reflects the political and, sometimes, personal tension between Ottley and other writers of his generation.

The version of *The Negro in New York* published by the Schomburg Library and Praeger Publishers in 1967 presents Black New York as a development of geography and racial politics leading to a complex social environment.

---

12. USWPA, "Statement of Stephen Naft Concerning the Book of the Negroes, 12 April 1938, Box A753, Social Ethnic Studies Folder: New York City, Negro, "The Negroes of New York."

13. See Mangione, *Dream and the Deal*, 155–190, and Bold, *WPA Guides*, 92–122, on communism on the NYC unit.

14. Baxter P. Leach, *New York Age*, 8 October 1938, 3.

15. Ellison, *Selected Letters of Ralph Ellison*, 197. Ellison also mentions a previous betrayal of Wright by Ottley, but the referent is unclear. Generally, Ellison's letters and interviews indicate that he did not think much of Ottley, and Ottley was fairly critical of Ellison's work as well.

Like many books of the time, it recognizes other neighborhoods but focuses heavily on Harlem. Its history of Black settlement in the city depicts socioeconomic geographic struggle intensified by race. After tracing the history of Black neighborhoods in upper Manhattan, it highlights the real estate wars between the Afro-American Realty Company and the Harlem Property Owner's Improvement Association, which had been organized to keep Black citizens from buying in the neighborhood. *The Negro in New York* study definitively splits from earlier histories in tracing the development of Harlem through the Depression downturn, which enables an assessment of the effects of both Depression decay and New Deal reforms.

Notably, the discussion of Harlem focuses less on racial conflict than on intragroup diversity within the neighborhood, even to a greater extent than the essay on Harlem in the *WPA Guide to New York City* had done. *The Negro in New York* reminds readers of the complex social identities hidden by race. It highlights the presence of Haitian, French Caribbean, and British West Indian immigrants, as well as Puerto Ricans, while illuminating the "Harlem Prejudice" of African Americans against West Indian immigrants. At the same time, it suggests that the West Indian immigrants have contributed culturally to the neighborhood, particularly to cuisine and music. Subtly dispelling interethnic tensions, one particularly interesting section attempts to draw connections between African Americans and Jews by noting the similarity between Black social clubs and Jewish *landsmanschaften*. This connection suggests that interaction among FWP staff generated recognition of commonalities among urban social groups and reinforces the civic pluralist vision of shared community.

Like the FWP guidebooks, *The Negro in New York* justifies liberal policies at the national and local level, yet the study differs from the New York guidebooks in that it portrays these policies as essentially reactive to pressure rather than as proactively planned interventions. The book notes the conditions arising from the Depression that Harlemites face: retreat back to tenement houses, reduction of work opportunities, increased crime. The section that deals with the early response to the Depression is titled ". . . While Rome Burns," suggesting the failure of "Federal, State and City administrations" to address Depression conditions in Harlem.[16] It highlights corruption in Mayor Jimmy Walker's administration, while citing the elections of Franklin Roosevelt and Fiorello La Guardia as a "vital" shift.[17] The text cites the March 1935 riot as an expression of anger in Harlem with "deep roots" that sparked atten-

---

16. FWP, *Negro in New York*, 274.
17. FWP, *Negro in New York*, 275.

tion from City Hall in the form of the Mayor's Commission on Conditions in Harlem.[18] The book credits the Federal Arts projects with taking the place of White philanthropy as the latter dried up during the Depression.[19] However, with this notable exception, the study suggests that reform initiatives generally respond to escalating conflicts rather than proactively creating social equity. Unlike the FWP guidebook, *The Negro in New York* does not credit public housing programs with a central role in reform.

While diverging from the New Deal interventionist ethos, *The Negro in New York* remains optimistic about the possibility of social justice. The concluding words of the study highlight key African American contributions, reinforcing their centrality in a participatory national frame:

> And so for more than three centuries, the record reveals, the Negro has struggled for integration into this community. During those years he has bequeathed song, dance, and laughter to a grim and busy new world society. His sweat has been mixed with the steel, brick, and mortar of this great city. American laws, customs, traditions, and institutions, as they are known today have been shaped with an awareness of the Negro's presence. It is therefore impossible to stand on the sidelines and ignore Negro life, so inextricably is it tied up with that of the city and the nation.[20]

Linking the fate of the nation and African Americans, the book nevertheless ends on a positive note. Eschewing *New York Panorama*'s warning tone, *The Negro in New York* exclaims: "Throughout his long American history, the Negro's faith has been in the ultimate triumph of democracy. At no time has this goal been as visible as it is today."[21] This certainty of justice, so typical of New Deal futurism, would be notably absent in many later texts about Black neighborhoods. However, it is important to recognize the rhetorical deferral of justice to a near future point without specifying an agent or method.

In his memoir of the project, Jerre Mangione noted that "Ottley's relationship to the thirty-five manuscript boxes that constituted the New York Project's effort in Black studies is a curious one."[22] Mangione, who wanted to tell the story of the FWP as a groundbreaking endeavor, refrained from fully detailing the odd fate of the manuscript. Ottley's stewardship of the project

---

18. FWP, *Negro in New York*, 280.

19. Hutchinson, *Harlem Renaissance in Black and White*, 23, contests the idea of a drought of White patronage in the 1930s.

20. FWP, *Negro in New York*, 293.

21. FWP, *Negro in New York*, 293.

22. Mangione, *Dream and the Deal*, 261.

108 · CHAPTER 4

was marred by an embarrassing plagiarism incident that delayed production. The catalyst for this event was Helen Boardman, a White NAACP member who was a sharp-eyed FWP editor. Boardman had already caused some tensions in the FWP group. Her attempt to join the communist-backed FWP Negro Authors' Guild in 1937 had been resisted by McKay, Ted Yates, and Ellen Tarry on the grounds that despite a CPUSA emphasis on integrated organizing, Black writers needed organizations of their own.[23] Letters among national editors also reveal tensions between Boardman and Ottley in 1938 over materials the New York unit had gathered. Boardman wanted to use these for a study titled "Negro Influence on American History" and complained that Ottley had been keeping the research and drafts at home, making access inconvenient.[24] Ottley sent a memo to NYC director Frederick Clayton in January of 1940 stating that the manuscript was ready after having been reviewed by a list of notable figures: Sterling Brown, prominent attorney Hubert Delany, folklorist Arthur Fauset, Abyssinian Baptist Church pastor Adam Clayton Powell Jr., historian and director of a FWP former slave interview project Laurence Reddick, NAACP head Walter White, and Richard Wright.[25] This is an impressive list, ostensibly representing the approval of a wide range of public intellectuals and activists who would have had a great deal of familiarity with African Americans, both in life and in print. However, when Boardman reviewed the manuscript of *The Negro In New York* in April, she discovered a number of unattributed quotes and paraphrase as well as structural similarities to other books. She alerted the national editors. An unsigned report states:

> We urge that more care be taken in the matter of quotation. We have discovered many passages uncomfortably close to some in James Weldon Johnson's *Black Manhattan* and *The Autobiography of an Ex-Colored Man,* and Sterling Brown's *Negro Poetry and Drama.* These passages, however, are not enclosed in quotation marks and are not properly attributed. We urge that the manuscript be scrutinized lest it be accused of not giving credit where it is due and of resembling too closely other works (many of them well known).[26]

---

23. Cooper, *Claude McKay,* 323–324.

24. United States Works Projects Administration Records, New York Guide Correspondence Memo, Stephen Naft to James Magraw, "Helen Boardman's Sub-Project," 31 October 1938, Library of Congress; United States Works Projects Administration Records, New York Guide Correspondence, Letter, James Magraw to Roi Ottley, 3 November 1938, Library of Congress.

25. FWP MACNY, Memo, Ottley to Clayton, 4 January 1940, Series 51: *Negroes of New York,* Roll 263.

26. Ellison Papers, "Editorial Report on State Copy," 25 April 1940, Box 21, Folder 1. This letter is also available in the FWP MACNY files, Series 51: *Negroes of New York,* Roll 263.

FWP records from April of 1940 reveal a flurry of communications among various local and national editors and Ottley over the plagiarism incident as they determined how to address it. Ottley remained the editor of the project in the meantime, but by August, he was complaining in a memo that he had been left out of editing decisions by a "high handed and arbitrary attitude."[27] Ralph Ellison, who had established a reputation for diligence and diplomacy, was called in to make corrections chapter by chapter, likely fueling the conflict with Ottley.[28]

A close reading of *The Negro in New York* material reveals that Boardman was correct in her assessment, though mitigating circumstances exist. The historical and geographical frameworks of *Black Manhattan* and *The Negro in New York* prior to the material on the Depression and New Deal in the FWP text are nearly identical. Much of the exposition is similar in particular passages, and some wording is nearly identical. For example: Johnson writes of Booker T. Washington's Atlanta Exposition speech: "By his Atlanta speech he had at a stroke gained the sanction and support of both the South and the North—the South, in general, construing the speech to imply the Negro's abdication of his claim to full and equal citizenship rights and his acceptance of the status of a contented and industrious peasantry."[29] Here is the corresponding FWP passage: "The South in general construed the speech as Negro abdication from claim to equal citizenship rights. For its conciliatory aspects indicated the black race's willingness to accept the status of contented and industrious peasants." Similar problems occur in passages about Fraunces Tavern, boxer Tom Molineaux, and Marcus Garvey, among others.

Why did no one catch this problem sooner? The FWP's process relied on many writers culling secondary and primary sources, and the subunit's editorial staff may have never recognized the extent of the similarities as they compiled their source material. Perhaps Boardman's earlier feuds with McKay and Ottley gave her a more critical perspective than other editors. It is difficult to trace lines directly from the notes gathered by individual project staff through the final manuscript, in part because of the thorough reorganization of the draft materials. Oddly, Johnson had served as a consultant for the FWP,

---

27. FWP MACNY, Memo from Roi Ottley to Frederick Clayton, 16 August 1940, Series 51: *Negroes of New York*, Roll 263.

28. FWP MACNY, Letter from Ralph Ellison to Sumner Smith, 22 April 1940, Series 51: *Negroes of New York*, Roll 263, indicates Ellison's role as the manuscript's fixer. Manuscript drafts with and without Ellison's corrections can be found in the Ellison Papers, Box 21. The continuance of these examples in the version of *The Negro in New York* published in the 1960s suggests that either Ellison's corrections were incomplete or were not included in the material Ottley turned over to the Schomburg Library.

29. Johnson, *Black Manhattan*, 131.

110 · CHAPTER 4

and perhaps he knew about these similarities. Borrowing and reference have long been central to African American literature as a means of preserving records and acknowledging influences, and maybe he saw it as a tribute to his authority. More likely, though, this may indicate that the plagiarism occurred in rewriting after Johnson's death in 1938, which would put responsibility more squarely on Ottley's shoulders. Whatever the origins of the plagiarism, the potential for public embarrassment was clear. As the editor and a journalist, Ottley had the responsibility to make certain the FWP book met ethical standards.

For the manuscript, the delay was fatal. Investigations by congressional subcommittees and wartime prioritization reduced FWP staffing. From December 1940 through 1941, the New York office tried various publishers but could not get any of them to commit to the manuscript without subvention.[30] Racial biases in the publishing industry likely played a part too, though FWP officials had indicated they believed the book would be timely. Naft notes that historian Carter G. Woodson had told Boardman that "during the last three years the interest for books on the Negro has risen considerably" and that "the whites are buying more such books than the Negroes."[31] The Book-of-the-Month Club success of Wright's *Native Son* also suggests a public appetite for books on African Americans at the time. However, publishing was not in the cards for the FWP manuscript. Due to budgetary and reorganizational fallout from the congressional hearings, the FWP shuttered many of the remaining projects. Ottley was let go along with several other employees.[32] He transferred some of the material from the subunit to the Schomburg Library in 1940, and project records indicate the New York office transferred other material there in 1942. At the Schomburg, they served researchers on several important postwar studies, notably historian Gilbert Osofsky's *Harlem: The Making of a Ghetto*.[33] In 1967 the Schomburg published the archived materials as *The Negro in New York: An Informal Social History, 1626–1940*, naming Ottley (posthumously) and Civil Rights journalism mainstay William J. Weatherby as its editors. Ironically, the FWP's demise would turn out to be Ottley's big break.

---

30. FWP MACNY, Series 51: *Negroes of New York,* Roll 263.

31. United States Works Projects Administration Records, "Statement of Stephen Naft Concerning the Book of the Negroes, 12 April 1938, Box A753, Social Ethnic Studies Folder: New York City, Negro, "The Negroes of New York."

32. Rampersad, *Ralph Ellison,* 116.

33. FWP, *Negro in New York,* viii.

## New World A-Coming

Following the collapse of the project, Ottley made two consequential, if ethically questionable, decisions. First, rather than turning over his subunit's project materials to the federal office, he decided to handle their dispensation himself. Ralph Ellison remembered that he understood Ottley had "the consent of [FWP NYC director] James Magraw."[34] On top of his sense of grievance from the plagiarism affair, other factors may have made Ottley question the materials' security in federal hands. Racial overtones in attacks on Federal One poisoned the political climate. Also, the resulting defunding of the FWP projects created chaos, and editors scrambled to find publishers for the remaining manuscripts. The National Archives Establishment, which now houses many of the FWP records, was new in 1940, its purview and permanence still uncertain. The Schomburg had, by contrast, an excellent and growing reputation as an archive of Black American history and would have presented an alternative that looked both reliable and responsible.

Ottley's second decision is perhaps best characterized as doubling down on the boondoggle. He used the FWP material to develop his own study of Harlem and published it in 1943 as *New World A-Coming*, which brought him celebrity as a public guide to African American life. Wright's *Native Son* and the work of the Julius Rosenwald Fund had helped to place sociological material about African Americans squarely in the public eye. Building on this momentum, Houghton Mifflin published *New World A-Coming* in its *Life in America,* Prize series. The book invites the reader, using the first-person plural, "to get a first-hand view of the intimate pattern of life in Black America," and it figured in between *Native Son* and *American Dilemma* as one of the most important books on Black America during the 1940s.[35] Its best-seller status earned it a place in other popular media as well. Inspired by the book, pianist Duke Ellington composed a song named after it in 1943, which in turn became the theme for a weekly eponymous radio program on WMCA in 1944 and 1945. The radio program's themes and content shifted in response to the needs of wartime and recovery, extending Ottley's material and his method of simultaneously highlighting injustices, foregrounding dissent, and asserting patriotism.[36]

Like its FWP predecessor, *New World A-Coming* provides an expansive and diverse portrait of African American urban life. Ottley did little to acknowledge the book's links to the FWP. As governmental documents, the materials

---

34. Mangione Papers, Interview with Ralph Ellison, 30 June 1969.

35. Ottley, *New World A-Coming,* 3.

36. Many of the radio plays for this program are archived in the Schomburg Library.

were not subject to copyright, which resolved any legal problem, though not the ethical one. Ottley's foreword contains a somewhat mystifying reference to "a number of people, who contributed to this work in a variety of ways," and the FWP project is referenced in the bibliography.[37] This deeply understates Ottley's debt to the FWP and to his staff who worked hours upon hours to pull together the material. Offering an understated critique of both Ottley's project management and his actions, Ellen Tarry wrote, "Even at the end of my work [at the FWP] I was not aware of the overall plan. Though we were aware that much of the same background was part of Roi Ottley's book."[38] Ellison told Jerre Mangione that he was "not too proud of the interpretations" in Ottley's book and that a group of FWP writers wanted to confront Ottley but decided against it.[39]

*New World A-Coming* departs substantially from its FWP source in its scope, method, and in its aims. Ottley primarily borrowed from the final two chapters of the FWP manuscript, the ones least indebted to Johnson and the ones that most frequently deployed an anecdotal method that Ottley found useful for his own project. With these anecdotes, the book addresses a broad range of contemporary Harlem social and cultural activities, contesting oversimplified understandings of Black urban experience. *New World-A Coming* asserts African Americans' belief in liberal democratic principles, while focusing on the need for national leadership in resolving economic inequality.

Indeed, the desire to assert both complexity and unity sets up a crucial tension within the book between sociological naturalism and an attention to the particularity of Harlem culture. The introduction prefigures the theme of frustrated democratic yearnings by expanding on the common idea of Harlem as "the capital of black America."[40] Here, the naturalist focus on ecology is in evidence. Reading like a statement of Zola-esque naturalism, Ottley's foreword suggests that "Harlem, the most complex of Negro communities, is used as a sort of test tube in which the germs of Negro thought and action are isolated, examined, and held up to full glare to reflect Black America."[41] Ottley goes on to claim, "By and large, I am concerned with the mass, not individuals," and continues, "Although the book is built on personalities, they are used only in

---

37. Ottley, *New World A-Coming*, vi.

38. FWP, *Negro in New York*, 10.

39. Mangione Papers, Interview with Ralph Ellison. In one telling moment in the interview with Mangione, Ellison alludes to Pig Foot Mary, who had seized an entrepreneurial opportunity in selling pigs feet to black Harlemites from the South. Ellison suggests he saw it instead as an "American success story," but notes Ottley's tendency to view such situations humorously, as a kind of light picturesque, and thereby miss their significance.

40. Ottley, *New World A-Coming*, 1.

41. Ottley, *New World A-Coming*, v.

so far as they reveal the influence of broad social factors."[42] From a reading of the foreword, a reader might well assume that they were going to encounter a social protest novel in the mold of *Native Son*.

Like these novels, *New World A-Coming* explores the way that race becomes a primary shaping force in struggles over space determining the "pattern of life in Black America."[43] After a brief history of Black New York that glosses the details of *Black Manhattan* and *The Negro in New York*, Ottley also highlights the racial property wars over Harlem. He extends the focus on race and space by noting the influence of large-scale development interests over the outcome. The book reveals that a settlement for the displacement of a Black church for the Pennsylvania Railroad's new midtown station secured several multifamily buildings on 135th Street for Black residents, which became the anchor for the emerging Harlem community.[44] Like the account of the Harlem real estate wars, this places an emphasis on Black activities, while highlighting social forces shaping the outcome. Ottley attributes many problems to the environmental conditions of Harlem. His chapter "The Slum-Shocked" begins with an account of the 1935 riot. Ottley notes the careful, "almost studied," targeting of White-owned businesses for looting and suggests that the uprising resulted from overcrowding caused by barriers to expansion that stimulated conditions of poverty and squalor in Harlem.[45]

However, Ottley's strategy has as much in common with Walt Whitman as it does with Wright. Wright's books are tightly controlled experiments; *New World A-Coming* by contrast resembles a laboratory in which the curiosities and oddities run amok. Ottley notes that his book "is a reporter's job relating the Negro's search for democracy. . . . Sometimes in the journey, we are led into curious, entertaining, and often bizarre corners."[46] Aided by the masses of material collected under the FWP, Ottley seems to have fallen in love with the life histories of Harlem's oddest citizens: charlatans and religious leaders, millionaires and street people. Ottley claims that Harlem evinces many extremes: squalor and beauty, celebration and anger, urban and folk culture. He noted that "[Harlem] is at once the capital of clowns, cults, and cabarets, and the cultural and intellectual hub of the Negro world. By turns Harlem is provincial, worldly, cosmopolitan, and naïve—sometimes cynical."[47] The book attempts to create legibility for this assembly, slotting the disparate ensemble

---

42. Ottley, *New World A-Coming*, v.
43. Ottley, *New World A-Coming*, 3.
44. Ottley, *New World A-Coming*, 32–33.
45. Ottley, *New World A-Coming*, 152.
46. Ottley, *New World A-Coming*, v.
47. Ottley, *New World A-Coming*, 1.

into a cast of characters with form and function. The balancing act between complexity and unity is a difficult one, and Ottley often has to editorialize to reel in his expanding frame.

*New World A-Coming* conducts its examination of multicultural Harlem over several chapters. The first of these chapters asks rhetorically "How Colored Is Harlem?" and answers by detailing the heterogeneity of the population while simultaneously claiming that the actual intermixing of groups and political expediency have created tight social bonds. Besides the African Americans, Ottley lists the various groups from Africa and the West Indies. Like the FWP study, Ottley focuses on the Ethiopian antifascist struggle and conflicts between West Indians and African Americans. He suggests that the latter was gradually being resolved as the two groups recognized their common position in American racial hierarchy. Ottley also takes note of the other Harlem ethnic groups: Puerto Ricans, Mexicans, and "Asiatics," highlighting their racial bind between Black and White. The chapter also offers a comparative focus on the Asian Americans between East Coast and West Coast racial relations in the wartime context. Ottley, however, defers most of his discussion of Japanese Americans until a later chapter.

The account of Harlem culture elides the Harlem Renaissance focus on fine arts in favor of evolving popular entertainments and religious expression. The reader finds very little discussion of Harlem's painters, writers, sculptors, and thespians as individuals. Instead, the text classifies them as part of a café society—a temporary group outside the petit bourgeoisie, middle class, and working class that mixes easily with Whites. Ottley views this group as an essential and unique part of the Harlem social landscape, but the absence of a more developed account reflects a devaluation of culturalism in favor of struggles over jobs, housing, and services.[48]

While he downplays the bohemian culture of the Renaissance, Ottley is more interested in the vernacular and mass cultural forms shaping everyday life in Harlem. The book figures popular entertainment as central to the majority of Harlem citizen's lives and their experience of race relations. Ottley dedicates a chapter to "Joe Louis and his people," crediting the prizefighter with restoring a faith in the American promise of opportunity and spurring a reinvestigation of African American sports history. The book discusses various aspects of Harlem's nightclubs, particularly their racial dynamics of inclusion and exclusion. In the section on the 1920s titled "Springtime in Harlem," Ottley singles out the all-White Cotton Club as an example of these dynamics.

---

48. See Foley, *Spectres of 1919,* for a discussion of many African American intellectuals' turn toward a culturalist strategy during the Harlem Renaissance.

He also discusses the troubles that mixed race couples faced when going out to clubs that cater to exclusively White or exclusively Black clientele. Overall, the book suggests that Harlem nightlife both stimulates and reflects citywide trends.[49]

Despite this openness to popular culture, Ottley at times adopts Wright's anachronistic view of folkways. He suggests that the Great Migration "was in fact a flight from a feudal to a modern way of life."[50] *New World A-Coming*'s analysis of religion also initially seems similar to that of *12 Million Black Voices.* Ottley suggests religious organizations meet a hunger for culture and community. However, Ottley contextualizes this hunger in the absence of an inclusive public sphere. He suggests that the church "will never completely lose its place in the Negro's life so long as the race is discriminated against. For, within its portals, Negroes find entertainment, culture, and self-expression as well as political guidance and spiritual nourishment."[51] Like Wright then, Ottley presents religious movements as largely compensatory, but he also leaves room for their role as vectors of political power both problematic and useful.

Ottley's portrayal of religion exceeds the anachronistic view precisely because of his fascination with peculiarity. The book's most vivid discussion of vernacular culture is its skeptical portrayal of the New Religious Movements (NRMs), generally referred to at the time as "cults" or "sects." Ottley discusses the success of High John the Conqueror, a "love-potion purveyor" and Harlem's Barefoot Prophet, and rent party staple Elder Clayborn Martin.[52] He focuses on the competition between Father Divine—whose believers pool wealth, attend "Get Happy" services, and live in a succession of colonies called "Heaven"—and the similarly styled Daddy Grace, whose grace did not extend to economic aid for his followers.[53] Ottley suggests that "cultists—jackals of the city jungles" take advantage of the desperation of others to set up lucrative religious organizations.[54] Crucially, however, while Ottley sees these organizations as predatory, he is compelled by the localized power these organizations create outside recognized structures.

Ottley more readily acknowledges the positive political potential of Harlem's mainstream churches for coalition-based leadership against racism. George Sorett notes, "If religion was to have any place moving forward it would have to be aligned with civil rights in the United States and with

---

49. Ottley, *New World A-Coming,* 66.
50. Ottley, *New World A-Coming,* 34.
51. Ottley, *New World A-Coming,* 224.
52. Ottley, *New World A-Coming,* 86.
53. Ottley, *New World A-Coming,* 91.
54. Ottley, *New World A-Coming,* 87.

116 · CHAPTER 4

democracy around the globe."[55] A chapter titled "Glamour Boy" highlights the political rise of Abyssinian Baptist Church pastor and New York City councilman Adam Clayton Powell Jr., suggesting that African Americans deeply supported the work Powell achieved through coalitions targeting employment, housing, and consumer discrimination. Ottley claims that that Powell's goal is to use his 1944 congressional bid to "seize national leadership of the Negro people."[56] However, echoing his concerns about NRM leadership, Ottley raises a concern about charismatic opportunism. The same chapter cites some Harlemites distrust of Powell because of his "frequently changing political alignments" and the difficulty of separating his successes as an activist from his public flair and personal ambitions.[57] Sharpening his critique, Ottley states that Powell "stirs the emotions, and drives people to action. But it is left to others to formulate concrete programs. Actually, Negroes are more dazzled than lifted by him—which indeed makes him a tough man to beat."[58] A 1945 letter from Ellison to Wright indicates Ottley himself had been dazzled by Powell at one time, suggesting that Ottley's tone here likely speaks personal disillusionment.[59]

*New World A-Coming*'s most prescient and rhetorically effective analysis occurs in its account of the rise of racial nationalism. Ottley foregrounds this early in the book with a discussion of Marcus Garvey's Universal Negro Improvement Association (UNIA). Many writers of the period recognized Black nationalism as important, while still castigating Garvey as a demagogue, and Ottley largely follows this script—tracing the history of its founder, the movement's aims to establish a Black empire, its links to earlier repatriation plans, and the financial mismanagement that doomed UNIA.

Ottley's conclusion, however, moves beyond the usual vague claims that the movement inspired lingering racial pride. It traces what he sees as constructive and destructive outgrowths of Garvey's nationalism through several developments in the 1930s and 1940s. Going further, it identifies the ways racial nationalism both amplifies and challenges the idea of an inclusive liberal community. It notes of Garveyism:

---

55. Sorett, *Spirit in the Dark,* 109. Sorett compares Ottley's depiction of religion to Richard Wright and Claude McKay.

56. Ottley, *New World A-Coming,* 87.

57. Ottley, *New World A-Coming,* 235.

58. Ottley, *New World A-Coming,* 235.

59. Ellison, *Selected Letters of Ralph Ellison,* 198. Rampersad, *Ralph Ellison,* 190, notes that Ellison saw Powell as being guilty of neglecting his duties in Congress. Sorett, *Spirit in the Dark,* 107, notes that Ottley had attended Abyssinian Baptist since he was young and was friends with Powell; that fact makes Ottley's criticism seem even more pointed.

Concretely, the movement set in motion what was to become the most compelling force in Negro life—race and color consciousness, which is today that ephemeral thing that inspires race loyalty; the banner to which Negroes rally; the chain that binds them together. It has propelled many a political and social movement and stimulated racial internationalism. It is indeed a philosophy, an ethical standard by which most things are measured and interpreted. It accounts for much constructive belligerency today.[60]

The book identifies social movements that draw on Garvey's legacy directly as well as those containing undercurrents of Black nationalism. Its invocation of "racial internationalism" anticipates arguments by Brent Hayes Edwards and Nikhil Pal Singh showing that Black nationalism has long been an international mode of affiliation that has gone through multiple incarnations, not all embodied in full-fledged movements.[61] Ottley claims, "The growth of a militant racial sentiment, and thus of racial solidarity, has produced leaders different from any period in the Negro's history."[62] Among these, he cites the popular pamphleteer Joel A. Rogers (who had also worked on *The Negro In New York* manuscript) and Elijah Muhammad's Islamic organizations as radical proponents of racial nationalism.

To highlight the stakes of liberal failure, Ottley links the rise of racial nationalism with the potential for wartime disunity. The book examines a debate over whether African Americans should support the war or should instead view the Japanese as the leader of a non-White power bloc that could challenge Western dominance. Ottley expresses support for American-born Japanese on the West Coast and notes the deep personal relationships that often formed between these Nisei and African Americans. However, he also warns readers about Japanese ambassadors' attempts to win over Black Americans to their cause. He notes the influence of some of these ideas and charges groups associated with Elijah Muhammad, Robert O. Jordan, Harry Fredericks, and Sufi Abdul Hamid with celebrating Axis victories and anti-Semitism. Ottley refutes the idea that African Americans would support the Axis powers but contends that the racial situation in America creates unnecessary divisions and serves as useful propaganda for the enemy.

If racial nationalism presents a threat in wartime disloyalty, it also offers a "constructive belligerency."[63] In a chapter titled "Who Are the Negro's Leaders?" Ottley links strident shifts in mainstream political advocacy organiza-

---

60. Ottley, *New World A-Coming*, 81.
61. Singh, *Black Is a Country*; Edwards, *Practice of Diaspora*.
62. Ottley, *New World A-Coming*, 237.
63. Ottley, *New World A-Coming*, 81.

tions like the NAACP, the National Urban League, and labor unions to Garvey and his followers, suggesting, "It is these wild currents that the Negro leaders are riding today."[64] Rather than specifying the most effective leaders or directions, the book here suggests a multi-headed wartime pragmatism pushing toward "unconditional equality with whites!"[65] Ottley lauds the role the CPUSA played, stating, "The party did more than any other agency in American life toward breaking down the rigid color barriers that had once existed between the races, through organizations in which the party's influence was a factor—youth, labor, unemployed groups, and in the cultural movements."[66] But he also notes, "As to the Communist Party's ultimate goal, the Negro's attitude is something else again."[67] Ottley suggests that Walter White at the NAACP and the head of the Brotherhood of Sleeping Car Porters A. Philip Randolph have assumed leadership in negotiating racial justice issues with the federal government. The chapter posits the 1941 March on Washington movement, which helped generate Executive Order 8802, the Fair Employment Act, as an important example of the power of national coalitions. The chapter also links national racial stridency in wartime to an increased global focus in racial consciousness. In particular, he cites the growing international concerns of African Americans with countries like Haiti, Jamaica, the Bahamas, and Ethiopia as symptomatic of a belief that "there is a tacit understanding among English and American leaders to limit democracy to white men only."[68] These approaches, in Ottley's account, pose a creative political response, driving demands for rights and backing them with pragmatic action.

In concluding his study, Ottley calls on the federal government to act to head off the threat of disloyalty by ensuring African American inclusion in a national community. The introduction asserts that Harlem's residents are ultimately united "on the question of their rights—moral, economic, and political."[69] Ottley draws on the rhetoric of the war for democracy abroad and the threat of social unrest at home to promote social reform. His closing statement echoes this assertion of unity:

> The Negro's cause will rise or fall with America. He knows well that his destiny is intimately bound to that of the nation. America stands today as a symbol of freedom! The loss of this symbol will undeniably mean the loss of

---

64. Ottley, *New World A-Coming*, 241.
65. Ottley, *New World A-Coming*, 240.
66. Ottley, *New World A-Coming*, 243.
67. Ottley, *New World A-Coming*, 244.
68. Ottley, *New World A-Coming*, 325.
69. Ottley, *New World A-Coming*, 3.

hope for white and black alike. This war, undeniably, belongs to the Negro as well as to the white man. To this extent, it may be called a "People's War"— for in spite of selfish interests a new world is a-coming with the sweep and fury of the Resurrection.[70]

The statement freely borrows from patriotism, the Popular Front, and Christian messianism, but Ottley proclaims that the problems of African Americans in Harlem are primarily economic ones the federal government could do much to resolve.

In closing, the book directly addresses the Roosevelt administration, citing the war as a moment when the president "must lift himself above the picayune racial concerns of Sikeston, Missouri and Atlanta, Georgia, or Meridian, Mississippi, and view the color problem in its broadest international terms."[71] Rather than recognizing the New Deal's modernization project, Ottley advocates the expansion of employment equity. He calls on the Roosevelt administration to clarify the intent of Executive Order 8802, which established the Fair Employment Practice Committee, a move Ottley views as "the opening wedge to economic equality that Negroes seek."[72] This act, he suggests, would signal a commitment to inclusion in the national community, one that would go far toward securing Black unity and loyalty behind the government during wartime.

## *The Negro in Illinois*

The Illinois branch of the FWP under the directorship of John T. Frederick, an author and Northwestern University professor, had one of the largest concentrations of writers after New York, and it had an especially robust representation of African American staff in its Chicago office.[73] While the Harlem Renaissance was in decline in the 1930s, Chicago's Black intellectual sphere was surging. A group of Black intellectuals and White allies that included writers, sociologists, and historians had been growing there since the 1920s, forming the backbone of the Chicago Renaissance. As FWP employees, several writers

---

70. Ottley, *New World A-Coming*, 347.

71. Ottley, *New World A-Coming*, 347.

72. Ottley, *New World A-Coming*, 293.

73. In 2013, Brian Dolinar, working with the Chicago Public Library (CPL) archivists, pulled together the manuscript holdings in the CPL and the chapters borrowed by Conroy and Bontemps and published them. His introduction to FWP, *The Negro in Illinois*, is the most useful guide to the composition of the Illinois unit and the work on its manuscript project.

affiliated with the South Side Writers' Group—including Arna Bontemps, Fenton Johnson, Willard Motley, Onah Spencer, Margaret Walker, and Richard Wright—worked to construct a multilayered sociohistorical study of African Americans in Chicago.[74] Under Bontemps's direction, the project expanded to focus on the entire state with a strong concentration on the metropolis.

Where *The Negro in New York* aligns its details in a broad historical sweep with anecdotes filling in the details, *The Negro in Illinois*'s framing works more like the essay sections at the beginnings of the FWP guidebooks. The first eight chapters trace out the social history of Black Illinois from slaves traded there by the French would-be miner Phillip Francois Renault and the 1724 *La Code Noir* to late nineteenth-century strategies of educational uplift. From there the manuscript focuses on specific contemporary concerns such as housing, business, recreation, and the arts, with a brief detour in Chapters 14 and 15, which focus on the Great Migration.

The historical elements of the book clearly reflect civic pluralism's participatory vision of the past. As Brian Dolinar notes, the decision to begin with Jean Baptiste Point du Sable, the mixed-race, possibly Haitian, trader who settled the area around Chicago, was by no means neutral. Making his story visible in the 1933 World's Fair had been the objective of a campaign among African American Chicagoans who sought to correct a White-washed account of Illinois history.[75] Point du Sable's primacy in the guides, then, serves as the equivalent of a representational victory lap. Much of the Illinois book's focus on history also serves to remind readers of African American participation in the national story both as historical figures and, through slavery and abolition, as subjects of history. It highlights how violence against abolitionist printers helped turn public sentiment toward an antislavery position. It also highlights the role of Black abolitionists such as John Jones, the Chicago businessman and county commissioner who the book calls "John Brown's Friend," alluding to the way that history promotes White figures while often relegating Black ones to support roles. These hidden relationships shaping history are important in the book. For example, it suggests that Abraham Lincoln's recognition of Haiti as an independent nation was due to his friendship with Springfield's "Billy the Barber," the Haitian American William de Fleurville.[76]

---

74. FWP, *Negro in Illinois*, x. Dolinar also notes that Kitty Chapelle, Robert Davis, Katherine Dunham, Richard Dunham, Robert Lucas, and George Coleman Moore were among the employed writers. Dolinar also remarks that while Frank Yerby worked for the Illinois FWP, there is no evidence that he contributed directly to *The Negro in Illinois*.

75. FWP, *Negro in Illinois*, xxix.

76. FWP, *Negro in Illinois*, 39.

The influence of Chicago sociology is evident in *The Negro in Illinois*'s descriptions of social geography. While it traces a wide range of African American social life, it is deeply concerned with the emergence of the racial ghetto. The discussion of "Housing" highlights the various ways that racism shaped urban morphology. It traces the impact of the Great Migration and World War on earlier patterns, situating them in a broader migratory landscape. The book suggests that while Black Chicagoans previously had the ability to shift neighborhoods as they changed class status, that the twin pressures of more migrants and wartime housing shortages led to increased resistance among White homeowners and realtors. Initially, this seems to cast racism as a reaction to economic pressure, but the book also describes the active impact of racial real estate covenants in reducing racial integration and creating a narrowed housing market for Black citizens:

> During the early years of the present century, 20 percent of Chicago's Negro population lived in areas where whites constituted 95 percent of the total. . . . Thirty years later 90 percent of all the Negroes in the city lived in areas where they constituted more than 50 percent of the total. Covenants have been far more effective than terrorism.[77]

Finally, they highlight the emergence of the kitchenette as a manifestation of racially created scarcity, citing surveys that associated the kitchenette with crime, health problems, and safety concerns.

Like other FWP books, *The Negro in Illinois* negotiates the tension between the sociological analytic that read urban vernacular culture as a symptom of pathology and a desire to highlight African American creativity. Significantly, the book's structure potentially replicates normative understandings by dividing high and low culture. One such split occurs in the book's treatment of music. The chapter "Music" focuses on African American participation in classical music and opera, as well as gospel music, which by the 1930s had become part of romantic nationalism. At the end of the cultural sections, a separate chapter titled "Rhythm" explores the dynamics of vernacular music and mass culture in ragtime, blues, and jazz. Unlike Wright, the editors refrain from suggesting that these developments are compensatory. As the last section in the book, the chapter suggests that they offer new directions in Black culture that shape the larger national culture.

At other points, the division of recognized and unrecognized elements combines with the focus on urban pathology to suggest some cultural ele-

---

77. FWP, *Negro in Illinois*, 162.

122 · CHAPTER 4

ments are effectively out of sync with modernization. For example, the chapter "Churches" focuses on mainline religious denominations and African American branches of these denominations. It is one of the first chapters following the historical overview and highlights the crucial ongoing role that the church plays in Black communities. Here the text eschews the tension Wright expressed in *12 Million Black Voices* over the question of religion's value and its modernity. The church clearly remains a vital political force.

In contrast, a later chapter on religion titled "And Churches" deploys a colloquialism for the difference between the recognized and the unrecognized to encompass the wide range of NRMs, often based in storefronts, that the editors refer to as "cults" and "sects," as Ottley had done. Much of this material was collected under the direction of Katherine Dunham, a dramatist and dancer who worked with both the FTP and FWP units in Illinois, along with anthropologist Mary Fujii and writer Frank Yerby. Jack Conroy later assumed direction of the research on NRMs when Dunham left.[78] The focus on these groups touched on a class schism within Chicago's Black communities. Storefront churches were a particular point of contention for the urban Black bourgeoisie, who saw them as backward, easy to caricature, and often corrupt—an embarrassing reminder of working-class culture.[79] *The Negro in Illinois* suggests that these religious movements exist largely as compensation for inequity, particularly as Black urban districts swell, and established churches are overwhelmed. As in *New World A-Coming,* they are portrayed as modern developments but problematic ones:

> An undeclared religious war exists between the two types of churches. Controversy centering around the issue has become so bitter and widespread that the storefront has assumed an importance it would not have had ordinarily. Many citizens of the community have expressed themselves on the matter; the pros contend that they are homier and a good influence, the cons that they are disseminators of superstition and little better than rackets.[80]

Though the Illinois guide refrains from settling this dispute directly, its repeated invocation of controversy highlights disunity. Similarly, in contrast with the earlier discussion of mainline churches focusing on their historical emergence and role, the research on storefront churches, some of which was performed through undercover infiltration, details beliefs and practices, sometimes with soft ridicule. Pointedly, the account of these organization's

---

78. FWP, *Negro in Illinois,* xxii
79. Kimble, *New Deal for Bronzeville,* 21.
80. FWP, *Negro in Illinois,* 210.

fragmentation and proliferation contrasts with the call to action in an editorial from the *Chicago Defender*, which serves to close the chapter. The editorial highlights the importance of the church as a political site, and calls for "collective, unified action by the Negro church as a whole."[81] *The Negro in Illinois* implicitly sides with this call. Its earlier recognition that many established denominations emerged as storefront concerns leaves a path open for the newer churches, but it clearly laments their fragmenting effect.

Even while rendering many cultural elements problematically, the Illinois Writers' Project (IWP) writers begin to make visible cultural and political connections that would play an important role in reshaping social and cultural politics and challenging the postwar liberal order. Significantly, the chapter on NRMs is preceded by a chapter titled "What Is Africa to Me?," a juxtaposition that suggests the connection between secular and spiritual politics. The chapter traces the emergence of racial nationalism in the Garvey movement into later manifestations such as the Peace Movement in Ethiopia and the African Pacific Movement of the Eastern World (APMEW). Black nationalism emerged concomitant to an interrogation of national racial politics and imperialism abroad, and the FWP book recognizes the international and anticolonial outlook of racial nationalism. It also deflects the charges made against the APMEW that it was a front for Japanese subversive activities. Eventually the essay traces Garvey's influence into Black Muslim groups headed by Noble Drew Ali, W. D. Fard, and Elijah Muhammad. As with the storefront churches, it often distances the reader from these groups in exploring their practices and terminologies, often uncritically literalizing symbolic and prophetic language. It highlights ideas like Muhammad's reinterpretation of Ezekiel's Wheel as a "Mother's Airplane" that would destroy White people or of social security numbers as a "mark of the Beast" identifying Black individuals to the White-controlled state and making them more susceptible to disempowerment, a process Muhammad labeled "Tricknollogy."[82] While *The Negro in Illinois* refuses the legitimacy of the political critique in these ideas, it still makes their presence visible and highlights a rationale for their persuasiveness in the pervasive ghetto conditions.

Like other New Deal books, *The Negro in Illinois* is as much prophecy as description. Unlike its New York counterpart, housing still serves as one of the major hallmarks of the New Deal vision. The Illinois book notes, "The Federal Housing Authority has answered some of the pleas of Negroes for adequate housing facilities" and cites the inclusive Jane Addams Houses, Julia C. Lath-

---

81. FWP, *Negro in Illinois*, 216.

82. FWP, *Negro in Illinois*, 207.

rop Houses, and Trumbull Park Homes.[83] It also notes the amenities of the Ida B. Wells Homes, which resembled those of Harlem River Houses:

> These modern, fireproof, brick and steel structures comprise 1,662 units, 868 in apartment buildings and 794 in rowhouses and garden apartments. Units consisted from two to six rooms, all equipped with electric refrigerators, modern gas ranges, cupboards, two-party laundry sinks in the kitchen and built-in bathtubs. There was a central heating plan for all the buildings.[84]

Why the relatively welcoming attitude toward housing in *The Negro in Illinois* as opposed to the silence of the New York book? The answer likely lies in the Illinois group's ties to sociology, and in the radical politics of the Chicago Renaissance. As sociologists caught the attention of or became New Deal policymakers, their scientific approach required measurable, implementable solutions, both of which housing reform offered through eliminating substandard units and building new affordable ones. Moreover, campaigns for access to public housing and associated jobs and recognition of Black history in the names of the housing projects had been foundational struggles in the Chicago scene, making their inclusion important as a marker of victories and ongoing struggles.[85]

Nevertheless, the IWP authors propose housing reform neither as a cure-all nor as an achieved fact. If anything, they stress the contingency of these measures, and, like the New York guidebooks, the essential reactiveness of governmental reform. Instead, the measures the book foregrounds depend on community self-reliance and activism. If it dismisses the storefront churches and Black nationalism, it nonetheless, like *New World A-Coming*, sees hope in organization. The book discusses the role of the radical Unemployed Councils in restoring evicted African Americans to their homes during the early 1930s. It also notes the fight to have the Ida B. Wells Homes reflect African American history in their name as one of the most unifying causes among Chicago's Black citizens in 1937–1938.

While neither the New York nor the Illinois FWP studies tie their cultural evaluations to political development as explicitly as does Wright's *12 Million Black Voices,* they nevertheless offer a cultural and political plenitude largely missing in Wright's analysis. They define some cultural elements as symptoms—not symptoms of an arcane way of life but of a deleterious urban social order. Crucially, this shifts the terms of discussion of culture from premodern

---

83. FWP, *Negro in Illinois,* 163.

84. FWP, *Negro in Illinois,* 164.

85. See Kimble, *New Deal for Bronzeville.*

survivals versus modern elements to questions of function and health. With this shift, they disjoin the coupling of temporality and politics that legitimates both communist and New Deal modernization and reopens the question of the future. Just as this reopening provided ground for Ottley to engage in a rhetorical dance with wartime liberalism in *New World A-Coming*, it also offered Arna Bontemps and James Conroy room to redevelop the Illinois FWP materials toward similar ends.

## *They Seek A City*

From the Midwest, Bontemps and Conroy watched Ottley's post-FWP success and sought to replicate it. Conroy noted in a letter, "It irks me to see Ottley wearing diamonds acquired from his utilization of material no better than ours. I don't mind Ottley's having the diamonds, of course, but I think we ought to have bigger and more sparkling ones."[86] Like the New York FWP study, *The Negro in Illinois* was largely complete but remained unpublished when the FWP ceased operations. The Rosenwald Fund, which had sponsored the project, hoped to locate a publisher. In the meantime, Bontemps and the Rosenwald Fund's Julia Waxman placed the manuscript materials with Vivian Harsh in the Special Negro Collection in the Hall Branch of the CPL.[87] Bontemps and Conroy secured permission to use the material, but the presses they approached were largely uninterested in a study focused on Black life in Illinois. However, one of the ideas from the proposal, Black migration, caught the attention of Bucklin Moon, a White author and editor at Doubleday, Doran & Company whose literary career was built on books about Black culture.[88]

Together, Conroy and Bontemps reworked the proposal into an exploration of Black migration into the Midwestern and Western states. Migratory networks became a useful frame for reimagining African American history along an axis that ran up the Mississippi to the Great Lakes, westward through Kansas and Oklahoma, and eventually followed wartime jobs to the Pacific coast. *They Seek a City* advances a view of the New Deal project as laudable but incomplete, offering examples of effective action by the federal government, but also showing the ways that such action might be undermined by racist politics. Like *New World A-Coming*, it constructs a historical framework that connects vernacular culture to political organizing, but its scope offers a more nuanced understanding of developments in Black nationalism that

---

86. Bontemps Papers, Correspondence, Conroy to Bontemps, 23 November 1943.

87. FWP, *Negro in Illinois*, xxxv.

88. See Jackson, *Indignant Generation*, 152–157, for discussion of Bucklin Moon's career.

126 • CHAPTER 4

would eventually lend the book a second life as a diagnostic of a more assertive era.

The organizing framework of the book provides a window into the complex motivations and adaptations that fueled Black migration from the South, while highlighting the contributions of Black Americans. The authors ran into the challenge faced by FWP editors generally—how to organize such a broad array of information. It is clear that they did not want to generate a mythic explanatory structure in the vein of *12 Million Black Voices*. Nor, despite the close relationship, did they adopt the IWP scheme of historical background and recent developments, though there are traces of *The Negro in Illinois*'s broader chapter order, and many chapters of *They Seek a City* are very similar to the original FWP material. Instead, like *New World A-Coming*, *They Seek a City* focuses on individual lives and movements, allowing history to speak through them. Such subject matter could generate satisfying arcs for individual chapters, but containing a subject defined by dispersion is difficult. The last third of the book reads like a laundry list of sites and people, and it certainly lends a sense of understanding for why Wright, and even Ottley, chose somewhat narrower frameworks. However, like both the FWP studies and *New World A-Coming*, the inclusiveness of *They Seek a City* enables both breadth and insight.

Like Ottley, Bontemps and Conroy are clearly drawn to odd tales, and they recognize the value of the anecdote as both entertaining and illuminating the complexity of African Americans' contribution to history. Much of their book focuses on tracing individual lives that expand and exploit Black migratory networks. Like the IWP book, the inaugural figure of their study is the mixed-race trader Jean Baptiste Point du Sable, who established his trading empire as the founding settlement of what is now Chicago. Freed from the concentration on Illinois, the books explore a broader array of figures and sites central to Black westward migration. Benjamin "Pap" Singleton, who made it his mission to lead African Americans en masse from the South to Kansas, Indiana, and other states, figures prominently. He was so effective, they note, he created a panic as his "exodusters" disrupted the Southern labor supply. Reflecting Bontemps and Conroy's Leftist backgrounds, the relationship between labor and migration continues as a focus throughout the study.

One of the book's most important contributions is tracing the historical impact of African Americans on American vernacular culture through migration. Both writers were deeply interested in the culture that traveled the Mississippi River corridor from New Orleans to Chicago. They collected jokes, songs, and folk tales, which they exchanged with each other and with

# AFRICAN AMERICA IN FWP SOCIAL HISTORIES AND INTERTEXTS · 127

Benjamin Botkin.[89] They also found an outlet for these in children's books. Throughout the 1940s, their 1942 children's story *The Fast Sooner Hound,* illustrated by Virginia Lee Burton and based on older folk tales, continued to sell well. Given this interest, it is unsurprising that *They Seek a City* devotes ample space to vernacular culture. One of the most interesting figures in the study is James Beckwourth, whose self-claimed exploits—including fur-trading, bigamy, frontier warfare, and leading the Blackfoot—helped set a pattern for Western narrative. Going beyond Wright's view of the church primarily as a reservoir of hope, Bontemps and Conroy note the importance of storefront churches as community anchors in the "readjustment process," while suggesting that participation in them "gave rise to a whole new body of gospel music."[90] The book also traces the movement of musicians and music up the Mississippi through Scott Joplin's ragtime, W. C. Handy's blues, and Jelly Roll Morton's jazz, creating the sonic landscape of vernacular culture.

This Whitmanesque view of vernacular culture goes hand-in-hand with the book's broad conception of political possibilities. Bontemps and Conroy explore both a range of organizational strategies and the conflicts that make them necessary. They also cite the rise of leadership from within Black migratory communities in their new homes. Borrowing on the extensive research for *The Negro In Illinois,* and particularly the material Dunham, Conroy, and Yerby had collected on Black nationalist religious movements, the book offers a more developed framework for understanding Garvey's influence as a working-class political phenomenon than *New World A-Coming* does, and the book traces post-Garvey networks to Detroit and Chicago, where they were having some of their most consequential developments through Wallace Fard Muhammad and Elijah Muhammad's Nation of Islam.

In contrast, despite both authors' different Leftist backgrounds, the book largely ignores communist organizing. Letters between Bontemps and Conroy reveal their general ambivalence about the CPUSA by this time.[91] However,

---

89. See correspondence between Bontemps and Conroy, and Bontemps and Botkin in the Jack Conroy Papers and Arna Bontemps Papers.

90. Bontemps and Conroy, *They Seek a City,* 145.

91. Conroy Papers, Letter from Bontemps to Conroy, 4 August 1944, Box 3, Bontemps notes Richard Wright's public disavowal of communism:

> Perhaps if Dick had worn communism as a loose garment, this sad story would have been less sad. But he gave his heart without reserve, and I doubt that a creative spirit can ever quite do that—to any organizational group—no matter how deep his sympathy. The creative mind is different; it doesn't ever exactly fit. At least, that is my impression. But that's his crown of thorns. Ours is a September deadline!

128 • CHAPTER 4

like many other writers who had affiliated with the radical Left, they remained interested in working-class politics and particularly policies of inclusion in unions. The Congress of Industrial Organizations's (CIO) policy of racial inclusion was one of their major foci in *They Seek a City*. Significantly, the book links labor activity among Black workers to political action at the local, state, and national level, signaling the growing interaction between organized labor and welfare state political organization.

Bontemps and Conroy offer a fairly sanguine view of welfare state liberalism, but they also signal awareness of the questions about racial equity the end of the war would bring. In a letter to Conroy, Bontemps suggested:

> If the war ends this year, the publishing picture may be somewhat changed, but I have a feeling that the change may be for the better—more paper, etc. I also think the subject of Negroes will be of GREATER interest, for many housing developments will be in the cards, the FEPC will be working harder than ever—in short, all the race relations business will be intensified.[92]

Their book uses the experience of Black Midwesterners and Westerners to highlight and challenge the limitations of New Deal liberalism. Like many FWP guidebooks, they cite the development of public housing approvingly, as a means to alleviate substandard housing conditions. In a passage that could have been lifted directly from a FWP guidebook, they write:

> Standing in close proximity to Chicago's most dilapidated slums, the spick-and-span Ida B. Wells housing project is a tiny island—an oasis with its brave young trees and green lawns and trim flower beds. It's only a small beginning—a drop in the bucket. The woman for whom it was named knew what it meant to build against opposition and discouragement from small beginnings.[93]

Clearly they approve of the intervention, and Bontemps wrote Conroy of a letter he had received from Frank Horne at the FHA who "[hopes] the book will become a sort of primer for all officials of this authority in all cities."[94] However, the last sentence of the passage invokes the organizing that lay ahead, not on the part of the government but by citizens working to ensure they would share in the benefits of welfare state liberalism.

92. Bontemps Papers. Correspondence, Bontemps to Conroy, 4 May 1944.
93. Bontemps and Conroy, *They Seek a City*, 82.
94. Conroy Papers, Incoming Correspondence, Bontemps to Conroy, 19 July 1945.

AFRICAN AMERICA IN FWP SOCIAL HISTORIES AND INTERTEXTS · 129

Illustrating this point further, they feature the recent conflict over whether African Americans would be able to occupy the FHA's Sojourner Truth housing project in Detroit after resistance from local homeowners pressed the FHA to make the project Whites only and change the name. Only the organizing of the NAACP and a combination of "various labor, church and civic groups" restored the intended occupants and name, and even then, there were protests on moving-in day. They sum up their view of sole reliance on government initiatives in a discussion of San Francisco's Westside Courts: "Public housing units offer a soupçon of relief, but the process is far too slow," and they note the danger that manifests when "local managers yield to pressure by segregationists."[95] Here, they get to the heart of many of the problems with the New Deal's tendency to rely on local power structures.

Similarly, they are cautious about the extent to which the New Deal framework of workers' rights would counteract racial divisions on its own, noting the National Labor Relations Board (NLRB) and FEPC struggle with the American Federation of Labor's (AFL) boilermakers' union over segregated local unions. The last line of the book, "Any place but *here!*" caps an anecdote in which three Black men at a mining camp, realizing that their White coworkers will eventually turn on them despite their shared union, escape on a train without knowing its destination.[96] Deeply ambivalent about future prospects, Bontemps and Conroy clearly showcase the ways that progressive liberalism could be undercut by systemic racial politics. The unresolved question for them is whether institutional policies could ameliorate entrenched inequities, or whether bureaucracies would succumb to deeply ingrained White supremacist beliefs and become part of their apparatus.

## Conclusion

While the FWP social histories meant to expand the reach of New Deal civic pluralism, these books find both points of agreement and disagreement with the terms of modernity offered in New Deal guidebooks. Though neither the social histories nor their documentary intertexts offer the character development, narrative arcs, or structural tension that made Wright's *Native Son* and other novels of the era so effective, they engage with similar problems. The writers of these intertexts, as novelists and journalists rather than historians or sociologists, sought to develop new interpretive frames that could speak

---

95. Bontemps and Conroy, *They Seek a City*, 240.
96. Bontemps and Conroy, *They Seek a City*, 252.

to a public seeking to understand African Americans' wartime responses and claims on justice. They used the documentary form to deploy a wide range of stories to capture a broader and more complex picture of African American life than novels of this era often do. They grappled with the persistence of urban poverty and the modes of describing it, building out the notion of the racial slum. They also foregrounded cultural complexity and reflected the New Deal–era conflicts over what cultural elements would form the background of a healthy society. Where Wright cautiously imagines a future built on worker alliances, these books generally align that future with a more robust liberalism, even while warning that the politics of race might again derail dreams of national community.

While they support liberalism, these books use the FWP's considerable resources to construct frames through which they interrogate the state's justice claims. The intertexts in particular draw on the FWP guidebook's characteristic mode of presenting historical and cultural details as a guide to future political developments. They show that focusing on African American urban experiences means not only restoring the visibility of Black social and cultural contributions but also reiterating and reckoning with a history of racial violence and the cultural elements generated in its shadow. These histories serve to warn readers that, however idealistic liberal initiatives might be, they could still be hijacked by racism, derailing the New Deal project.

As with in other books in this study, this reminder undercuts the FWP guidebooks' certitudes about the efficacy of planning and development. While imagining a wide range of political futures for African Americans, these books point out potential alternatives to state-engineered national community in local initiatives, communism, and racial nationalism. Though the FWP books on African America, *New World A-Coming*, and *They Seek A City* all shared a commitment to the liberal project, the documentary intertexts emphasize its incompleteness and highlight paths forward that would require substantive commitments toward guaranteeing African Americans' civil rights. My final chapter explores how Ann Petry and Ralph Ellison utilized these lessons to reconceptualize Harlem space, culture, and liberal citizenship for the Civil Rights era.

CHAPTER 5

# Patterns of Modernity

*The Urban Folk, State Power, and*
*Citizenship in Petry and Ellison*

In 1948, Ralph Ellison wrote "Harlem Is Nowhere," an essay intended for '48 magazine, to be published alongside photographs by Gordon Parks, who had established his reputation as a photographer for the Farm Securities Administration under Roy Stryker.[1] Many Harlemites refer to their neighborhood as "nowhere," the essay explains, because of the feeling that "they have no stable, recognized place in society. . . . One 'is' literally, but one is nowhere; one wanders dazed in a ghetto maze, a 'displaced person' of American democracy."[2] Lamenting this displacement, at once social and psychological, "Harlem Is Nowhere" joined the host of New Deal intertexts by African American writers serving as diagnostics of urban Black life while prefiguring the notion of invisibility in the novel Ellison was writing at the same time.[3] The FWP found it necessary to make urban space legible to articulate its vision of citizenship and

---

1. Ellison's essay was published eventually in *Shadow and Act* and then modified for *Harper's Magazine* in 1964.

2. Ellison, *Collected Essays of Ralph Ellison*, 325.

3. In his working notes for *Invisible Man*, Ellison, *Collected Essays of Ralph Ellison*, 343–344, suggests that invisibility emerged out of the ghettoized psychological condition he observed in "Harlem Is Nowhere." He argues, "Out of this conflict personalities of extreme complexity emerge," which are necessitated by the daily hardships of racial oppression. This complexity is invisible to Whites, who tend to see Blacks as types, and this allows Blacks to operate in the "blind spot" of Whites.

132 · CHAPTER 5

social justice. Ellison's essay raises the question: What kind of citizen could come from nowhere?

The following year, Ann Petry, building on the authority of her 1946 Harlem novel *The Street,* was offered another public opportunity to define the neighborhood. She published an essay on the neighborhood in the April edition of *Holiday* magazine in an issue focusing on New York. Though she was not a FWP employee, Ann Petry was no stranger to New Deal cultural work.[4] She participated in the American Negro Theatre, which grew out of the Federal Theatre Project, and her husband Frank had worked for the New York City FWP unit. Moreover, Ann Petry's work at the *Amsterdam News,* Adam Clayton Powell Jr.'s *People's Voice,* and a children's after-school program exposed her to a wide range of information about Harlem. Although Petry was not a Communist Party member, Wald notes that Petry's alignment with *People's Voice* from 1941 to 1944 as a reporter, editor, and columnist mark her as leaning well to the Left politically during the 1940s.[5] Her *Holiday* essay, sandwiched oddly between essays on Little Italy and the Lower East Side, begins like Wright's *12 Million Black Voices,* with a suggestion that outsiders cannot read Black life because "the shadow of the past hangs heavily over Harlem, obscuring its outlines, obliterating its true face."[6] Again, the issue of legibility is crucial. As the essay moves forward, it links the physical and social environments of Harlem to the lives of its diverse citizens while advocating for their needs.

This chapter rereads Petry's *The Street* and Ellison's *Invisible Man* as FWP intertexts that explore questions of vernacular culture, social justice, and liberal citizenship as the postwar liberal order and welfare state were established. In both novels, figures of legibility and patterning in Harlem space and folk culture link the protagonists' concerns to those of the New Deal and enable an interrogation of liberalism. Like *12 Million Black Voices, The Street* frames these questions in the tension between its sociological and vernacular elements, offering a dual reading that refuses easy resolution. While it ultimately reaffirms the sociological diagnosis of urban pathology, its assertion of folk perspective and foregrounding of women's experiences undercuts faith in the state as an agent that can generate justice and, by extension, the kinds of citizens hailed by New Deal civic pluralism. Ellison, in turn, utilized cultural

---

4. See Holladay, *Ann Petry,* for a biography of Ann Petry. For a more though account of Ann and George Petry's activities on the Left, see Wald, *Trinity of Passion,* 114–128, and *American Night,* 179–200.

5. Wald, *Trinity of Passion,* 115; *American Night,* 197. Several critics have remarked on Petry's protective stance about her political identity, and she even upbraided the Negro Labor Victory Committee, an organization with which she likely had shared views, for including her name in a list of members.

6. Petry, "Harlem," 112.

URBAN FOLK, STATE POWER, AND CITIZENSHIP IN PETRY AND ELLISON • 133

ideas he had encountered through the FWP to rework the idea of folk history and then to performatively refashion liberal citizenship in a mode attentive to the experience of past injustices and attuned to creative resistance.

## Patterns in the Wind

Written as a postwar housing crisis was beginning to reshape urban politics, *The Street* focuses on the violence of the racial ghetto on both individuals and African Americans as a group. Though a discussion of public housing is absent in *The Street,* housing is a central concern of the novel. In her work for the progressive *People's Voice,* which covered a wide range of equity issues in Harlem, Petry would have had significant engagement with activism over housing policy and other areas of discrimination. Petry's *Holiday* essay recognizes this demand. It notes that New York Mayor Fiorello LaGuardia would send for the Reverend John Johnson of Harlem's St. Martin's Protestant Episcopal Church to ask him, "Well, Johnnie what do they want now?" Johnson replies, "More houses, Mr. Mayor. More houses." The narration editorially affirms Johnson: "They still want more houses. Need more houses."[7]

This response is especially notable because it is a concrete way to solve a problem that Petry chooses to figure through a folk abstraction. In the essay, housing provides a potential solution to a problem the essay calls "Hawkins." Harlemites invoke this presence, also known as "Old Man Hawk" or just "The Hawk," in windy, winter conditions.[8] Petry, however, suggests a broader meaning, with the weather serving as an allegory for social conditions. Consider this passage on the fictional Harlem everyman George Jackson, whose pragmatic politics and religious faith are central to his identity:

> As George Jackson walks slowly to and from his church, he tries to arrive at an honest conclusion about Harlem. He knows there is too much fear around—fear of the police, and an equally great fear of one's neighbors, as evidenced by the special locks on the doors of the apartments and iron bars at the windows that open on fire escapes, He admits, uneasily, that there are too many children playing in the streets, night and day—his own and other

---

7. Petry, "Harlem," 168.

8. As compiled on the website of etymologist Barry Popik, entries in the *Dictionary of American Regional English,* 925, and the *Random House Historical Dictionary of American Slang,* 48, suggest "Hawkins" is used from Baltimore to Chicago and may have traveled up from the South with early jazz players. Potential origins vary from a pirate named Hawkins who raided Cornish coastal towns to Sir John Hawkins, the sixteenth-century British admiral and slave trader.

134 · CHAPTER 5

people's children. His final conclusion might be contained in one short sentence: "Hawkins is here."[9]

The passage suggests that "Hawkins" can refer to "a bone-chilling wind" or to "the chilling statistics on Harlem."[10] In Petry's essay, Hawkins is a folk figuration of misery so deep-seated that it is almost impossible to separate from the natural environment. If housing can ameliorate the Hawk, then the government has on hand powerful tools with which it can reshape the lives of its hardest hit communities.

As my second chapter notes, New Dealers intended WPA housing programs to have a broadly transformative impact on urban communities. That notion of community was tied to specific expectations of citizenship and domestic roles. The New Deal continued the practice of governmental support for a family form centered around a male wage-earner and female caregiver, while setting conditions for nuclearization of the family. Artwork on the grounds of the Harlem River Houses reflects this position. *The WPA Guide to New York City* notes:

> At the southern end of the plaza is a statue of a Negro laborer, while at the opposite end is a group depicting domesticity: mother and child with a dog. These pieces, ideally suited for their setting, are carved of pink and black marble.[11]

The statues emphasize the gendered domestic norms that public housing and other New Deal provisions meant to reinforce. However, in these statues' pedagogical presence, it is also easy to read more specific racial anxieties regarding the activities of unemployed Black men, the form of the Black family, and Black sexuality. Even as different paths were set for Black and White Americans in housing, and while Black women were able to access more stable employment than Black men, the government's idealization of men as wage-earning workers and women as family caregivers remained a constant.

---

9. Petry, "Harlem," 166. Wald, *Trinity of Passion*, 121, suggests that George Jackson's approval of Harlem communist leader and city councilman Ben Davis likely indicates Petry's own continuing support for communist positions even after Powell had moved to anticommunist ones. However, Petry, "Harlem," 165, is clear that Jackson "was likely pursuing his usual political course and voting for a man, not a political party." The essay does seem to reflect the appeal of 1940s Progressivism, which, like the big tent Popular Front before it, often blurred the lines between liberal positions and ones further to the Left.

10. Petry, "Harlem," 166, 168.

11. FWP, *WPA Guide to New York City*, 398. Section 31 of the United Sates Housing Act of 1937 allowed tenants to own pets.

*The Street* presents the image of a deserving family in crisis, while challenging readers to recognize that the state apparatus is built around the same racism that generates and sustains the ghetto. In the 1930s, reformers who had pushed for a range of social welfare programs based on their experience with urban immigrants sought to expand their efforts to African American families.[12] The group of progressive women who helped determine New Deal welfare policy from the Children's Bureau and the Department of Labor Women's Bureau was instrumental in developing what we now call welfare or public assistance. When these programs were realized in New Deal programs, however, they often fell victim to national race politics and gendered expectations. For example, the longstanding dependence of wealthy White families on Black women's work as hired domestic laborers led to the categorical exclusion of these workers from beneficial social welfare policies. Black mothers' need for work in the absence of a labor market that provided equitable employment for Black men also problematized the domestic ideals that these activists sought to strengthen. One significant problem that welfare proponents inherited from the nineteenth-century tradition of charitable aid was distinguishing deserving from undeserving mothers.[13]

The idea of the deserving poor had, of course, been a mainstay of how novels managed readers' sympathies as well. As a single working mother, Lutie Johnson represents a central concern of both New Deal reform and the social protest novel, but *The Street* challenges the terms of both by exposing and undercutting their narrative conventions. The novel forecloses the New Deal preference for a male-earned family wage by highlighting the unavailability of work for Lutie's husband due to race and then linking his marriage-ending affair to his feelings of diminished self-worth. Lutie struggles to make ends meet while maintaining her child's welfare and her own independence on 116th Street. Petry sets Lutie up as a virtuous mother who is determined to provide for her child, Bub, while protecting herself from sexual exploitation. However, rather than rescuing her family from poverty and the slum environment, Lutie's actions yield perverse effects that place both mother and son in danger, while the dynamics undercutting her efforts remain invisible to a state that can only see her as aberrant.

---

12. See Gordon, *Pitied but Not Entitled*, 111–306; Kessler-Harris, *Out to Work*, 250–272; Mink, *Wages of Motherhood*, 123–150, for discussions of the relationship between motherhood, work, and social welfare policy in the New Deal.

13. See Gordon, *Pitied but Not Entitled*, for discussion of this tradition. Policymakers eventually settled on the children of single women as the ideal subjects for aid since this eliminated the need to make distinctions between worthy and unworthy mothers at the federal level, leaving such distinctions to state and local authorities.

136 · CHAPTER 5

Though Petry leaves Hawkins unnamed in *The Street,* the novel invokes the folk concept almost immediately, signaling the novel's focus on the ecology of Harlem. As the book opens, a "cold November wind" blows through 116th Street in the block between Seventh and Eighth Avenues where Lutie and Bub live. Lutie claims, "She never really felt human until she reached Harlem," but she also views the environment as dangerous.[14] She claims that the ghetto's influence has caused the downfall of her parents, as well as Mrs. Hedges, Min, and Superintendent Jones. Most of all, Lutie fears the effects of the street on her child, Bub, who has to navigate it in her work absence. Lutie believes that "the street had pushed [Superintendent Jones] into basements away from light and air until he was being eaten up by some horrible obsession."[15] Thinking about her street, Lutie realizes, "It was a bad street. And then she thought about the other streets. It wasn't just this street that she was afraid of or that was bad. It was any street where people were packed together like sardines in a can."[16] Crucially, Lutie moves from sensory moral judgment to identify a source that has causes and could potentially be relieved.

Lutie's belief is reflected later in the novel by a lawyer, who suggests that he could easily paint for the jury a picture of 116th Street as "any street. . . . Any place where there's slums and dirt and poverty you find crime."[17] Lutie, going further, recognizes the racial component driving the making of slums:

> It was any city where they set up a line and say black folks stay on this side and white folks on this side, so that the black folks were crammed on top of each other—jammed and packed and forced into the smallest possible space until they were completely cut off from light and air.[18]

Here, Petry repeats the analysis of slum congestion in the FWP guidebooks and moves to link Harlem to all racial ghettoes. Like Wright's South Side, Harlem is drawn from a concrete place, but it is seen as interchangeable with other Black urban districts in the North, a far cry from the portrayals of Harlem as a unique cultural capital, productive autonomous zone, or entertainment district.

Petry's critique of housing also highlights the distinction between expectations and available opportunities. Facing housing options advertised as "reasonable," Lutie muses,

---

14. Petry, *Street,* 57.
15. Petry, *Street,* 57.
16. Petry, *Street,* 206.
17. Petry, *Street,* 391.
18. Petry, *Street,* 206.

> Reasonable—now that could mean almost anything. On Eighth Avenue it meant tenements—ghastly places not fit for humans. On St. Nicholas Avenue it meant high rents for small apartments; and on Seventh Avenue it meant great big apartments where you had to take in roomers in order to pay the rent. On this street it could mean almost anything.[19]

Lutie notes the absence of sunlight and the weak defenses of the buildings on 116th Street against seasonal temperatures. Later, once she has rented an apartment, Lutie echoes housing reformers' criticisms of tenements when she suggests that her apartment, and the others like it, are "dirty, dark, filthy traps."[20] The effects of this are evident in the reading of Superintendent Jones as a naturalist trope—a monstrous character twisted by his environment. Throughout the novel, the narrator focuses on Jones's lust for women as an irrational, compelling hunger. When he attempts to rape Lutie in the hallway of the building, Mrs. Hedges repels him, claiming, "You done lived in basements so long you ain't human no more."[21] As the Superintendent is linked to Bub throughout the book, through their friendship and their common worship of Lutie, the threat Lutie understands is that her own son will be reduced to monstrosity.

Readings of Petry's novel often turn on the extent to which it reinforces or undercuts Lutie's understanding of her environment as a malevolent force.[22] As Donald Pizer argues, highlighting the limitations of subjective knowledge was particularly important to the naturalist lens, which developed in conjunction with complex power relationships that were incomprehensible to individuals whose lives were affected by them.[23] Readers of such novels must be careful not to privilege any single character's understanding of their environment. However, the novel provides a structure of subjective and objective information that allows the reader to weigh perspectives and to see connections between local and global phenomena.

---

19. Petry, *Street*, 4.

20. Petry, *Street*, 73.

21. Petry, *Street*, 237.

22. Critics have generally taken two approaches to the novel. Some contend that *The Street*'s insistence that racism operates like an environmental force links it to *Native Son* as a naturalist novel. See Bell, "Ann Petry's Demythologizing of American Culture and Afro-American Culture," 105; Hicks, "This Strange Communion." Critics following Pryse, "Pattern against the Sky," have used the novel's many references to Benjamin Franklin's *Autobiography* as a means to highlight its interrogation of the boundaries of national community. These, critics have suggested that the novel connects Lutie's eventual failure to her naïve embrace of Franklinian ideals of thrift and virtue that are continually frustrated by environmental and social realities. See Winter, "Narrative Desire in Ann Petry's *The Street*"; Wurst, "Ben Franklin in Harlem," for accounts of *The Street* that expand on Pryse.

23. Pizer, *Theory and Practice of American Literary Naturalism*, 21.

138 • CHAPTER 5

Marjorie Pryse's influential essay "Pattern against the Sky" exposes one of the limits of Lutie's perspective, introducing a folk alternative in the novel's street-smart characters. Pryse suggests that *The Street* constantly undercuts Lutie's adherence to principles of self-determination and individual uplift through self-improvement, thrift, and hard work that the novel links referentially to Benjamin Franklin. It highlights a division between Lutie, who sees only chaos in the environment, and other characters who read its pattern. To claim that Lutie's perception is faulty suggests that other characters might read the environment in more productive ways and potentially offer alternatives to the sociological view of the ghetto. Mrs. Hedges, for example, sees the street as unique rather than typical:

> [Mrs. Hedges] knew so much about this particular block that she came to regard it as slightly different from any other place. When she referred to it as "the street," her lips seemed to linger over the words as though her mind paused at the sound to write capital letters and then enclosed the words in question marks—thus setting it off, and separating it from any other street in the city, giving it an identity, unmistakable and apart.[24]

Mrs. Hedges knows *this* street, and she knows how to operate on it. Indeed, other characters, like Min, Boots, and Junto, also have a more developed street sense than Lutie and engage more directly with its working-class culture. Pryse suggests that these foils serve as "the strongest evidence of a lingering cultural cohesion among the black community."[25] She argues:

> *The Street* does offer its readers an alternative in the vision of a black community which might embrace its grandmothers, its folklore, and the survival of human feeling, a street which might become, and thereby transform, "any street in the city"—even the street in Lyme, Connecticut, on which Petry shows us white people, like Mr. Chandler's brother, blowing their brains out.[26]

In this reading, Lutie fails to recognize that there is a Black, working-class folk culture just as available to her as it is to these other, more successful figures and that this street, recognized clearly, might have transformative powers.

The novel offers plenty of evidence to question such a hopeful reading. The characters Pryse identifies all find ways to work within localized power relations, but *The Street* does not suggest they offer an efficacious means of

24. Petry, *Street*, 252.
25. Pryse, "Pattern against the Sky," 125.
26. Pryse, "Pattern against the Sky," 129.

URBAN FOLK, STATE POWER, AND CITIZENSHIP IN PETRY AND ELLISON • 139

challenging the ghetto or a political community. Superintendent Jones is, as Kari J. Winter has suggested, a figure driven beyond self-control by an inability to fulfill desire.[27] Boots is similarly driven by passions that eventually lead to his death. Even Min, who finds independence from Jones through conjure work, does not move on to self-determination; instead, she moves in with, quite literally, the first man she sees on the street. While Mrs. Hedges is an entrepreneurial businesswoman, her business is the exploitation of women like Lutie. The book emphasizes the elements of control, rather than economic self-determination, in prostitution. One might as well read the exploitative White bar owner Junto, whose name evokes the group of Philadelphia businessmen Franklin organized both to exchange ideas and to coordinate business activities, as the novel's model of success. The novel never portrays a community on which Lutie could rely to meet her needs that would also provide a satisfactory counterbalance to the simultaneously local and national problem of the racialized ghetto.

However, the alternate frameworks of perception and agency that these characters represent are significant, and Pryse is correct that the complicated turns of folk culture offer at least a vision of a more humane order. To keep Jones from throwing her out, Min seeks the Prophet David, a root doctor who offers folk remedies for both physical and interpersonal ailments. The doctor's hoodoo prescription combines the display of Christian iconography with occult use of a potion. The cure works, but not in the way Min intends. Petry shows how the symbols induce a paralyzing sense of guilt that prevents Jones from throwing Min out of the apartment or physically abusing her. Indeed, the rituals are perhaps as important for giving Min space to develop a sense of self as they are for her protection. By the end of the novel, Min recognizes that she is no longer dependent on Jones, and, aided by this self-recognition, abandons him.

Throughout the novel, vernacular culture provides a sphere where hopes can be articulated and felt if not realized and where the trauma of daily life in the ghetto can be made bearable. *The Street* surveys a broad swath of African American urban vernacular culture, including dancing, singing, and musicianship. These activities are presented as a balm to the harshness of urban life. Lutie's brief singing career offers a glimpse of the interaction between folk culture, mass culture, and community. At the bar where she goes to escape her troubles, Lutie begins to croon after the end of a song:

---

27. Winter, "Narrative Desire in Ann Petry's *The Street*," 108–110.

## 140 · CHAPTER 5

> Her voice had a thin thread of sadness running through it that made the song important, that made it tell a story that wasn't in the words—a story of despair, of loneliness, of frustration. It was a story that all of them knew by heart and had always known because they had learned it soon after they were born and would go on adding to it until the day they died.[28]

Petry connects the blues with a shared experience of suffering, one that connects all of the African Americans in the room. In this connection, a utopian yearning remains. Lutie explicitly pins her dreams of escape from the ghetto on her performance and expresses them in it:

> Though she sang the words of the song, it was of something entirely different that she was thinking and putting into the music: she was leaving the street with its dark hallways, its mean, shabby rooms; she was taking Bub away with her to a place where there were no Mrs. Hedges, no resigned and disillusioned little girls, no half human creatures like the Super. She and Bub were getting out and away, and they would never be back.[29]

The elicited utopian vision is important to Lutie's ability to continue negotiating her daily trials. At the end of the song, she feels remorse for losing herself in the daydream, but the applause of both audience and orchestra shows that the feeling is what makes the song important to them as well. Here the novel affirms the importance of an imaginative folk culture where suffering and hopes can be expressed.

Moreover, Petry challenges Wright's positioning of the folk in the past by troubling the division between folk survivals and a modern urban culture. Foregrounding the mass cultural economic conditions on which folk culture rests, Petry complicates the distinction between popular expression and mass cultural commodification. Shared feeling provides Lutie a commercial opportunity as Boots Smith notices her talent and asks her to front his band. This opportunity involves costly exchanges. At the bar, Lutie calculates how much her drinks and the rent cost of that space cut into the savings that are meant to remove her family from the ghetto. When Boots enlists Lutie as a singer, her success depends on navigating his sexual demands. Not only is the performance a commodity, but Lutie also becomes part of the spectacle. While culture offers emotional support, communal feeling, and a potential path to economic independence and emotional sustenance, the novel shows that the

---

28. Petry, *Street*, 148.
29. Petry, *Street*, 222.

last path is unstable and transactional.[30] Ultimately, as Gayle Wurst has noted, Lutie faces a nearly impossible balance between virtue and autonomy.[31] Lutie's body and her family's security are the stakes in her cultural participation. She is determined to support her family, but in order to maintain her position in the band, the novel suggests, she would have to be willing to negotiate Boots's sexual demands, to become Junto's mistress, and eventually to become a prostitute. In order to increase her dependence, Junto orders Boots to keep her off salary. Without a stable income, Lutie is unable to make long-term decisions that would allow her to move. Critics often read Junto as the symbol of White power in the novel. Junto's Whiteness is troubled by the novel's repeated insistence that Junto views African Americans as his social equals.[32] However, this contradiction can be resolved by recognizing that Junto is essentially an agent, working in an already emplaced racist and capitalist power structure. In consequence, Junto becomes, by turns, the cultural benefactor, employer, and economic oppressor of Black Harlemites.

Crucially, the novel does not end with Lutie's subversion of Junto's power but instead with a vision of state paternalism gone wrong. Jones triumphs by finding a means to guide state power through predetermined racial channels as retribution for Lutie's rejection of his sexual advances, placing Bub beyond Junto's money and sphere of protection:

> This was the way to get the kid. Not even Junto with all his money could get the kid out of it. The more he thought about it, the more excited he became. If the kid should steal letters out of mail boxes, nobody, not even Junto, could get him loose from a rap like that. Because it was the Government.[33]

Like New Dealers, *The Street* presents the state as an institution with the power to curtail or circumvent local power. However, it is not just or benevolent. Instead, it is, at best, blind to its own racial biases and perhaps even will-

---

30. Nor does mass culture present a viable alternative. Like Lutie's venture to the bar, the movies offer Bub real solace, but are not without consequences. As Hicks, "This Strange Communion," 32, argues, Bub's inability to distinguish between the mystery films he watches and reality leads to his downfall.

31. Wurst, "Ben Franklin in Harlem," 17.

32. Pryse, "Pattern against the Sky," 118, notes that Junto, as a reference to the Philadelphia organization of business leaders Franklin founded, stands for the other side of Franklinian enterprise, the cultivation of exclusive relationships that aid only a few in their rise. See Hicks, "This Strange Communion," 29, for a discussion of Junto's "colorblindness."

33. Petry, *Street*, 91.

142 • CHAPTER 5

fully malevolent.[34] Rather than reinforcing the power of the family, the federal government isolates a child from his mother.

The racial bias shaping the case is clear. Jones depends on the law's willingness to see Bub and other Black children like him as potentially criminal. In the eyes of the law, Lutie is also seen as a poor mother. A detective waiting for her suggests that she is "probably some drunken bitch. They usually are."[35] The structure of the legal system is also unfair; Lutie cannot afford a lawyer who wants to charge $200 for a service that even he believes will be unnecessary. Reflecting on the situation, Lutie makes the crucial connections between her condition and racial practice: Whites won't employ her husband, so she herself must go to work. This situation strains the family relationship, and in consequence "the women work and the kids go to reform school."[36] When she kills Boots Smith in self-defense, she knows her actions will reflect on Bub negatively. In a last act of motherly caring and self-preservation, Lutie flees, knowing that her action seals her image as the undeserving mother the White public already assumed that she was. In the split between Lutie's motivation and the perception of her actions, the novel highlights the resulting damage when state power is refracted through assumptions about race and gender.

What divides *The Street* and Petry's *Holiday* essay are their visions of governmental efficacy. If the essay invokes governmental provision of housing as the way to combat Old Man Hawk, the novel offers a much more skeptical view. *The Street*'s vision of Harlem is unrelenting, and its vision of governmental agency is deeply pessimistic. Public housing is nowhere in view as a solution in *The Street*. Alan Wald notes that Petry insisted, following a view of political writing advanced by Albert Maltz, that novelists should have the ability to present realistic social diagnoses without having to offer a picture of social totality or satisfying political trajectories. He argues that *The Street* works by "subtraction," assuming the reader's familiarity with "a general view of potential solutions," and withholding "positive resolution" while demonstrating the inevitability of negative outcomes without those solutions.[37] Perhaps, then, the essay's relative optimism reflects a genre that seeks to offer answers along with diagnoses.

Still, Petry's "Harlem" essay ends with an accusatory turn that ties its outlook somewhat more closely to *The Street* and to earlier FWP intertexts. The essay invokes the many views of Harlem by "sociologists, anthropologists, pol-

---

34. See Hicks, "This Strange Communion," 32, for a more thorough account of Jones's decision.

35. Petry, *Street*, 387.

36. Petry, *Street*, 388.

37. Wald, *Trinity of Passion*, 118–119, 127.

iticians" and notes of their attempts to make the neighborhood legible, "It has been turned and twisted, to the right and to the left; prettied up and called colorful and exotic; defamed and labeled criminal."[38] Yet the essay suggests that

> looked at head on, its thousand faces finally merge into one—the face of a ghetto. In point of time, it belongs back in the Middle Ages. Harlem is an anachronism—shameful and unjustifiable, set down in the heart of the biggest, richest city in the world.[39]

Seeing Harlem directly, Petry suggests, requires recognizing the pattern, the irony of its setting amidst American affluence. Like the documentary texts in the previous chapter, then, the essay leverages the rhetoric of modernity and democracy to invoke the urgency of state action. Public housing is needed. But the figure of Hawkins haunts the essay as a marker of the state's continuing failure to act effectively, or even worse, to act in ways that exacerbate problems. Here, Petry's work has much in common with the FWP social histories and their documentary intertexts.

Both *The Street* and Petry's "Harlem" essay deploy folk figures to communicate multiple perspectives and messages, even while the novel questions the efficacy of the folk as a means of generating scalable political agency or community. In this tension, these works highlight the necessity of seeing complexity and pattern simultaneously. Though this focus seems to echo the FWP guidebooks' attempts to discern hidden spatial logics, it refuses their depiction of benevolent state modernization. Instead, while recognizing the government as a crucial agent in social change, Petry's resolutions also point back to the federal government as bearing responsibility for Black citizens' curtailed opportunities. Petry highlights possibilities of action but forgoes the assurances of the FWP texts or even the sincere hopes of *New World A-Coming* and *They Seek a City*. Drawing on his experiences as an FWP writer, Ralph Ellison would also advance a desire to maintain both pattern and complexity in his own novel exploring national history and Black citizenship.

## Citizens from Nowhere

When Jerre Mangione asked Federal Writer #700846 about what he took from his work on the FWP, Ralph Ellison replied, "I became a writer."[40] Though

---

38. Petry, "Harlem," 168.
39. Petry, "Harlem," 168.
40. Mangione Papers, Interview with Ralph Ellison, 30 June 1969.

some FWP writers felt ambivalence about project work, Ellison was at the beginning of his career, and he acknowledged having much to gain from his work there. In this regard, he was like Ellen Tarry, Margaret Walker, Frank Yerby, and many other young Black writers, whose access to the publishing world was limited and for whom the FWP served as an important apprenticeship. Though critics often note Ellison's recognition of the FWP as a formative experience, its influence yet remains relatively underanalyzed; critics generally posit Ellison's engagement with Richard Wright and the interwar Left as his key intellectual context in the 1930s and 1940s. Though some critics have considered the role of the FWP in providing images and folk material for the book, relatively few have considered how these materials shaped its political outlook. Jerrold Hirsch has offered one of the most useful summations of the FWP's influence on *Invisible Man,* stating that Ellison

> found a way to create a work of art that in its very structure wrestled with all the issues that had preoccupied the FWP: the nature of the relationship between the individual and the folk group, provincialism and cosmopolitanism, tradition and modernity, the fact of diversity and the need for unity.[41]

These gaps offer an opportunity to reexamine Ellison's activities while on the project and to resituate *Invisible Man* in the nexus of FWP work and the conversation in FWP intertexts. A focus on the New Deal illuminates the broad field of liberal discourses with which Ellison engaged. In particular, *Invisible Man*'s deployment of vernacular culture and history attacks both sociological discourses and the utopian underpinnings of planning advanced by the FWP and other New Deal agencies. As this book has argued, these discourses were central to the New Deal national imaginary before World War II and remained important in domestic and international frameworks afterward.[42]

Through its deployment of vernacular culture as the basis of a revised understanding of history, *Invisible Man* refashions liberal citizenship to perform critical pluralism, a mode of citizenship that was antiutopian and cautious in outlook. The ideal citizen of the New Deal welfare state as imagined in its own documents was historically knowledgeable, socially progressive, and oriented toward modernization. Ellison's novel brackets each of those ide-

---

41. Hirsch, "Cultural Pluralism and Applied Folklore," 54–55. Sara Rutkowski also includes an excellent chapter on Ellison and the FWP in *Literary Legacies of the Federal Writers Project.* For other accounts of links between Ellison's FWP work and the novel, see O'Mealy, *Craft of Ralph Ellison*; Baron, "I Saw Mrs. Saray Sitting on a Bombalerry."

42. This chapter's discussion of Ellison clarifies and extends my analysis in Butts, "Pattern and Chaos."

als, highlighting the ways that positivist overconfidence tended to disguise prejudice, to elide stories that spoke to ongoing dispossession, and to posit uncertain teleological speculation as facts. It calls into question the recognized causal patterns of historical narrative, opening up other modes of connection, both historical and symbolic. With these connections, it emphasizes local knowledge and claims on justice against broader plans for reform and modernization. *Invisible Man* simultaneously maintains critical distance from welfare state liberalism even while supporting many of its core ideas.

Ellison applied for WPA relief status in 1937 and was hired in June 1938. His duties, as stated in his WPA reclassification notice were "to gather historical, cultural, commercial, educational, and other data for presentation to the staff editor as a comprehensive, authoritative, well-written survey of the subject assigned."[43] Ellison's prior work experience fit well with the FWP. His references included letters from the psychoanalyst Harry Stack Sullivan, for whom Ellison worked as a clerk and receptionist, and William Sturgis of the *Champion,* where Ellison had worked as a member of the editorial staff and as a freelance reporter. It also includes one for Ellison's publicity work for Adam Clayton Powell Jr.'s organization, the Greater New York Coordinating Committee for Employment, which carried out several successful campaigns to integrate utility companies, Harlem stores, and the 1939 World's Fair.[44] In his biography, Arnold Rampersad characterizes Ellison as adept at navigating the complex politics of the New York FWP office, where labor struggles, political factionalism, and anxiety over the continuing existence of the project fueled everyday interpersonal disputes.[45] Ellison's ratings as an employee were consistently "Excellent," and he was promoted to senior newspaperman in October 1938.[46]

Since Ellison joined the FWP relatively late, he missed most of the work on the New York guidebooks. Instead, Ellison took on general editorial work, research, and reporting for various subprojects: a *Famous Trials* manuscript, the Negro History Group, and the Living Lore group, one of Botkin's folklore projects. The Living Lore work is the most widely recognized FWP influence on Ellison's writing. Heavily shaped by the ideas of Benjamin Botkin and Sterling Brown, this project rejected the idea of folklore as an anachronism, whether as a fading holdover from the past or, as John Lomax had argued, a

---

43. Ellison Papers, Reclassification Notice, John Cody to Ralph Ellison, 20 October 1938, Box 19, Folder 6.

44. See Ellison Papers, Box 1, Folder 17. See also Greenberg, *Or Does It Explode,* 133–139.

45. See Bold, *WPA Guides,* 92–122; Mangione, *Dream and the Deal,* 155–192, for discussion of these arguments on the New York City FWP unit.

46. Ellison Papers, Box 19, Folder 6.

146 • CHAPTER 5

residual cultural resistance to industrial capitalism. Living Lore instead demonstrated that folklore was being re-outfitted for urban existence, and new folkways were emerging within urban life.[47] The productive presence of vernacular culture was a crucial insight for *Invisible Man,* and documented Living Lore moments are visible throughout the text, among these: a chant about Buckeye the Rabbit that Ellison heard on a Harlem playground; the story of the invisible trickster "Sweet-the-Monkey" told to Ellison by Leo Gurley; and a line from an excised chapter in which Mary Rambo talks about being in New York without New York being in her, which Ellison picked up in an anonymous oral interview in 1939 at Eddie's Bar.[48]

Though archival records indicate that Ellison's work for the Negro History Unit consumed more of his time, critics have given that project less recognition than the Living Lore work. In part this is because in the critical divide between Wright's sociological approach and Ellison's vernacular approach, the material from the Living Lore project seems to resonate more clearly in the distinctive narrative dynamics of *Invisible Man.* The Living Lore and other New Deal folk projects yielded insights about culture and, more importantly, documents of culture in the form of oral histories, songs, and stories that formed the basis of much of postwar American popular culture and counterculture, as well as the memory/recovery of African American culture during the Civil Rights era. By contrast, many of the social histories remained unpublished until 1967, limiting recognition of their impact. As my previous chapter demonstrated, the contribution of the social history work was indirect, appearing primarily in the postwar flourishing of sociological and documentary studies of African America.

A quick scan of Ellison's Negro History project assignment titles—"Short story of Negroes of New York on swimming as an amusement"; "Problems of early Negroes during English occupation, etc."; "Short history of Dutch using Negroes to fight Indians"; "Trace deed of Madison Square to the city by one Annie Angola"—reveals a grouping that initially seems scattershot. However, in the diversity and richness of African American experience, Ellison was developing an alternate notion of American history. He openly recognized his debt in a 1977 interview with Ann Banks:

> For me, being on the Writers' Project was a way to broaden my knowledge of Afro-American culture. I'd always liked the stories and things, and I couldn't hear enough of them, so this was throwing me into my own history. Once

---

47. Hirsch, "Cultural Pluralism and Applied Folklore."
48. These interviews can be found in NARA, RG69, Box A648.

you touched the history of blacks in New York then you were deep into American history.[49]

Ellison's reminiscent evaluation captures an important dynamic of *Invisible Man* reflected in its preoccupation with depth and the hidden, captured so adeptly in the idea of "lower frequencies" on which the novel ends—the difference between the national historical myths of American history and "touch[ing]" the materials that form its "deep" elements.[50]

Ellison would have been aware of historical misrepresentation and mythmaking before his FWP employment, of course, but his research in historical material and folk stories revealed both telling details and important counternarratives. What Ellison took from both the folklore and social history projects was their joint assertion of the continuous presence of African American culture, which was more than merely participatory in the civic pluralist sense.[51] Instead it highlighted the gaps in the national narrative, even while contributing directly to American culture. Demonstrating its potential for building counternarrative, Eli Luster, one of Ellison's interview subjects, charted a course through American history built on a series of correspondences centered on the sinking of the *Titanic*. In African American folklore, the *Titanic's* sinking is not portrayed as tragedy or a metaphor for technological hubris, but instead is recast as comeuppance for the ship's owners refusal of passage to the boxer Jack Johnson because of his race.[52] Luster's scattered telling connects it to George Washington's active suppression of African Americans and to the coming World War, as a reminder of the limits of White civilization and its pretensions to inclusion, order, and civility.[53] For Ellison this presence ultimately conflicted with the certainties of the narrative of modernization advanced in the American Guides by revealing the deep patterns of racism within national history, which he would call in *Invisible Man* "the pattern within the chaos."[54]

When Irving Howe critiqued *Invisible Man* for failing to offer a systematic analysis of the ghetto in the manner of Petry or Wright, he was partially right:

---

49. Ellison Papers, Interview with Ann Banks.

50. Ellison, *Invisible Man*, 581.

51. Morrison, *Playing in the Dark: Whiteness and the Literary Imagination,* makes a similar point about the deep shaping of national meaning through literal and figurative blackness.

52. Ellison Papers, Box 19, Folder 6. As the song "The Titanic" by Huddie "Lead Belly" Ledbetter illustrates, this was a common motif.

53. Ellison Papers, Interview with Eli Luster, Box 19, Folder 6. Barbara Foley also discusses this interview and links it to the character Peter Wheatstraw. See Foley, *Wrestling with the Left*, 204.

54. Ellison, *Invisible Man*, 580.

148 · CHAPTER 5

*Invisible Man* does not showcase the deterministic effect of the physical environment on psychology evident in the more sociological sections of *The Street* or *Native Son.* Instead, *Invisible Man* often portrays Harlem as a symbolic, even surreal, landscape, one in which individuals negotiate their position in society through images and materials, highlighting a different view of psychological formation. Ellison prefigured this approach in "Harlem Is Nowhere," and Arnold Rampersad has shown that themes from the essay echo throughout the landscape of *Invisible Man.*[55]

Beginning with its "mazelike" underground journey to reach the Lafargue Psychiatric Clinic, the essay's introduction reads similarly to the kind of prose that FWP editors expected. The essay seeks to understand "a character that arises from the impact between urban slum conditions and folk sensibilities."[56] The essay spins out a series of "surreal fantasies" in sketching "a character that arises from the impact between urban slum conditions and folk sensibilities":

> A man ducks in and out of traffic shouting and throwing imaginary grenades that actually exploded during World War I; a boy participates in the rape-robbery of his mother; a man beating his wife in his park uses boxing "science" and observes Marquis of Queensberry rules (no rabbit punching, no blows below the belt); two men hold a third while a lesbian slashes him to death with a razor blade.[57]

Though Ellison's depiction of Harlem is far more violent than Ottley's version, there is a similar representational strategy at work in the presentation of "slum-shocked" figures whose peculiarities mark social and psychological dynamics.[58]

In both "Harlem Is Nowhere" and *Invisible Man,* Ellison echoes a crucial question of the New Deal critique of slums: *What kind of citizen comes from nowhere?* The question of citizenship has long been one of the key fault lines in critical approaches to *Invisible Man.* In the epilogue, the narrator asserts the possibility that "even an Invisible Man has a socially responsible role to play."[59] However, Ellison's meaning is notoriously difficult to pin down. The book often undercuts the narrator's claims to knowledge, and its first chapter highlights "social responsibility" as coded language for docility. Should

---

55. See Rampersad, *Ralph Ellison,* 219–222.

56. Ellison, *Collected Essays of Ralph Ellison,* 321.

57. Ellison, *Collected Essays of Ralph Ellison,* 321–322.

58. Ellison, *Collected Essays of Ralph Ellison,* 325. Langston Hughes in "Down Under in Harlem," also used this term.

59. Ellison *Invisible Man,* 581.

readers take seriously the claim, or is it just "buggy jiving"?[60] If the former, then the novel seems to be gesturing toward a mode of citizenship consonant with the liberal welfare state. The latter reading questions whether liberalism is a framework in which racial inequity can be addressed. *Invisible Man's* reworking of American history through the "stuff" Ellison encountered as a member of the FWP provides a lens through which the question of the novel's approach to liberalism and citizenship can be resolved.

Discussing his experience interviewing people for the project, Ellison noted, "You didn't have to encourage them too much before this stuff began to come out."[61] "Stuff" is a decidedly awkward word, not to mention an ambiguous one, but here it has a specific historical and institutional context. "Stuff" was a popular term in the Federal Arts lexicon and served as a folky, humorous reference to the immense range of phenomena in American history and culture. The 1937 collection of literature by FWP writers was even named *American Stuff*. In *Invisible Man*, Ellison's Harlem is riotous, filled with noise, chaotic action, and typological characters like those of *New World A-Coming*. Ellison created an allegorical landscape in which stuff, in the form of vernacular material, directly intervenes in the present. Throughout the novel, folkways, historical objects, and other forms of vernacular culture call into question historical narrative as an authoritative pattern, giving shape to the past, present, and future.

Ellison's thinking on vernacular culture developed significantly after his FWP experience. Robin Lucy demonstrates that Ellison's 1930s discussions on the folk largely accord with Wright's discussion in "Blueprint for Negro Writing," but Ellison's essays throughout the 1940s reflect the growth of a conception of the folk engaged with modern politics. Lucy argues that his 1941 essay "Recent Negro Fiction," "intimates that the expressive forms of the urban working-folk embody cultural energies and insights that express a concomitant political desire or direction."[62] As Ellison reckoned with the importance of the folk material he had gathered in Harlem for the FWP and the antiracist and anticolonial movements he was chronicling in *Negro Quarterly*, he began to see the folk as more than just reactive expression. Ellison viewed the blues, jazz, zoot suits, and other elements of Black culture as modes of signification yielding political possibilities while asserting the simultaneous individual and collective nature of Black experience in America. This was precisely what sociologists were missing in their accounts of Black communities. Without

---

60. Ellison, *Invisible Man*, 581. See Larkin, "Postwar Liberalism, Close Reading, and 'You'" for an excellent summation of the sides and stakes of this debate.

61. Ellison Papers, Interview with Ann Banks.

62. Lucy, "Flying Home," 272.

it, Ellison argued in his attack on Gunnar Myrdal's *An American Dilemma* in nearly the same language Ellison would later use to describe the condition of invisibility, African Americans too often ended up "a nightmarish fantasy of the white American mind."[63] The intervention of vernacular material serves a crucial role in Ellison's novel, creating the possibility of a creative engagement based in Black history and culture.

*Invisible Man* often marks these interventions with temporal intrusions, in which stuff suddenly disrupts the expected framework of time and its attendant values and hierarchies. As a musician and an audiophile, Ellison was well aware of the power of time as a patterning and disorganizing phenomenon. From the discussion of the local yokel beating the scientific boxer and the time-slowing powers of marijuana and jazz in the prologue to the surreal riot scene at the end of the story, the novel is filled with references to slipping into alternative temporalities. Most often, this state is referred to as being "out of history," a phrase that suggests both being outside history and emerging from it. In each of these cases, Ellison imagines a temporality outside the efficient beat of science and progress that allows for action beyond recognized etiological vectors and enables new possibilities of movement.[64]

In particular, two moments of temporal intrusion indebted to Ellison's FWP work mark the narrator's awakening from the shattered dream of Washingtonian uplift. In the factory-hospital scene, where the doctor interrogates him after he wakes up, he is surprised when he is asked who his mother is. Mishearing it as a Mama joke, the narrator draws on the politics of respectability and responds in his head "I don't play the dozens," seeing the game as beneath his dignity.[65] But when he is asked about Buckeye the Rabbit, the narrator has a realization:

> Somehow *I* was Buckeye the Rabbit . . . or had been, when as children we danced and sang barefoot in the dusty streets:
>
> > *Buckeye the Rabbit*
> > *Shake it, shake it*
> > *Buckeye the Rabbit*
> > *Break it, break it . . .*[66]

---

63. Ellison, *Collected Essays of Ralph Ellison*, 328. See also Lucy, "Flying Home," 264–266.

64. Baker, "To Move without Moving" discusses folk figurations of unrecognized possibilities of action in the novel.

65. Ellison, *Invisible Man*, 241.

66. Ellison, *Invisible Man*, 241–242.

Though the chant is from the narrator's Southern hometown, Ellison picked it up verbatim from the playgrounds of a public school in Harlem.[67] The image collapses temporalities and spaces, linking them as it makes the narrator aware of the way repressed experiences shape his identity and its possible forms. Suddenly, the narrator *is* playing the dozens, drawing on vernacular culture to offer a retort: "He was your mother's backdoor man."[68] Here, American stuff helps the narrator regain elements of identity he has repressed in his attempt to be a socially responsible citizen.

Fragmentary history returns as a force in the eviction scene where the narrator first begins to use rhetoric as a tool of authority. As he views the objects of the elderly couple's past, things with meanings unrecognized by the state that is literally uncovering and dispossessing them, it seems the power of stuff compels him to empathy and action:

> I turned and stared again at the jumble, no longer looking at what was before my eyes, but inwardly-outwardly, around a corner into the dark, far-away-and-long-ago, not so much of my own memory as of remembered words, of linked verbal echoes, images, heard even when not listening at home. And it was as though I myself was being dispossessed of some painful yet precious thing that I could not bear to lose. . . .[69]

If the factory-hospital scene is the point at which folkways bring the narrator to a new form of self-consciousness, the anachronistic congeries in the eviction scene in Harlem materialize the folk, allow the narrator to touch history, and hail him as a citizen of a social body. Mark C. Conner contends,

> The things in *Invisible Man* do not simply exist in present time and space; rather they are portals to a larger concept of time, history, and identity than is otherwise available to the Invisible Man. . . . Ellison's objects do not merely point the Invisible Man toward a larger universe—they create that universe and make it exist in the present moment.[70]

---

67. NARA, RG69, Ellison, "Folklore, Harlem Children's Rhymes." 15 December 1939, Box A648, Folklore Project Folder, WPA Records. The draft indicates Ellison interviewed and recorded songs near PS89 at 134th St. and 135th St.

68. Ellison, *Invisible Man,* 243.

69. Ellison, *Invisible Man,* 273.

70. Conner, "Litany of Things," 172–173. Conner also ties in this passage to the narrator's cognizance of community.

As it does in Walter Benjamin's "Theses on the Philosophy of History," the detritus of the past here serves as a material record of, and entry into, the suppressed elements of history. It also invokes an intergenerational debt premised on justice.[71] The narrator does not recognize the full import the pile of stuff has for the older couple; he only knows the necessity of acting to prevent their dispossession and displacement.

For Wright, folkways provided a coded language of survival in agrarian environments and ameliorated suffering in urban ones. While the new generation of "Men in the Making" Wright envisioned would ostensibly cast off folk knowledge, Ellison understood the power in Wright's evocation of a folk history, as he clearly indicated in his enthusiastic response to *12 Million Black Voices,* but *Invisible Man* resolves the tension between tale and telling by reworking the understanding of the folk.[72] In *Invisible Man,* folk knowledge, drawn out by material remnants, by *stuff,* is precisely what makes the narrator able to engage with his environment in a way that evades its patterning. *Invisible Man* grants a continuously generative presence to folk history consonant with the Living Lore approach. In turn, its presence disrupts the selective patterns of national mythology that legitimate White supremacy.

Problematizing the concept of history as a selective pattern that tends toward justice is crucial to the book's critique of New Deal development narrative. The Brotherhood with its "scientific history" serves as selective history's most visible champions in the novel. A clear reference to the Communist Party—if one that creates a straw version of its dynamic presence in Harlem—the Brotherhood offers a unilineal, progressive account of history that temporally sorts individuals and groups. Brother Jack, the Brotherhood's leader, suggests to the narrator that the sympathy that he feels for the elderly couple who were being evicted is misplaced. Jack tells him, "History has passed them by. Unfortunate, but there's nothing to do about them. They're like dead limbs that must be pruned away so that the tree may bear young fruit or the storms of history will blow them down anyway."[73] *Invisible Man* notes the seductiveness of the idea for the narrator, and for a time he adopts it, studying its logic to see how it might be useful.

However, the Brotherhood's idea of history does not square with the narrator's experience. Ellison clearly develops an understanding of the folk as useful, even necessary, as the narrator forges a political identity. When asked

---

71. Conner, "Litany of Things," 173, also makes this link to Benjamin. See Benjamin "Theses on the Philosophy of History," 253–264.

72. See Ellison, *Selected Letters of Ralph Ellison,* 143–146, for his response to *12 Million Black Voices.*

73. Ellison, *Invisible Man,* 291.

to perform a gospel tune for a Brotherhood party by a White member who sees all Black people as naturally endowed entertainers, the narrator acknowledges the racial stereotyping but also muses that there should be a way that he could be able to participate in singing since he enjoys it. In Harlem as the spokesperson for the Brotherhood, the narrator's activities center on building an organized community, and he turns to folk culture to achieve this aim. He finds inspiration in the leg iron of a chain gang escapee, which he keeps on his desk and which another Brotherhood member instinctively recognizes as a threat to Brotherhood teachings. The events that the narrator organizes in Harlem draw on popular activities like high-step marching and music. He even adopts the stump speech technique utilized by the Brotherhood's popular enemy, Ras the Exhorter. All of these activities put him at odds with the Brotherhood since they evoke racial experiences and community.

Barbara Foley and Lawrence Jackson have shown that Ellison's novel once contained a more positive representative of Left politics as well.[74] A merchant marine named Leroy, a boarder at Mary Rambo's house, leaves a journal behind with militant internationalist views that play a significant role in the political education of the narrator. Leroy's journal is a reminder of how deep Ellison's commitments to international and national Left politics ran. Ellison cut it in 1951 on the advice of editors who saw it as prolix, dispersing fragments into the epilogue.[75] In the absence of this positive figuration, communism as a whole comes under fire, and the novel tacks away from the kind of labor-oriented community suggested by Wright in *12 Million Black Voices*. The expungement changed the plot structure of the book as well as its political outlook. As Foley notes, the novel trades a politics of organized resistance for one focused on nation, individual citizenship, and diversity.[76] However, that does not mean that the novel loses its political efficacy. Instead, its orientation decidedly becomes more liberal and national in focus. The novel enacts an understanding of political power emerging from within Black American culture, aligning with the political movements of the postwar era that sought to hold the nation to account for the promises of the New Deal.

In this regard, Progressive liberalism is not off the hook for its blindness to the fundamental racial elements shaping its understandings of history. Ellison's novel contests Progressive teleological claims often on the same grounds as its attack on the Brotherhood, though its critique is less direct. As Alan Nadel argues, Ellison also took a shot at Progressive thinker and planner Lewis Mumford by referencing his *The Golden Day: A Study in American*

---

74. Foley, *Wrestling with the Left*, 221–236, 342–349; Jackson, *Ralph Ellison*, 414–428.

75. Jackson, *Ralph Ellison*, 416.

76. Foley, *Wrestling with the Left*, 345.

*Literature.* Mumford's nostalgic focus on the preindustrial eras in most of his 1930s criticism was meant to remind the reader that a greater future was possible by reference to more organic past societies, while his utopian visions and activities as a critic and planner sought to call that future into being. Mumford's critique helped elevate Herman Melville, Ralph Waldo Emerson, Walt Whitman, Nathaniel Hawthorne, and Henry David Thoreau to the liberal democratic pantheon, but the fact of slavery provided a glaring counterpoint to the freedom these authors invoked.[77] Ellison's essay "Twentieth Century Fiction and the Black Mask of Humanity" exposed the extent to which slavery informed the discussions of freedom in literature. Clearly, Mumford's blindness provoked Ellison's ire: the bar in *Invisible Man* that bears the name of Mumford's book is filled with African American veterans who have attempted to claim citizenship, have been cast aside as psychologically ill, and who are staging a revolt against their attendant, Supercargo, whose name references supervision of transported slaves. *Invisible Man* reminds readers of the human toll of Mumford's celebrated preindustrial era and the Progressive debt to the fantasy of republican subjectivity.

Ellison also challenges a selective cultural nationalism that affirms Black identity to the exclusion of broader political alliances. Ras the Exhorter, like Marcus Garvey, a West Indian advocate of Black nationalism, is the primary counterbalance to the Brotherhood and serves as a potential for a politics founded on Black vernacular history. Ellison's decision to anachronistically juxtapose these elements—Garvey was most powerful in the 1920s, the Communist Party in the 1930s—spoke to the continuing influence of Black nationalism beyond Garvey. Like Ottley, Bontemps, and Conroy, Ellison was frank about the seductiveness of Black nationalism. Ras generates large crowds through public speeches and appeals to Black solidarity, challenging the Brotherhood for popular leadership in Harlem. To the Brotherhood, Ras is simply a man outside history, who cannot see the possibility of cross-racial alliances, but in the text, he serves as a potent reminder of the continuing importance of race as a framework of meaning and potential political alliances. Ellison also shows how easily racial nationalism is co-opted. When the Brotherhood allows conditions in Harlem to deteriorate, Ras gains in power. Claiming the title of Destroyer, he precipitates a riot. For the narrator, the image of Ras on horseback armed with spear and shield is at once terrifying and absurd. However, the narrator quickly figures out that Ras is doing exactly what the Brotherhood had hoped he would do, bringing conditions in Harlem into crisis.

---

77. Nadel, *Invisible Criticism*, 86.

Exposing the hidden elements and the will to power in selective history carries a political risk: it might encourage cynicism. "What if," the narrator asks when he encounters Rinehart's zoot suiters, "history was not a reasonable citizen, but a madman full of paranoid guile and these boys his agents, his big surprise! His own revenge?"[78] The zoot suiters represent a sartorial revolt against wartime fabric quotas, a kind of anticitizenship in the face of attacks by servicemen on Black, Latino, and Filipino individuals. Rinehart's own multiplicity of identities all work to take advantage of chaos, allowing him to operate in multiple places and in multiple guises. Within Rinehartism lies the possibility of smooth action, hidden and highly individual motives—a stylistic engagement for which the Brotherhood has no category. However, the novel suggests it does not allow for an ethical engaged politics, as the narrator suggests in a semantic slip when he responds that the Brotherhood's opportunistic politics amount to "Rinehartism—cynicism."[79]

The final riot scene, which the narrator unintentionally spurs, raises the same specter of political disinvestment that the FWP guides had raised to cement the novel's disavowal of cynicism. The Brotherhood's sudden, calculated withdrawal from Harlem enflames both Black nationalist and more cynical passions, and forms an interesting analogue with the role of the federal government in urban disinvestment. The FWP had blamed pre–New Deal leadership failures for the conditions leading to the 1935 Harlem riot, but Ellison had both the 1935 and 1943 Harlem riots as inspiration, and the government could not dodge responsibility for the latter.[80] Wartime scaling back of both the FWP and the New Deal's more ambitious community projects had begun to undercut what goodwill had been garnered.

In the riots, the crucial figure representing disenchantment is Dupre, who attempts to burn the tenements. Dupre remains one of the more underrepresented figures in criticism of the novel, despite his prominence as the final in the succession of figures the narrator encounters. George E. Kent, in a passage that casts Dupre in the same vein as Rinehart, contends,

> The dramatic and symbolic function of Dupre and his followers is to reflect the folk ability to move with poise amidst chaos and in contradiction to the

---

78. Ellison, *Invisible Man*, 441. See Jimoh, *Spiritual, Blues and Jazz People in African American Fiction*, 148–150, for a discussion of Rinehartism as an idea that the narrator rejects as a philosophy of citizenship while maintaining awareness of its useful evasive and critical stance.

79. Ellison, *Invisible Man*, 504.

80. See Capeci, *Harlem Riot of 1943*, for a history of the 1943 uprising.

156 • CHAPTER 5

flat rational assumptions of the Brotherhood concerning its mission as planners for others. The rioters move with a plan that directly confronts Reality.[81]

This idea nicely illustrates the possibility of folkways for generating action. However, the primary aim in the arson is destruction of the offending structure; little thought is given to what will come next. Indeed, Dupre's arson achieves slum clearance with remarkable efficiency at little cost to the state. While Rinehart and Dupre figure as useful vernacular alternatives to the Brotherhood's scientific history, they do not offer solutions to the novel's concerns about citizenship. Instead, like the specters of dissent in the FWP guides and documentary intertexts, they offer warnings about the cynicism in the face of political abandonment.

Ultimately, the question is whether an understanding of citizenship can be formed that recognizes the broader stuff of history, while rejecting both cynicism and the idealized citizenship envisioned by New Dealers. As the narrator considers how he should approach his return in the epilogue, he reflects on his grandfather's advice: "Could he have meant—hell, he *must* have meant the principle, that we were to affirm the principle on which the country was built and not the men, or at least not the men who did the violence."[82] While it might be tempting to view this as an acceptance of foundational national myths, as it seemed to many critics in the 1960s, Charles Banner-Haley correctly argues that Ellison's work takes far too much notice of historical damage to fold this statement into a bland romantic nationalism.[83] Instead, *Invisible Man* modifies civic pluralism, placing an emphasis on caution and creation to advance a narrative in which African Americans are central participants in the development of a national democratic culture.

The epilogue suggests how a critical liberal citizenship might be approached when the narrator makes this provocative claim:

And the mind that has conceived of a plan of living must never lose sight of the chaos against which that pattern was conceived. That goes for societies as well as for individuals. Thus, having tried to give pattern to the chaos within the pattern of your certainties, I must come out, I must emerge.[84]

This passage highlights the narrator's aim: to expose the phantasmagoric elements of Western fantasies by narrating the return of material and discursive

81. Kent, "Ralph Ellison and the Afro-American Folk and Cultural Tradition," 54.
82. Ellison, *Invisible Man*, 574.
83. Banner-Haley, "Ralph Ellison and the Invisibility of the Black Intellectual," 164.
84. Ellison, *Invisible Man*, 580–581.

elements rendered obsolete or invisible by modernization. In the process, it has shown those fantasies as being based not so much on progress but rather on brutal, willful repression. The displaced elements of history remain, though often in fragmentary form or attached to discourses that make their presence difficult to see; even the concept of the folk itself can obscure the continuity and modernity of vernacular culture. The critical citizenship Ellison proposes, on the other hand, would need to keep the stuff of history in view, recognize their presence and the debts owed, and thus resist their permanent incorporation into political narratives disguising a will to power and exclusion. The simultaneous view of pattern and chaos offers a perspective from which the narratives structuring power can be viewed and understood as contingent.

Ultimately, Ellison's invocation of living on the "lower frequencies" signals a style of citizenship—as the narrator's grandfather suggests, a mode of engagement with power embedded in narrative, rather than a set "plan of living." Hirsch suggests:

> Like FWP officials the *Invisible Man* argues for pluralism and a way of preserving democratic liberalism in an increasingly totalitarian world. Ellison's *Invisible Man* uses an image Franklin Roosevelt had employed: "America is woven of many strands and I would recognize them and let it so remain."[85]

The novel's concluding statements clearly indicate espousal of a form of civic pluralism, yet embracing a "cosmopolitan view of the world," which Hirsch suggests is the resolution to the narrator's and the New Deal's dilemmas, does not fully capture the novel's critical engagement with questions of liberalism and citizenship.[86] The novel invokes democratic pluralism and cosmopolitanism as desirable ends, but it also privileges experience and lived engagement over ideals. The narrator claims that what African Americans have to offer is not just material cultural contributions but an understanding of how to live in a pluralist environment structured by differential power relations. The narrator suggests, "We were older than they, in the sense of what it took to live in the world with others."[87] African Americans' long experience with the darker side of liberalism provides attunement to both the nuances and the aporia of a pluralistic society, especially its tendency to disguise racial power relations in universal presumptions and to design policies built on those assertions. Black vernacular culture offers a way of identifying the patterns of a social system that produces both conceptual equality and material inequity simultaneously.

---

85. Hirsch, "Cultural Pluralism and Applied Folklore," 61.
86. Hirsch, "Cultural Pluralism and Applied Folklore," 61.
87. Ellison, *Invisible Man*, 574.

*Invisible Man* never really offers a model citizen, or more precisely, the several models it offers—from Bledsoe to Dupre—all fail. Instead, the narrator's telling, right down to its ambiguities and ironies, use vernacular resources to perform critical citizenship, creatively keeping alive "the chaos" while bringing it into a visible pattern.[88] By emphasizing the need to see power interests involved in planning the future, the way that narratives are recruited to serve it, and, most importantly, the persistence of alternatives to that pattern, *Invisible Man* effectively theorizes and actualizes Wright's dark mirror as a performance of citizenship. *Invisible Man*'s most obvious targets are the patterns of American history and liberal psychology. Its folk history undercuts these, revealing the discordant elements in the pattern that in turn reveal a will to power.

Modernization, as a narrative built on these patterns, necessarily comes under Ellison's critique as well. Against it, Ellison radicalizes civic pluralism to undercut Progressive faiths in objective measurement and technocratic positivism. Ellison reminds us that they will mask a will to power with perverse ends. However, while *Invisible Man* is not a utopian novel, it cannot be seen as a stand against planning either. *Invisible Man* does not cynically reject patterns and plans altogether but instead shows how their codification tends to erase people from history and, by extension, futurity. The narrator's planned emergence suggests a new approach, one that requires an expansive, particularized view of history and culture, and active participation to ensure that the patterns of being and becoming remain open to experience and intervention. *Invisible Man*'s mode of citizenship insists on the possibility of more equitable and more pluralistic approaches.

## Conclusion

Petry and Ellison offered pointed critiques in their fictional and nonfictional prose as the postwar recovery revealed that the promise of civic pluralism was giving way to a consumer's republic and that the modern opportunities promised by the New Deal would not be fully available to African Americans. Like Wright and Hurston before them, both authors developed texts that performed a crucial tension through their use of vernacular elements. Their attention to pattern and disruption of pattern recast the focus on urban and racial legibility in the New Deal cultural projects. Putting the interplay of pat-

---

88. Ellison's emphasis on chaos, like Benjamin's moment of crisis in "Theses on the Philosophy of History," suggests possible forms of intelligibility that preserve not only awareness but also the value of those things that fall outside modernization schemes.

tern and chaos on display, these writers addressed the blind spots of New Deal liberalism on race and, in Petry's case, on gender as well. In both writers' work, folkways remained vital to the ability to articulate social wrongs, and while they differed in their representation of how folkways might provide paths forward, Black vernacular culture in both remains a living force holding open the possibility of alternative futures.

Crucially, neither writer offers a conception of politics rooted in concerted and connected political action in their fiction, and in this regard, both reflect not just the deep-seated ambivalence in Black literature over modernization but also the dilemma many left-leaning authors found themselves in at midcentury, caught between the welfare/warfare state's broken promises and political ideas that seemed marginal or bankrupt. Petry's article on Harlem suggests the need for government intervention in housing, signaling an acceptance of the liberal state as agent of justice. However, her insistence on the independence of the novel from articulating solutions and *The Street*'s pessimistic vision of the state leave in doubt whether governmental solutions are sufficient to the challenge.

Ellison's novel leaves open the question of whether the narrator's promised reengagement offers a means of political action beyond the individual citizen's critical engagement, though its insistence on understanding the histories embedded in a shifting vernacular culture suggests a need to understand collective as well as individual experiences. Moreover, in at least two ways, Ellison's ideas connected with postwar political dynamics. Though they were split in their assessment of *Invisible Man,* the New York Intellectuals who helped develop a new intellectual style for Cold War liberalism liked Ellison's suspicion of technocratic authority, his insistence on keeping complexity—the tensions between the universal and the particular—in view. They saw this as according with their own stance as a means of resisting both forms of totalitarianism and an American complacency. Although journals associated with this group took up issues of race, for the most part they never developed a sustained engagement with African American vernacular culture or fully reckoned with the way it opened up political possibilities, and Ellison frequently pointed to this limitation in his essays.[89]

Second, Black vernacular culture, in both real and fantasized versions, served as a language of individual and group resistance for both Black and White Americans throughout the postwar period. Often the Black vernacular served as a marker of individual style, sometimes manifesting problematically in White social groups. However, it also provided a collective structure of feel-

---

89. See Teres, *Renewing the Left,* 204–229.

ing that served as the basis for more collective politics, opening challenges to normative liberal culture from citizens from a wide range of social group backgrounds.[90] The conclusion of this book addresses the fate of New Deal modernization and civic pluralism, and explores the ways that the dominant critiques of the welfare state misrecognized the important limitations and possibilities detailed in Black countermodern intertexts.

---

90. See Browder, *Slippery Characters*, 203–230; Jackson, *Indignant Generation*, 411–431; Medovoi, *Rebels*, for discussions of how Black vernacular culture became a marker for countercultural identities in the postwar era.

# CONCLUSION

# Irony and Liberalism

As Christine Bold points out, the FWP guidebooks were often wrong in their prognoses of the nation's future. The hopeful vision of modernization in the "Democracity" exhibit that the guidebooks lauded in their account of the 1939 World's Fair ran aground on wartime and postwar developments that rebuilt the nation around mass consumer culture and recentered Whiteness. Arguably, New Deal civic pluralism eased the acceptance of many immigrants and second-generation White citizens. However, wartime recovery programs combined with postwar economic growth likely contributed just as much. Lizabeth Cohen convincingly details the emergence of a postwar society aided by government programs promoting social insurance and family-based consumer activity for White citizens. In its expansion of racial inequity, this development contrasted with the progressive ideals of inclusion and active participatory citizenship.

Still, the New Deal's civic pluralist vision survived in demands for inclusion both in civil rights movements and in elements of postwar counterculture. The New Deal had centered the federal government as a site of leverage for civil rights campaigns, and the Supreme Court's increasing willingness to assert the federal government's authority to challenge Jim Crow bore out that strategy. The sense of a lost opportunity also fueled civil rights movements, causing some Black citizens to develop community-based political strategies while others questioned the government's willingness and ability to challenge

White supremacy. As a new pluralist ethos set in during the 1960s, the histories and cultural elements preserved by the FWP served as a cultural pathway for building identity, authority, and political power through shared social group experience, fueling a wave of identity-based assertiveness in the late 1960s. These would bolster Black nationalist and internationalist movements that sought to address the gaps in welfare/warfare state social provisions and were sometimes openly oppositional to the federal government. These movements would have profound effects in literature and other arts, setting in motion a new critical focus on pluralism that would challenge selective cultural traditions. Revived for this moment, many of the books in this study promoted their alternative understandings of history and culture long after the specific political initiatives they sought to connect with had faded. As the 1960s republication of Bontemps and Conroy's study, the renewal of interest in Hurston and Petry, or the long-acknowledged legacies of Wright and Ellison all suggest, these works could speak to new political and cultural contexts. Indeed, the New Deal-echoing rhetoric of progressive Democrats and Social Democrats and regular calls for a renewal of New Deal-style arts patronage suggest the continuing appeal of a more robust and inclusive liberal culture.

State-directed modernization was highly effective in generating immediate social and demographic change in metropolitan areas and beyond, even though the results were often locally and generationally problematic. While modernization may have provided important benefits for many citizens, the disparity in its application across racial lines exacerbated relative inequity and reinforced social tensions. Programs encouraging White city dwellers to move to the suburbs simultaneously increased racial divisions and deprived cities of the revenue needed to maintain commitments to social welfare. The FWP guidebooks clearly promoted a future the New Deal did not and, perhaps, could not deliver.

While some elements of this story, particularly its generational effects on racial inequity, are still being elaborated, one line of attack that would be used effectively against the liberal welfare state was articulated by the English writer W. H. Auden in a FWP intertext. Anzia Yezierska's 1950 memoir, *Red Ribbon on a White Horse,* included an introduction in which Auden seized the moment to condemn welfare state patronage and point out a fundamental irony:

> The Arts Project of W. P. A. was, perhaps, one of the noblest and most absurd
> undertakings ever attempted by any state. Noblest because no other state has
> ever cared about whether its artists as a group lived or died. . . . Yet absurd
> because a state can only function bureaucratically and impersonally—it has

to assume that every member of a class is equivalent or comparable to every other member—but every artist, good or bad, is a member or class of one.[1]

Auden captures the nostalgic longing for an America that cares about culture through which many on the Left today approach the New Deal cultural project. However, he quickly heads this off. Auden's state, however nobly intentioned, is profoundly impersonal, anathema to artistic creativity and, by extension, to the individual. It inevitably reduces individuals to generalities and statistics, interest groups and consumers, yielding a tragic irony. Auden's critique anticipates the condemnation of the welfare state in the libertarian strain of postwar White counterculture, which imagined a misguided therapeutic state regulating and containing the creative resistance of individuals and communities.

Ironically, just as Leerom Medovoi has shown that the idea of the rebel was made to serve Cold War nationalist political aims, countercultural suspicion of the state echoes in conservative attacks on the welfare state today. Combined with an antitotalitarian rhetoric expanded to include the welfare state and White racial resentment, conservatives found the attack on state overreach effective in reconstituting both a critique of interventionist liberalism and a politics of top-down resource distribution anchored in White voting blocs. Although the United States has a comparatively weak social welfare framework, conservatives attack attempts to bolster or even maintain that framework, charging its proponents with fiscal irresponsibility, enabling freeloaders, or even full-blown socialism. Inevitably this attack points to unintended consequences, both real and imagined: housing projects figure as breeding grounds of both criminality and social breakdown; highways and suburbs contribute to the decline of community; government subsidization of housing and, later, healthcare elevate costs. A smug fatalism often goes hand-in-hand with pointing out these failures. They suggest that irony is inevitable, that the contingencies of history must necessarily expose the hubris of large-scale planning activity. Though social insurance entitlements and military buildup became the welfare state's primary expenditures, the comparatively modest efforts of the federal government to target social inequity have become its Achilles heel. Like Hurston's Moses, though, this substitutes one political myth of history (and space) for another—in place of the welfare state: the essential fairness of the market, the sacral functionalism of traditional institutions, the virtue of the small and local, Western Civilization.

---

1. Yezierska, *Red Ribbon on a White Horse*, 17.

This myth's racial strings have been showing for a long time. When Ronald Reagan famously reiterated a popular 1970s joke, "The nine most terrifying words in the English language are: I'm from the government, and I'm here to help," while charging that the welfare state had created legions of "poverty pimps" and "welfare queens," he captured and capitalized on the White suburban ressentiment that fueled the rollback of the liberal welfare state. He also unwittingly illustrated just how prescient Wright, Petry, and Ottley had been in suggesting that racialized, impoverished urban neighborhoods would become the crux of the welfare state's imagined national community. While citing social complexity as a cause of the inevitable collapse of reform, conservative critics often ignore or deny the systemic racial biases and practices these writers identified as factors shaping persistent inequity.

Liberals have been guilty of repeating this blindness, too, often by failing to recognize the role race plays in shaping value and ignoring the specific effects of policies on Black neighborhoods. The implementation of principles for creating more livable urban environments distilled from Jane Jacobs's critique of modernist planning, often gathered loosely under the term New Urbanism, have shifted the image of cities away from postwar dysfunction to hubs of creative activity and connection. They have helped to attract investment, development, businesses, and young professionals to urban neighborhoods—from Harlem to the Deep Deuce neighborhood in Oklahoma City where Ellison grew up. However, Jacobs would likely have been appalled at gentrification's displacement of existing populations, its tendency to develop spaces serving narrow race and class interests, and its co-optation of distinctive group histories as symbolic markers of authenticity that drive profits. Ellison would certainly have grasped the failure here in the drive to codify a "plan of living" without examining the social costs of that plan.[2]

Irony is a tool of revelation, but irony can quickly become an anti-analytic, a way of avoiding responsibility for further discovery and basking in the pleasure of exposure. However satisfying irony may be as a narrative mode, it fails to fully account for both the New Deal's successes and failures, which are perhaps better characterized by the complexities and tensions the New Deal inherited. Liberals welcomed a range of previously excluded voices and still expected a high degree of conformity to normative frameworks in building the future. The expanded welfare state both opened up new ground for civil rights movements and furthered disparities in wealth and opportunity. The early housing projects provided crucial modern housing, and in tandem with suburbanization, they impoverished and racialized cities. The tensions

---

2. Ellison, *Invisible Man*, 580.

between these terms reflect the historical ties that bind the history of liberalism, and the Enlightenment project more generally, to imperialism and the creation of race as a means of domination.

One of the most important contributions of African American New Deal intertexts, then, is the way their critical reflection of American culture reconfigures the postwar thematics of the welfare state, intercepting ironic fatalism and replacing it with a more nuanced understanding of the interplay between power and race. The greatest irony of the welfare state is not the myth of unintended results but rather the New Deal's practice of gathering voices but failing to connect them to its futuristic vision. Heard correctly, these voices could have offered alternative understandings, local knowledges, a deep understanding of race, and, perhaps most importantly in the interplay of pattern and chaos, course corrections—indeed, a *wiser* geolatry.[3] Black FWP intertexts highlight alternate ways of imagining and structuring community, history, and modernity. They call into question the warrants of New Deal modernization and challenge the liberal state to deal more equitably with African Americans or to risk its legitimacy. Their critiques of the welfare state's new patterning of American life repurpose vernacular modes of storytelling to keep in view both pattern and chaos, to illuminate the way that race structures social relations "on the lower frequencies."[4]

The sheer number and complexity of FWP texts and their intertexts is a reminder that there is more work to be done. In its vast project records, manuscripts, lists of contributors, and correspondence, the FWP serves as an archive of writers and texts, both those already known and those yet to be discovered. Many of the excellent studies of the 1930s Left mention only briefly the role of the FWP in authors' lives. More scholarship is needed on these writers *as* FWP writers. While several of the unpublished FWP studies of African American social history have been published with commentary, more could be done to illuminate their wealth as cultural resources and literary artifacts. Catherine Stewart's work shows that even on relatively welltrodden paths like the FWP slave narratives, there are new perspectives to be gained by paying attention to specific histories and cultural aesthetics. The focus on cities in this book offers one approach to exploring crucial sociodemographic changes, but it leaves open the possibility of research on the rural

---

3. Community-based Great Society initiatives, particularly those developed through the short-lived Office of Economic Opportunity, represented a recognition of some of the New Deal's failings in their attempts to develop communities through local organizations. However, these programs' dismantling illustrates the continuing susceptibility of program funding to racially divisive politics.

4. Ellison, *Invisible Man*, 581.

and small-town focused texts. More work is needed on FWP writers from different social groups as well. Development remains an underexplored socio-cultural phenomenon connecting performative narratives on national, international, and personal levels.

More ambitiously, scholars, writers, and politicians could recognize and correct Auden's error. An artist is not a member or class of one. Collaboration is not the death of the artist. Nor is the state necessarily anathema to cultural production. The explosion of creativity from the FWP suggests that we need institutions and movements actively seeking to produce and record culture primarily as a source of meaning rather than as a source of profit. In these sites, we may find ideas and practices that allow us to see more clearly the links between ourselves and others, as well as those that maintain distance. Through the images in that dark mirror, we might learn to build more inclusive communities and govern more justly.

# BIBLIOGRAPHY

## Manuscript Collections

Arna Bontemps Papers. Bird Library Special Collections. Syracuse University. Syracuse, NY.

Federal Writers' Project Negro Group Papers. Beinecke Research Library. Yale University. New Haven, CT.

Federal Writers' Project New York City Records. Municipal Archives of the City of New York. New York, NY.

Federal Writers' Project Administrative Records. National Archive and Records Administration. College Park, MD. Record Group 69.

Henry Lee and Mollie Moon Papers. Schomburg Research Library. New York, NY.

Jack Conroy Papers. Newberry Library. Chicago, IL.

Jerre Mangione Papers. University of Rochester. Rochester, NY.

Ralph Ellison Papers. Library of Congress. Washington, DC.

Radio Scripts Collection. Schomburg Research Library. New York, NY.

Richard Wright Papers. Beinecke Research Library. Yale University. New Haven, CT.

United States Works Projects Administration Records. Library of Congress. Washington, DC.

Writers' Program, New York. Negroes of New York Collection. Schomburg Research Library. New York, NY.

## Primary and Secondary Sources

Abu-Lughod, Janet. *NY, Chi, LA*. Minneapolis: U of Minnesota P, 1999.

Allred, Jeff. *American Modernism and Depression Documentary*. New York: Oxford UP, 2012.

# 168 • BIBLIOGRAPHY

Armstrong, Ellis L. "Public Housing." *History of Public Works in the United States, 1776–1976.* Chicago: American Public Works Association, 1976.

Baker, Houston A., Jr. "To Move without Moving: An Analysis of Creativity and Commerce in Ralph Ellison's Trueblood Episode." *PMLA* 98, no. 5 (Oct 1983): 828–884.

Banner-Haley, Charles "Pete." "Ralph Ellison and the Invisibility of the Black Intellectual: Historical Reflection on *Invisible Man*." *Ralph Ellison and the Raft of Hope: A Political Companion to Invisible Man.* 158–170. Edited by Lucas E. Morel. Lexington: UP of Kentucky, 2004.

Baron, Robert. "'I Saw Mrs. Saray Sitting on a Bombalerry': Ralph Ellison Collects Children's Folklore." *Children's Folklore Review* 32 (2010): 23–52.

Bauer, Catherine *Modern Housing.* New York: Houghton Mifflin, 1934.

Bell, Bernard W. *The Afro-American Novel and Its Tradition.* Amherst: U of Massachusetts P, 1987.

———. "Ann Petry's Demythologizing of American Culture and Afro-American Culture." *Conjuring: Black Women, Fiction and Literary Tradition.* 105–115. Edited by Marjorie Pryse and Hortense J. Spillers. Bloomington: Indiana UP, 1985.

Benjamin, Walter. "Theses on the Philosophy of History." *Illuminations.* Translated by Hannah Arendt. New York: Schocken Books, 1968.

Berman, Marshall. *All That Is Solid Melts into Air.* New York: Simon and Schuster, 1982.

Blake, Cary Nelson. *Beloved Community.* Chapel Hill: U of North Carolina P, 1990.

Blakey, George T. *Creating a Hoosier Self-Portrait: The Federal Writers' Project in Indiana, 1935–1942.* Bloomington: Indiana UP, 2005.

Blow, Charles. "Bernie Sanders and the Black Vote." *New York Times.* 12 September 2015.

Bold, Christine. *The WPA Guides: Mapping America.* Jackson: UP of Mississippi, 1999.

Bontemps, Arna, and Jack Conroy. *Anyplace but Here.* New York: Hill and Wang, 1966.

———. *They Seek a City.* Garden City, NY: Doubleday, Doran & Co, 1945.

Boyd, Valerie. *Wrapped in Rainbows: The Life of Zora Neale Hurston.* New York: Scribner, 2003.

Brinkley, Alan. *Liberalism and Its Discontents.* Cambridge, MA: Harvard UP, 1998.

Brooks, Gwendolyn. "They Call It Bronzeville." *Holiday* (October 1951): 6–67, 112–116.

Browder, Laura. *Slippery Characters: Ethnic Impersonators and American Identities.* Chapel Hill: U of North Carolina P, 2000.

Butts, J. J. "New Deal Discourses." *African American Literature in Transition, 1930–1940.* Vol. 12. Edited by Ayesha Hardison and Eve Dunbar. New York: Cambridge UP, Forthcoming.

———. "New World A-Coming: African-American Documentary Intertexts of the Federal Writers' Project." *African American Review* 44, no. 4 (Winter 2011): 649–666.

———. "Pattern and Chaos: Ralph Ellison and the Federal Writers' Project." *American Studies* 54, no. 3 (2015): 35–49.

———. "Writing Projects: New Deal Guidebooks, Community, and Housing Reform in New York City." *The Space Between: Literature and Culture, 1914–1945* 2, no. 1 (2006): 113–138.

Capeci, Dominic J., Jr. *The Harlem Riot of 1943.* Philadelphia: Temple UP, 1977.

Cappetti, Carla. "Sociology of an Existence: Richard Wright and the Chicago School," *MELUS* 12, no. 2 (Summer 1985): 25–43.

———. *Writing Chicago: Modernism, Ethnography, and the Novel.* New York: Columbia UP, 1993.

Caro, Robert. *The Power Broker: Robert Moses and the Fall of New York.* New York: Vintage, 1974.

Cayton, Horace, and St. Clair Drake. *Black Metropolis: A Study of Negro Life in a Northern City.* New York: Harcourt, 1945.

Cohen, Lizabeth. *A Consumer's Republic: The Politics of Mass Consumption in Postwar America*. New York: Alfred A. Knopf, 2003.

Conkin, Paul. *Tomorrow a New World: The New Deal Community Program*. Ithaca, NY: Cornell UP, 1959.

Conner, Mark C. "The Litany of Things: Sacrament and History in *Invisible Man*." *Ralph Ellison and the Raft of Hope: A Political Companion to Invisible Man*. 171–192. Edited by Lucas E. Morel. Lexington: UP of Kentucky, 2004.

Cooper, Wayne. *Claude McKay: Rebel Sojourner in the Harlem Renaissance, A Biography*. Baton Rouge: Louisiana State UP, 1996.

DeMasi, Susan Rubenstein. *Henry G. Alsberg: The Driving Force of the New Deal Writers' Project*. Jefferson, NC: McFarland Press, 2016.

Denning, Michael. *The Cultural Front: The Laboring of American Culture in the Twentieth Century*. New York: Verso, 1998.

Dewey, John. *Individualism: Old and New*. Amherst, NY: Prometheus, 1999.

*Dictionary of American Regional English*. Vol 2. Cambridge, MA: Belknap Press, 1991.

Dolinar, Brian. *The Black Cultural Front: Black Writers and Artists of the Depression Generation*. Jackson: U of Mississippi P, 2012.

Duck, Leigh Anne. "Go there tuh know there": Zora Neale Hurston and the Chronotype of the Folk Author(s)." *American Literary History* 13, no. 2 (Summer 2001): 265–294.

———. *The Nation's Region: Southern Modernism, Segregation, and US Nationalism*. Athens: U of Georgia P, 2009.

———. "'Rebirth of a Nation': Hurston in Haiti." *Journal of American Folklore* 117 no. 454 (2004): 127–146.

Edmunds, Susan. *Grotesque Relations: Modernist Domestic Fiction and the US Welfare State*. New York: Oxford UP, 2008.

Edwards, Brent Hayes. *The Practice of Diaspora: Literature, Translation, and the Rise of Black Internationalism*. Cambridge, MA: Harvard UP, 2003.

Edwards, Erica R. "Moses, Monster of the Mountain: Gendered Violence in Black Leadership's Gothic Tale." *Callaloo* 31, no. 4 (Fall 2008): 1084–1102.

Ellison, Ralph. *The Collected Essays of Ralph Ellison*. Edited by John F. Callahan. New York: Modern Library, 2003.

———. *Invisible Man*. New York: Vintage, 1989.

———. *The Selected Letters of Ralph Ellison*. Edited by John F. Callahan and Marc C. Conner. New York: Random House, 2019.

Fairbanks, Robert B. *Making Better Citizens: Housing Reform and the Community Development Strategy in Cincinnati, 1890–1960*. Urbana: U of Illinois P, 1988.

Favor, J. Martin. *Authentic Blackness: The Folk in the New Negro Renaissance*. Durham, NC: Duke UP, 1999.

Federal Writers' Project. *American Stuff*. New York: Viking, 1937.

———. *Cavalcade of the American Negro*. Chicago: Diamond Jubilee Exposition Authority, 1940.

———. *Drums and Shadows: Survival Studies among the Georgia Coastal Negroes*. Athens: U of Georgia P, 1940.

———. *The Florida Negro: A Federal Writer's Project Legacy*. Edited by Gary W. McDonogh. Jackson: UP of Mississippi, 1993.

———. *Illinois: A Descriptive and Historical Guide*. Chicago: A. C. McClurg & Co., 1939.

# BIBLIOGRAPHY

———. *Jewish Hometown Associations and Family Circles in New York: The WPA Yiddish Writers' Group Study*. Edited by Hannah Kliger. Bloomington: Indiana UP, 1992.

———. *The Negro in Illinois: The WPA Papers*. Edited by Brian Dolinar. Chicago: U of Illinois P, 2013.

———. *The Negro in New York: An Informal Social History, 1626–1940*. Edited by Roi Ottley and William J. Weatherby. New York: Praeger, 1967.

———. *The Negro in Virginia*. New York: Hastings House, 1940.

———. *New Orleans City Guide*. Boston: Houghton Mifflin, 1938.

———. *New York Panorama*. Reprint. New York: Pantheon, 1984.

———. *Philadelphia: A Guide to the Nation's Birthplace*. Philadelphia: William Penn Association of Philadelphia, 1937.

———. *The WPA Guide to New York City*. New York: Pantheon Books, 1982.

———. *The WPA History of the Negro in Pittsburgh*. Edited by Laurence Glasco. Pittsburgh: U of Pittsburgh P, 2010.

———. *Yiddish Families and Family Circles in New York*. New York: Yiddish Writers' Union, 1939.

———. *The Yiddish Landmanschaften of New York*. New York: Yiddish Writers' Union, 1938.

Foley, Barbara. *Radical Representations: Politics and Form in US Proletarian Fiction, 1929–1941*. Durham, NC: Duke UP, 1993.

———. *Spectres of 1919: Class and Nation in the Making of the New Negro*. Urbana: U of Illinois P, 2003.

———. *Telling the Truth: The Theory and Practice of Documentary Fiction*. Ithaca, NY: Cornell UP, 1986.

———. *Wrestling with the Left: The Making of Ralph Ellison's Invisible Man*. Durham, NC: Duke UP, 2010.

Foucault, Michel. "What Is Enlightenment?" *Foucault Reader*. 32–50. Edited by Paul Rabinow. New York: Pantheon Books, 1984.

Gallagher, Julie A. *Black Women and Politics in New York City*. Urbana-Champaign: U of Illinois P, 2011.

Gates, Henry Louis, Jr., ed. *Reading Black, Reading Feminist: A Critical Anthology*. New York: Meridian Books, 1990.

Gelernter, David. *1939, The Lost World of the Fair*. New York: Avon Books, 1995.

Gelfand, Mark I. *A Nation of Cities: The Federal Government and Urban America 1933–1965*. New York: Oxford UP, 1975.

Georgia Writers' Project. *Atlanta: A City of the Modern South*. New York: Smith & Durrell, 1942.

Gerstle, Gary. *American Crucible: Race and Nation in the Twentieth Century*. Princeton, NJ: Princeton UP, 2001.

Gilman, Nils. *Mandarins of the Future: Modernization Theory in Cold War America*. Baltimore: Johns Hopkins UP, 2003.

Goetz, Richard. *New Deal Ruins: Race, Economic Justice, and Public Housing Policy*. Ithaca, NY: Cornell UP, 2013.

Gordon, Linda. *Pitied but Not Entitled: Single Mothers and the History of Welfare, 1890–1935*. New York: Free Press, 1994.

Gotham, Kevin Fox. "Racialization and the State: The Housing Act of 1934 and the Creation of the Federal Housing Administration." *Sociological Perspectives* 43, no. 2 (2000): 291–317.

# BIBLIOGRAPHY · 171

Greenberg, Cheryl Lynn. *Or Does It Explode: Black Harlem in the Great Depression.* New York: Oxford UP, 1991.

Griswold, Wendy. *American Guides: The Federal Writers' Project and the Casting of American Culture.* Chicago: U of Chicago P, 2016.

Harrison, Helen A. *Dawn of a New Day: The New York World's Fair, 1939/40.* New York: Queens Museum and New York UP, 1980.

Hicks, Heather. "'This Strange Communion': Surveillance and Spectatorship in Ann Petry's *The Street.*" *African-American Review* 37, no. 1 (Spring 2003): 21–37.

Hirsch, Arnold. *Making the Second Ghetto: Race & Housing in Chicago 1940–1960.* New York: Cambridge UP, 1983.

Hirsch, Jerrold. "Cultural Pluralism and Applied Folklore: The New Deal Precedent." *The Conservation of Culture: Folklorists and the Public Sector.* 46–67. Edited by Burt Feintuch. Lexington: UP of Kentucky, 1988.

———. *Portrait of America: A Cultural History of the Federal Writers' Project.* Chapel Hill: U of North Carolina P, 2003.

Holladay, Hilary. *Ann Petry.* New York: Twayne, 1996.

Hughes, Langston. "Down Under in Harlem." *New Republic.* 26 March 1944.

———. "The Negro Artist and the Racial Mountain." *The Portable Harlem Renaissance Reader.* Edited by David Levering Lewis. New York: Viking, 1994.

Hughes, Rupert. *The Real New York.* Illustrated by Henry Mayer. New York: Smart Set Publishing Company, 1904.

Hurston, Zora Neale. *Go Gator and Muddy the Water: Writings by Zora Neale Hurston for the Federal Writers Project.* Edited by Pamela Bordelon. New York: W. W. Norton, 1993.

———. *Moses, Man of the Mountain.* New York: Harper Perennial, 2009.

———. *Mules and Men.* New York: Harper Perennial, 2008.

———. "A Negro Voter Sizes up Taft," *Saturday Evening Post* 224, no. 3 (December 8, 1951): 29.

———. *Tell My Horse: Voodoo and Life in Haiti and Jamaica.* New York: Harper Perennial, 2008.

———. *Their Eyes Were Watching God.* New York: Harper Perennial, 2006.

Hutchinson, George. *The Harlem Renaissance in Black and White.* Cambridge, MA: Belknap P of Harvard UP, 1995.

Irwin, Will. *Highlights of Manhattan.* New York: Century Co., 1927.

Jackson, Kenneth. *Crabgrass Frontier: The Suburbanization of the United States.* New York: Oxford UP, 1985.

Jackson, Lawrence P. *The Indignant Generation: A Narrative History of African American Writers and Critics, 1934–1960.* Princeton, NJ: Princeton UP, 2011.

———. *Ralph Ellison: Emergence of Genius.* New York: John Wiley & Sons, 2002.

Jacobs, Jane. *The Death and Life of Great American Cities.* New York: Modern Library, 1961.

Jimoh, A. Yemisi. *Spiritual, Blues and Jazz People in African American Fiction.* Knoxville: U of Tennessee P, 2002.

Johnson, James Weldon. *Black Manhattan.* New York: Da Capo Press, 1991.

Kadlec, David. "Zora Neale Hurston and the Federal Folk." *Modernism/Modernity* 7, no. 3 (September 2000): 471–485.

Kent, George E. "Ralph Ellison and the Afro-American Folk and Cultural Tradition." *The Critical Response to Ralph Ellison.* 51–57. Edited by Robert J. Butler. Westport, CT: Greenwood Press, 2000.

Kessler-Harris, Alice. *Out to Work: A History of Wage-Earning Women in the United States.* New York: Oxford UP, 1982.

Kimble, Lionel, Jr. *A New Deal for Bronzeville: Housing, Employment, and Civil Rights in Black Chicago, 1935–1955.* Carbondale: Southern Illinois UP, 2015.

*King's Handbook of New York City.* Edited by Moses H. King. Boston: Moses H. King, 1892.

Klein, Marcus. *Foreigners: The Making of American Literature, 1900–1940.* Chicago: U of Chicago P, 1981.

Konzett, Delia Caparoso. *Ethnic Modernisms: Anzia Yezierska, Zora Neale Hurston, Jean Rhys, and the Aesthetics of Dislocation.* New York: Palgrave Macmillan, 2002.

Lackey, Michael. "Moses, Man of Oppression: A Twentieth-Century African American Critique of Western Theocracy." *African American Review* 43, no. 4 (Winter 2009): 577–588.

Larkin, Lesley. "Postwar Liberalism, Close Reading, and 'You': Ralph Ellison's Invisible Man." *LIT: Literature Interpretation Theory* 19, no. 3 (2008), 268–304.

Lowe, John. *Jump at the Sun: Zora Neale Hurston's Cosmic Comedy.* Urbana-Champaign: U of Illinois P, 1996.

Lucy, Robin. "'Flying Home': Ralph Ellison, Richard Wright, and the Black Folk during World War II." *Journal of American Folklore* 120, no. 477 (2007): 258–259.

Mangione, Jerre. *The Dream and the Deal: The Federal Writers' Project, 1935–1943.* New York: Avon, 1972.

Manzo, Kate. "Modernist Discourse and the Crisis of Development Theory." *Studies in Comparative International Development* 26, no. 2 (Summer 1991): 3–36.

Martin, Edward Winslow. *The Secrets of the Great City: A Work Descriptive of the Virtues and the Vices, the Mysteries, Miseries and Crimes of New York.* Philadelphia: Jones Brothers & Co. 1868.

Maxwell, William. *New Negro, Old Left: African-American Writing and Communism Between the Wars.* New York: Columbia UP, 2000.

McCann, Sean. *Gumshoe America: Hard-Boiled Crime Fiction and the Rise and Fall of New Deal Liberalism.* Durham, NC: Duke UP, 2000.

———. *A Pinnacle of Feeling: American Literature and Presidential Government.* Princeton, NJ: Princeton UP, 2008.

McKay, Claude. *Amiable with Big Teeth,* Edited by Jean-Christophe Cloutier and Brent Hayes Edwards. New York: Penguin, 2017.

———. *Harlem: Negro Metropolis.* New York: E. P. Dutton & Co., 1940.

Medovoi, Leerom. *Rebels: Youth and the Cold War Origins of Identity.* Durham, NC: Duke UP, 2005.

Mink, Gwendolyn. *The Wages of Motherhood: Inequality in the Welfare State, 1917–1942.* Ithaca, NY: Cornell UP, 1995.

Moon, Bucklin. *Primer for White Folks: An Anthology of Writings by and about Negroes from Slavery Days to Today's Struggle for a Share in American Democracy.* New York: Doubleday, 1945.

Moon, Henry Lee. *Balance of Power: The Negro Vote.* New York: Doubleday, 1948.

Moore, Jack B. "The Voice in *12 Million Black Voices.*" *Mississippi Quarterly* 42, no. 4 (Fall 1989): 415–424.

Morrison, Toni. *Playing in the Dark: Whiteness and the Literary Imagination.* New York: Vintage, 1993.

Mullen, Bill. *Popular Fronts: Chicago and African American Politics, 1935–1946.* Urbana: U of Illinois P, 1999.

Mumford, Lewis. *The Culture of Cities.* New York: Harcourt, Brace, & World, 1938.

———. *The Golden Day: A Study in American Literature and Culture*. New York: W. W. Norton, 1933.

Murphy, James. *The Proletarian Moment: The Controversy over Leftism in Literature*. Urbana-Champaign: U of Illinois P, 1991.

Myrdal, Gunnar. *An American Dilemma: The Negro Problem and Modern Democracy*. New York: Harper & Bros., 1940.

Nadel, Alan. *Invisible Criticism: Ralph Ellison and the American Canon*. Iowa City: U of Iowa P, 1988.

Nelson, Cary. *Repression and Recovery: Modern American Poetry and the Politics of Cultural Memory, 1910-1945*. Madison: U of Wisconsin P, 1989.

Nicholls, David. *Conjuring the Folk: Forms of Modernity in African America*. Ann Arbor: U of Michigan P, 2000.

O'Meally, Robert G. *The Craft of Ralph Ellison*. Cambridge, MA: Harvard UP, 1980.

Osofsky, Gilbert. *Harlem: The Making of a Ghetto, Negro New York, 1890-1930*. 2nd ed. Chicago: Elephant Paperbacks, 1966.

Ottley, Roi. *Black Odyssey: The Story of the Negro in America*. New York: Charles Scribner's Sons, 1948.

———. *New World A-Coming: Inside Black America*. Boston: Houghton Mifflin, 1943.

———. *No Green Pastures*. New York: Scribner, 1951.

———. *Roi Ottley's World War II: The Lost Diary of an African American Journalist*. Edited by Mark A. Huddle. Lawrence: U of Kansas P, 2011.

———. *White Marble Lady*. New York: Farrar, Straus & Giroux, 1965.

Page, Max. *The Creative Destruction of Manhattan: 1900-1940*. Chicago: U of Chicago P, 1999.

Penkower, Monty Noam. *Federal Writers' Project: A Study in Government Patronage of the Arts*. Urbana: U of Illinois P, 1977.

Petry, Ann. "Harlem." *Holiday* 3, no. 4 (April 1949): 110–115+.

———. *The Street*. Boston: Beacon Press, 1974.

Pizer, Donald. *The Theory and Practice of American Literary Naturalism*. Carbondale: Southern Illinois UP, 1993.

Plunz, Richard. *A History of Housing in New York City*. New York: Columbia UP, 1990.

Pryse, Marjorie. "'Pattern against the Sky': Deism and Motherhood in Ann Petry's *The Street*." *Conjuring: Black Women, Fiction and Literary Tradition*. 116–131. Edited by Marjorie Pryse and Hortense J. Spillers. Bloomington: Indiana UP, 1985.

Rabinowitz, Paula. *American Pulp: How Paperbacks Brought Modernism to Main Street*. Princeton, NJ: Princeton UP, 2015.

———. *Labor and Desire: Women's Revolutionary Fiction in Depression America*. Chapel Hill: U of North Carolina P, 1991.

———. *They Must Be Represented: The Politics of Documentary*. New York: Verso, 1994.

Rampersad, Arnold. *Ralph Ellison: A Biography*. New York: Vintage, 2008.

*Random House Historical Dictionary of American Slang*. Vol 2. Edited by J. E. Lighter. New York: Random House, 1997.

Retman, Sonnet. *Real Folks: Race and Genre in the Great Depression*. Durham, NC: Duke UP, 2011.

Reynolds, Guy. *Apostles of Modernist: American Writers in the Age of Development*. Lincoln: U of Nebraska P, 2008.

Riis, Jacob. *How the Other Half Lives*. New York: Dover, 1971.

Rodgers, Daniel T. *Atlantic Crossings.* Cambridge, MA: Belknap P of Harvard UP, 1998.

Rothstein, Richard. *The Color of Law: A Forgotten History of How Our Government Segregated America.* New York: Liveright, 2017.

Rowley, Hazel. *Richard Wright: The Life and Times.* Chicago: U of Chicago P, 2001.

Rutkowski, Sara. *Literary Legacies of the Federal Writers' Project: Voices of the Depression in the American Postwar Era.* New York: Palgrave, 2017.

Schindler-Carter, Petra. *Vintage Snapshots: The Fabrication of a Nation in the W. P. A. American Guide Series.* New York: Peter Lang, 1999.

Schwartz, Joel. *The New York Approach: Robert Moses, Urban Liberals, and Redevelopment of the Inner City.* Columbus: The Ohio State UP, 1993.

Scott, James C. *Seeing Like a State: How Certain Schemes to Improve the Human Condition Have Failed.* New Haven, CT: Yale UP, 1998.

Shackleton, Robert. *The Book of New York.* Philadelphia: Penn Publishing Company, 1920.

Shaffer, Marguerite S. *See America First, Tourism and National Identity, 1880–1941.* Washington, DC: Smithsonian Institution, 2001.

Singh, Nikhil Pal. *Black Is a Country: Race and the Unfinished Struggle for Democracy.* Cambridge, MA: Harvard UP, 2004.

Sitkoff, Harvard. *A New Deal for Blacks: The Emergence of Civil Rights as a National Issue.* New York: Oxford UP, 1978.

Sklaroff, Lauren Rebecca. *Black Culture and the New Deal: The Quest for Civil Rights in the Roosevelt Era.* Chapel Hill: U of North Carolina P, 2009.

Smith, Matthew Hale. *Sunshine and Shadow in New York.* Hartford, CT: J. R. Burr and Co., 1869.

Smith, Virginia Whatley. "They Sing the Song of Slavery: Frederick Douglass's *Narrative* and W. E. B. Du Bois's *The Souls of Black Folk* as Intertexts of Richard Wright's *12 Million Black Voices.*" *The Souls of Black Folk One Hundred Years Later.* 85–129. Edited by Dolan Hubbard. Columbia: U of Missouri P, 2003.

Sorett, Josef. *Spirit in the Dark: A Religious History of Racial Aesthetics.* New York: Oxford UP, 2016.

Stansell, Christine. *American Moderns.* New York: Metropolitan Books, 2000.

Stewart, Catherine. *Long Past Slavery: Representing Race in the Federal Writers' Project.* Chapel Hill: U of North Carolina P, 2016.

Stott, William. *Documentary Expression and Thirties America.* Chicago: U of Chicago P, 1973.

Susman, Warren. *Culture as History: The Transformation of American Society in the Twentieth Century.* New York: Pantheon, 1973.

Szalay, Michael. *New Deal Modernism.* Durham, NC: Duke UP, 2000.

Taylor, David A. *Soul of a People: The WPA Writers' Project Uncovers Depression America.* Hoboken, NJ: Wiley, 2009.

Teres, Harvey. *Renewing the Left: Politics, Imagination, and the New York Intellectuals.* New York: Oxford UP, 2001.

Thompson, Mark Christian. "National Socialism and Blood-Sacrifice in Zora Neale Hurston's *Moses, Man of the Mountain.*" *African American Review* 36, no. 3 (2004): 395–415.

Twelve Southerners. *I'll Take My Stand: The South and the Agrarian Tradition.* Baton Rouge: Louisiana State UP, 2006.

Vale, Lawrence J. *From the Puritans to the Projects: Public Housing and Public Neighbors.* Cambridge, MA: Harvard UP, 2000.

Wald, Alan. *American Night: The Literary Left in the Era of the Cold War.* Chapel Hill: U of North Carolina P, 2012.

———. *Exiles from a Future Time: The Forging of the Mid-Twentieth Century Literary Left.* Chapel Hill: U of North Carolina P, 2002.

———. *Trinity of Passion: The Literary Left and the Anti-Fascist Crusade.* Chapel Hill: U of North Carolina P, 2014.

Wall, Cheryl A. "Zora Neale Hurston's Essays: On Art and Such." *S&F Online* 3, no. 2 (Winter 2005): n.p.

Walzer, Michael. *What It Means To Be an American.* New York: Marsilio, 1992.

Warren, Kenneth W. *What Was African American Literature?* Cambridge, MA: Harvard UP, 2011.

White, Norval, and Elliott Willensky. *The AIA Guide to New York City.* New York: Three Rivers Press, 2000.

Winter, Kari J. "Narrative Desire in Ann Petry's *The Street.*" *Journal X* 4, no. 2 (Spring 2000): 101–112.

Woller, Joel. "First-Person Plural: The Voice of the Masses in Farm Security Administration Documentary." *JNT: Journal of Narrative Theory* 29, no. 3 (Fall 1999): 340–366.

Wood, Edith Elmer. *The Housing of the Unskilled Wage Earner: America's Next Problem.* New York: Macmillan, 1919.

Wright, Gwendolyn. *Building the Dream: A Social History of Housing in America.* New York: Pantheon Books, 1981.

Wright, Richard. *12 Million Black Voices: A Folk History of the Negro in America.* New York: Thunder's Mouth Press, 1941.

———. "Blueprint for Negro Writing." *The Portable Harlem Renaissance Reader.* 194–205. Edited by David Levering Lewis. New York: Viking, 1994.

———. "I Tried To Be a Communist." *Atlantic Monthly* 174, no. 2. (August 1944): 48–56.

———. *Native Son.* New York: Harper & Bros., 1940.

Wurst, Gayle. "Ben Franklin in Harlem: The Drama of Deferral in Ann Petry's *The Street.*" *Deferring a Dream: Literary Sub-Versions of the American Columbiad.* 1–23. Edited by Gert Buelens and Ernst Rudin. Boston: Birkhauser Verlag Basel, 1994.

Wye, Christopher G. "The New Deal and the Negro Community: Toward a Broader Conceptualization." *New Deal: Conflicting Interpretations and Shifting Perspectives.* Edited by Melvyn Dubofsky. New York: Garland, 1992.

Yezierska, Anzia. *Red Ribbon on a White Horse: My Story.* New York, Persea, 2004.

# INDEX

African Americans: Caribbean immigrants and, 106, 114; FWP reporting on Black culture, 68; Great Migration, 87–88, 121, 125–27; in New York guidebooks, 43–46; public housing and, 58–61; real estate exclusion, 48, 58–59, 89, 106, 121; separate guidebook essays, pattern of, 32; in Southern cities and New Orleans guidebook, 42–43; as voters, 15, 79, 91; World's Fair (1939) and, 62, 64. *See also specific writers*

Algren, Nelson, 8–9

Ali, Noble Drew, 123

Allred, Jeff, 97

Alsberg, Henry G.: about, 8, 12; Hurston and, 70; Negro History Unit (New York) and, 103; New York guides and, 34, 36–37, 40; Wright and, 83

American Guide series (FWP): about, 7, 9–11; description and prescription, conflation of, 52; interpretive contention over, 20; narration in, 43. *See also specific guide-books by location*

American Negro Theatre, 132

architectural modernism, 54–56. *See also* housing projects, public

assimilation, 17, 33–34, 39, 42

Attaway, William, 85

Auden, W. H., 162–63, 166

Baker, Jacob, 10

Banner-Haley, Charles, 156

Barrett, Mary, 35

Bell, Bernard, 85

Bellow, Saul, 8–9

Benjamin, Walter, 152, 158n88

"Big Boy Leaves Home" (Wright), 84

Black Belt Nation thesis, 94

Black Cabinet (Black Brain Trust), 14–15, 50

*Black Manhattan* (Johnson), 108–9, 113

Black nationalism, 116–18, 123, 154, 162

Blow, Charles, 79

"Blueprint for Negro Writing" (Wright), 94–96, 149

Boardman, Helen, 108–10

Boas, Franz, 12

Bodenheim, Maxwell, 9, 36n24

bohemianism, 12–13

# 178 · INDEX

Bold, Christine, 7, 11, 22–23, 29n3, 42, 45–46, 52, 161

Bontemps, Arna, 8–9, 83, 98, 120; *They Seek a City* (with Conroy), 102, 125–29

Botkin, Benjamin, 127; folk culture approach and, 68; FWP and, 8; Hurston and, 71, 72; Living Lore project and, 145

Bourne, Randolph, 12, 14n32

Brinkley, Alan, 50–51

Brooks, Gwendolyn, 101n3

Brown, Sterling: folk culture approach and, 68; FWP and, 8, 15; Living Lore project and, 145; *The Negro in New York* and, 108; *Negro Poetry and Drama*, 108; Wright and, 44, 83; Yiddish subgroup and, 101

*Brown v. Board of Education,* 81

Bryan, Lewis, 103

Burnham, Daniel, 55

Burton, Virginia Lee, 127

business ownership, Black, 44

capitalism: folk culture and, 145–46; Hurston on, 77; World's Fair (1939) and, 63–64; Wright on, 87–88, 89, 94, 96

Cappetti, Carla, 93

Cayton, Horace, 16–17, 83, 101n3

Census, US, 35–36n23

Cheever, John, 8–9

Chicago: housing projects, 123–24, 128; real estate exclusion, 58–59; South Side Writers Group, 82–83, 120; World's Columbian Exposition (1893), 55. *See also* Illinois guidebook

Chicago Renaissance, 119–20, 124

Chicago School sociology, 16–17, 19, 82–83, 89, 121

children and urban life, 90–91

children's books, 127

citizenship, in Ellison's *Invisible Man,* 144–45, 148–49, 156–58

civic pluralism. *See* pluralism, civic

Clarke, Joe, 76

Clayton, Frederick, 108

Cohen, Lizabeth, 161

communism: critical focus on, 21–22; Negro History Unit (New York) and, 105; Petry and, 132; Popular Front, 84, 119; Wright and, 22, 83–84, 127n91

Communist Party, American (CPUSA): Bontemps and Conroy on, 127–28; Ellison's *Invisible Man* and, 152–54; FWP and, 21; Ottley on, 118; Wright and, 84

Conkin, Paul, 49

Conroy, Jack, 8–9, 122, 125; *They Seek a City* (with Bontemps), 102, 125–29

consumerism and World's Fair (1939), 62, 64

corporations, 62, 63–64

Corse, Carita Dogget, 70

countermodernities, 4–6

Crane, Stephen, 30

Crawford, Ruth, 37

Cronyn, George, 8, 34

Cultural Front model, 21–22

cultural history, 20–21

cultural networks, Black, 13

culture, folk. *See* folk, vernacular culture, and folkways

*Culture of Cities, The* (Mumford), 36

Cumberbatch, Charles, 104–5

Davis, Frank Marshall, 83

de Fleurville, William, 120

Delano, Frederic A., 49

Delany, Hubert, 108

De Mille, Arnold, 1, 43

Democratic Party: civic pluralism and, 14; Southern Democrats, 29, 77, 91

deserving poor, the, 135

Dies, Martin, 29

documentary culture, New Deal, 71, 85–86, 102

documentary intertexts. *See* intertexts

Dolinar, Brian, 120

Drake, St. Clair, 16–17, 101n3

Du Bois, W. E. B., 12; *Home to Harlem,* 45

Duck, Leigh Anne, 23, 73, 76–77

Dunham, Katherine, 122, 127

Duvalier, François, 73

Edmunds, Susan, 22

Edwards, Brent Hayes, 117

Edwards, Erica, 79, 80

Eliot, Charles W., II, 49

Ellington, Duke, 111

Ellison, Ralph: FWP and, 8–9, 143–47; "Harlem Is Nowhere," 2, 131–32, 148; Negro History Unit (New York) and, 103, 146; *The Negro in New York* and, 109; on Ottley, 105, 111, 112, 116; "Twentieth Century Fiction and the Black Mask of Humanity," 154. See also *Invisible Man*

employment: African American, 44, 46, 134–35; anti-Semitism and, 40; Fair Employment Practices Committee, 119, 128; gender and, 134–35; literary in FWP, 8, 9, 21; Ottley on, 119; public housing projects and, 60n29; World's Fair and exclusion in, 64

"Ethics of Living Jim Crow, The" (Wright), 84, 95

family norms, 134

Fard, W. D. (Wallace Fard Muhammad), 123, 127

Farm Security Administration (FSA) photography, 85

Fauset, Arthur, 108

Fearing, Kenneth, 8

Federal One, 8, 54, 111

Federal Writers Project (FWP): about, 7–11; congressional criticism of, 29; demise of, 110; folk culture, view of, 67–68; Living Lore project, 145–46, 152; Negro History Unit, New York, 103–5, 145–46; personnel roster and list of writers, 8–9; subunits, 16, 100–102; Yiddish Writers Group subunit, New York, 100. See also *specific guidebooks by location*

Fisher, Vardis, 8

Foley, Barbara, 153

folk, vernacular culture, and folkways: about the folk, 5; African American impact on, 126–27; civic pluralism and, 12, 15–16; Ellison on, 146, 149–50; FWP views of, 16, 67–68; Hurston on, 71–72; intertexts, countermodernity and, 5–6; Living Lore project, 145–46; in New Orleans, 43; Ottley's *New World A-Coming* and, 115;

Petry's *The Street* and, 136, 139–40, 143; postwar period and, 159–60; *Titanic* in Black folklore, 147; Wright's *12 Million Black Voices* and, 86–89, 93–97, 152

Foucault, Michel, 4

Fouilhoux, André, 62

Franklin, Benjamin, 137n22, 138

Frazier, E. Franklin, 16–17

Frederick, John T., 98, 119

Fredericks, Harry, 117

Fuchs, Daniel, 41

Fujii, Mary, 122

Garvey, Marcus, 44, 109, 116–18, 123, 127, 154

Gellert, Lawrence, 103

gender: Hurston's *Moses* and, 73n11, 78, 80; Petry on domestic norms and, 134; Petry's *The Street* and, 135, 142

Gerstle, Gary, 12

Gody, Lou, 37

Goetz, Edward, 61

*Golden Day, The* (Mumford), 153–54

Great Migration, 87–88, 121, 125–27

Great Society initiatives, 165n3

Griot movement, 73, 77

Griswold, Wendy, 8

guidebooks, FWP. See American Guide series; *specific guidebooks by location*

guidebooks, urban (late 19th century), 29–31

Halpert, Herbert, 72

Hamid, Sufi Abdul, 117

Hanau, Stella, 35

Hansberry, Carl, 58–59

Harlem: Du Bois's *Home to Harlem*, 45; Ellison's "Harlem Is Nowhere," 2, 131–32, 148; in Ellison's *Invisible Man*, 148–49, 153, 155; Harlem River Houses, 58–61, 65–66, 134; "Negro Harlem," 45–46; *The Negro in New York* on, 106–7; Ottley's *New World A-Coming*, 112–16; Petry's "Harlem" (*Holiday*), 101n3, 132, 133–34, 142–43; "Portrait of Harlem," 1–2, 43–45; riots (1935 and 1943), 44, 46, 93, 106–7, 113, 155–56

180 · INDEX

Harris, Reed, 8

Harrison, Wallace K., 62

Harsh, Vivian, 125

Haywood, Harry, 94

Himes, Chester, 85

Hirsch, Jerrold, 12, 22, 67, 144, 157

Horne, Frank, 128

Houseman, John, 70

housing: gentrification, 164; kitchenettes, 89–90, 121; Ottley on, 121; Petry on, 133–34, 136–37; racial exclusion in, 48, 58–59, 89, 106, 121. *See also* suburbanization

housing projects, public: about, 57; Bontemps and Conroy on, 128–29; crime rates in, 65–66; in Detroit and San Francisco, 129; Harlem River Houses, 58–61, 65–66, 134; Ida B. Wells Homes, Chicago, 124, 128; in New York, 41–42; Ottley on, 123–24; racial inequity and, 18, 58–59, 61; Williamsburg Houses, Brooklyn, 57–58. *See also* slums and slum reform

"How 'Bigger' Was Born" (Wright), 85n45, 95

Howe, Irving, 147–48

Howells, William Dean, 30

*How the Other Half Lives* (Riis), 31

Hughes, Langston, 94

Hughes, Rupert, 30

Hurston, Zora Neale: on *Brown v. Board of Education*, 81; *The Florida Negro* manuscript and, 70–71; on folk culture, 71–72; FWP and, 8–9; in Jamaica and Haiti, 70, 73; on modernization, 76; *Moses, Man of the Mountain*, 6, 20, 69–70, 73–81; *Mules and Men*, 70, 101n3; Negro Theater Project (FTP) and, 70; on New Deal and centralization, 72, 77–78, 81; *Tell My Horse*, 71, 73, 76–77; *Their Eyes Were Watching God*, 71, 72, 76; Wright, disagreement with, 69

Hutchinson, George, 13

Ickes, Harold, 14

Illinois guidebook (*Illinois: A Descriptive and Historical Guide*): architecture essay, 55, 56–57; grouping by national origin, 32; Wright and, 83. *See also* Chicago

Illinois Writers' Project (IWP), 123

immigrants: in New York, 32–33, 106, 114; Sacco and Vanzetti case, Boston, 28–29

indigenous Americans, 32

intertexts: about, 18–20, 100–103; countermodernities and, 4–6; folk materials and, 5–6; *Moses, Man of the Mountain* (Hurston), 6, 20, 69–70, 73–81; *The Negro in Illinois* (ed. Dolinar), 83, 119–25, 127; *The Negro in New York* (ed. Ottley and Weatherby), 83, 103–10; *New World A-Coming* (Ottley), 102, 105, 111–19; social and cultural networks and, 4; *The Street* (Petry), 6, 20; *They Seek a City* (Bontemps and Conroy), 102, 125–29. See also *Invisible Man* (Ellison); *12 Million Black Voices* (Wright)

*Invisible Man* (Ellison): countermodernity and, 6; epilogue, 156–58; final riot scene, 155–56; FWP's influence on, 144–47; interpretive contention over, 20; Petry's *The Street* compared to, 158–59; postwar political dynamics and, 159; tensions over culture and modernity and, 6; themes, 147–58

"I Tried To Be a Communist" (Wright), 84n43

Jackson, Lawrence, 4, 9, 13, 21, 23, 153

Jacobs, Jane, 53, 66, 164

James, Henry, 30

Jews: cultural influence of, 39–40; *landsmanschaften* (hometown organizations), 100, 106; in New York guidebooks, 37–42; Yiddishkeit, 8, 40, 100

Johnson, Fenton, 83, 120

Johnson, James Weldon, 8, 44, 112; *Black Manhattan*, 108–9, 113

Johnson, John, 133

Jones, John, 120

Jordan, Robert O., 117

Kadlec, David, 71

Kallen, Horace, 12, 14n32

Kellock, Katherine, 8, 10, 11

Killens, John O., 85

Kimble, Lionel, 19, 59

Kohn, Robert D., 49, 62

labor organizing, 92–93, 127–28, 129

LaGuardia, Fiorello, 106, 133

*landsmanschaften* (Jewish hometown organizations), 100, 106

Leach, Baxter P., 105

*Left Front,* 82

legibility of space: FWP and, 33–34, 49, 53–54, 131–32; Hurston's *Moses* and, 99; Ottley's *New World A-Coming* and, 113–14; Petry's "Harlem" and, 132, 143; state intervention and, 53–54; World's Fair (1939) and, 62; Wright's *12 Million Black Voices* and, 96–97, 99

liberalism: African American experiences, White supremacy, and, 79; Black writers on, 69; Bontemps and Conroy on, 128–29; citizenship and, 144–45; Cold War, 159; Ellison, Mumford, and Progressive liberalism, 153–54; Ellison's *Invisible Man* and, 144–45, 157–58, 159; Hurston on, 81; irony and, 164–65; Rooseveltian and African American, 19; universalist ambitions vs. racial exclusion in, 2–3

Lincoln, Abraham, 120

Lippman, Walter, 64

Living Lore project (FWP), 145–46, 152

Locke, Alain, 12, 87, 93

Lomax, Alan, 72

Lomax, John, 8, 67–68, 145–46

Long, Huey, 73

Lowe, John, 74, 78, 80

Lucy, Robin, 5, 97, 149

Magraw, James, 111

Maltz, Albert, 142

Mangione, Jerre, 8, 107, 112, 143

Martin, Edward Winslow, 30–31

Massachusetts guidebook, 28–29

McCann, Sean, 22, 75–79

McHugh, Vincent, 34

McKay, Claude: FWP and, 8–9; Negro History Unit (New York) and, 103–5; *The Negro in New York* and, 108–9; "Portrait of Harlem" draft, 1, 43; Wright and, 83

Medovoi, Leerom, 163

Merriam, Charles E., 49

Minus, Marian, 84, 94

modernity: community vs., 11–12; Ellison's *Invisible Man* and, 144; folk culture and, 5–6, 19–20, 68–69, 157; Foucault on, 4; FWP subunits and, 100, 101; *The Negro in Illinois* and, 122; New Deal and, 10, 24; Petry's "Harlem" and, 143; racializing discourses in the construction of, 18–19; Wright's *12 Million Black Voices* and, 82, 87; Wright's "Blueprint for Negro Writing" and, 94

modernization: documentary intertexts and, 102; Ellison's *Invisible Man* and, 158; failure of, 18; Hurston's *Moses,* nation-building, and, 75–81; Jews and, 39; pluralism and, 3–4, 17–18; race and, 3–4, 48. *See also* housing projects, public; urban and regional planning

Moon, Bucklin, 125

Moon, Henry Lee, 9, 79, 103, 104

*Moses, Man of the Mountain* (Hurston), 6, 20, 69–70, 73–81

Moses, Robert, 50

Motley, William, 120

Muhammad, Elijah, 117, 123, 127

Muhammad, Wallace Fard (W. D. Fard), 123, 127

*Mules and Men* (Hurston), 70, 101n3

Mumford, Lewis: *The Culture of Cities,* 36; FWP and, 8; *The Golden Day,* 153–54; on Harlem River Houses, 65; regionalism and, 14, 54; Regional Planning Association of America and, 62

music: blues, in Petry's *The Street,* 139–40; Bontemps and Conroy on, 127; Ellison and, 150; Ottley on, 121; Rockefeller Center and, 56

Myrdal, Gunnar, 2, 150

Nadel, Alan, 153–54

Naft, Stephen, 105, 110

National Association for the Advancement of Colored People (NAACP), 64, 91, 104, 108, 118, 129

nationalism: Black or racial, 116–18, 123, 154, 162; Hurston on, 77; romantic, 12, 156

national origin, grouping by, 32

## 182 · INDEX

nation-building: Hurston on, 73, 76–81; Wright on, 81–82

*Native Son* (Wright), 85, 95, 98–99, 110, 111, 129

naturalism, Black, 85

Negro Authors' Guild (FWP), 108

*Negro in Illinois, The* (ed. Dolinar), 83, 119–25, 127

*Negro in New York, The* (ed. Ottley and Weatherby), 83, 103–10

*Negro Poetry and Drama* (Brown), 108

Negro Theater Project (FTP), 70

New Deal: documentary intertexts and, 102–3; Ellison's *Invisible Man* and, 144; guidebooks, propaganda function of, 7; Hurston on centralization and, 72, 77–78, 81; irony and, 164–65; Jews and, 38; modernism and, 54–56; public housing and, 57; urban planning and, 49–52; Wright on worker alliances vs., 91–93. *See also* liberalism; welfare state

New Orleans guidebook, 42–43

New Religious Movements (NRMs), 115–16, 122–23

*New World A-Coming* (Ottley), 6, 102, 105, 111–19, 149

New York City: 19th-century guidebooks, 30–31; 1930 US Census and division of, 35–36n23; Master Plan, 50; Negro History Unit, FWP, 103–5, 145–46; Williamsburg Houses, Brooklyn, 57–58; Yiddish Writers Group (YWG) FWP subunit, 100. *See also* Harlem

New York City guidebooks (*New York Panorama* and *WPA Guide to New York City*): African Americans, 1–2, 43–46; civic pluralism and, 31–33, 46; immigrants in, 32–33; Jews and the Lower East Side, 37–42; "Negro Harlem," 45–46; *The Negro in New York* compared to, 106–7; "New World Symphony," 33, 38–39, 43; outer boroughs, 36–37; pluralist vision and, 28; "Portrait of Harlem," 1–2, 43–45; public housing and, 59–61; sectional organization of, 33–37; urban planning and, 53–54; World's Fair in, 61–64; Wright's *12 Million Black Voices* as rereading of, 93

New York Writers' Alliance, 84

Nicholls, David, 5

*Noirisme* movement, 73, 77

Osofsky, Gilbert, 110

Ottley, Roi: about, 104; Conroy on, 125; FWP and, 9; Negro History Unit (New York) and, 103–5; *The Negro in New York* and, 107–11; *New World A-Coming*, 6, 102, 105, 111–19, 149

Paradise Valley housing project, San Francisco, 129

Park, Robert E., 16–17

Parks, Gordon, 131

Petry, Ann: Black naturalism and, 85; "Harlem" (*Holiday* essay), 101n3, 132, 133–34, 142–43; *The Street*, 6, 20, 132, 133, 135–43, 158–59

Philadelphia guidebook, 32

Pizer, Donald, 137

planning. *See* urban and regional planning

Plunz, Richard, 57

pluralism, civic: about, 11–17; Black life in Southern cities and, 42–43; Black New Yorkers in Harlem, 43–46; controversy and criticism, 28–29; defined, 2; Ellison's *Invisible Man* and, 156–58; FWP guidebooks and (overview), 31–33, 46–47; Hurston on, 77; intertexts and, 102; Jews in new york, 37–42; local movements vs. nationalism, 13–14; modernization and, 3–4, 17–18; Ottley's *New World A-Coming* on, 120; in postwar era, 161–62; sectional organization of the New York guidebooks and, 33–37; urban guidebooks of 19th century and, 29–31; urban networks and, 12–13; Wright on, 93

Point du Sable, Jean Baptiste, 120, 126

"Portrait of Harlem" (Wright), 1–2

Poston, Ted, 9, 103

Powell, Adam Clayton, Jr., 108, 116, 132, 134n9, 145

power: in Ellison's *Invisible Man*, 152, 153–58; folk culture and, 68; FWP and, 9, 162; Hurston on, 72–73; in Hurston's *Moses*, 73–81; interplay between race and, 165; legibility and, 53; local, 129; New Deal pluralism and, 14–15; organizational, 56; Ottley on, 115, 117–18; in Petry's *The Street*, 137–38, 141–42; of women, in Hurston's *Moses,* 80; Wright on, 86–87, 91, 95; in Wright's *12 Million Black Voices,* 92, 96, 99

Price-Mars, Jean, 73

primitivism, 45

Pryse, Marjorie, 137n22, 138

public housing projects. *See* housing projects, public

race: civic pluralism and, 33, 47; in Ellison's *Invisible Man,* 154–55; folk culture and, 68, 92; FWP and, 18–20, 67; Hurston on, 78, 81; interplay between power and, 165; modernization and, 49; *The Negro in New York* on, 106; New Deal politics and tensions over, 14; Ottley on, 113–17; in Petry's *The Street,* 135, 142; postwar conservatives and liberals and, 164; World's Fair (1939) and, 62, 64; Wright on, 82–83, 98–99; Wright on racial logic of value, 89

racial inequity and exclusion: Bontemps on WWII and, 128; housing projects and, 18, 58–59, 61; liberalism and universalism vs., 2–3; modernization programs and, 3–4; New York guidebooks on racial injustice, 44–45; suburbanization and, 48; welfare state criticism and, 164; Wright on, 98–99

Rahv, Philip, 8

Rampersad, Arnold, 145, 148

Randolph, A. Philip, 118

Reagan, Ronald, 164

*Real New York, The* (Hughes), 30

Reddick, Laurence, 108

regionalism, 34, 36, 54

religion: African American, in New York, 44, 46; Bontemps and Conroy on, 127; Jews in New York and, 38–39; New Religious Movements (NRMs), 115–16, 122–23; Ottley on, 115–16, 122–23; Wright on, 88

Renault, Phillip Francois, 120

Republican Party, 15, 72, 91

Retman, Sonnet, 15, 23

Rexroth, Kenneth, 8

Riis, Jacob, 31

Roane, Carita V., 59

Rockefeller Center, New York, 54–56

Rogers, Joel A., 103, 117

Rollins, William, Jr., 9

Roosevelt, Eleanor, 14

Roosevelt, Franklin D., 59, 77, 106, 119, 157

Rosenwald Fund, 111, 125

Ross, James, 59

Rosskam, Edwin, 85

Roth, Henry, 41

Royse, Morton, 68

Rutkowski, Sara, 16, 21, 23, 69

Sacco, Nicola, 28–29

Scott, James C., 53

*Secrets of the Great City, The* (Martin), 30–31

Seeger, Charles, 8

Shaw, Harry, 37

Singh, Nikhil Pal, 2, 3, 7, 117

Singleton, Benjamin "Pap," 126

Sklaroff, Lauren Rebecca, 22–23, 29

slavery, 86–87, 154

slums and slum reform: architecture and, 56–57; Black writers and, 69; Bontemps and Conroy on, 128; Ellison's *Invisible Man* on, 148; New York and, 41; Petry on, 136; in Wright's *Native Son* and *12 Million Black Voices,* 46, 92. *See also* housing projects, public

Smith, Matthew Hale, 30–31

social history. See *Negro in Illinois, The; Negro in New York, The*

Sojourner Truth housing project, Detroit, 129

Sorett, George, 115–16

Southern United States: Black life in Southern cities, 42–43; Southern Democrats, 29, 77, 91; Wright on Black folkways in, 86–87

South Side Writers Group, Chicago, 82–83, 120

Spencer, Onah, 120

Stansell, Christine, 12–13

Stewart, Catherine, 9, 22–23, 42, 68, 165

Strauss, Harold, 103

*Street, The* (Petry), 6, 20, 132–33, 135–43, 158–59

184 • INDEX

Stryker, Roy, 85, 131

suburbanization, 39, 48, 50, 66

Suburban Resettlement Administration, 50

Susman, Warren, 61–62

Sutherland, Edwin, 17

Szalay, Michael, 21–22, 54

Tarry, Ellen, 9, 103, 112, 144

*Tell My Horse* (Hurston), 71, 73, 76–77

Tennessee guidebook, 52–53

Terkel, Studs, 8

*Their Eyes Were Watching God* (Hurston), 71, 72, 76

*They Seek a City* (Bontemps and Conroy), 102, 125–29

Tugwell, Rexford, 50

*12 Million Black Voices* (Wright): about, 70, 81–82; on Black folk culture, 86–89, 93–97, 152; on children and urban life, 90–91; conclusion of, 97; countermodernity and, 6; dark mirror image in, 26, 97–98, 158; documentary style and FWP influence on, 85–86; Ellison's *Invisible Man* compared to, 153; on Harlem, 45; interpretive contention over, 20; Ottley's *New World A-Coming* compared to, 115; Petry's "Harlem" and *The Street* compared to, 132; political narrative and folk history, tensions between, 98–99; on racial slums, 46; on urban living conditions and the kitchenette, 89–90; worker alliances vs. New Deal in, 91–93

"Twentieth Century Fiction and the Black Mask of Humanity" (Ellison), 154

*Uncle Tom's Children* (Wright), 84

universalism vs. liberalism and race, 2–3

urban and regional planning: development as justice, 56–61; modernization and, 49, 52–54; New Deal and, 49–52; results of, 65–66; Rockefeller Center and New Deal aesthetic, 54–56; slum reform discourse, 41, 46, 56–57; Suburban Resettlement Administration and Greenbelt towns, 50; welfare state and, 16; World's Fair (1939) and, 61–64. *See also* housing projects, public; modernization

urban ecology, 17, 89, 92

Vanzetti, Bartolomeo, 28–29

vernacular culture. *See* folk, vernacular culture, and folkways

voters, African American, 15, 79, 91

Wald, Alan, 99, 132, 134n9, 142

Walker, Margaret, 8–9, 83, 120, 144

Warren, Kenneth, 20, 23, 102

Washington, Booker T., 16, 109

Waxman, Julia, 125

Weatherby, William J., 110

Weaver, Robert C., 59, 104

welfare state: Bontemps and Conroy on, 128–29; cultural politics and, 27; development of public assistance, 135; history from below and, 16; Hurston on, 72; ideal citizen in Ellison's *Invisible Man,* 144–45, 149; irony and, 165; liberalism and, 2–3; modern literary aesthetics and, 22; postwar attacks on, 162–64; urban and regional planning and, 16. *See also* housing projects, public; modernization

West, Dorothy, 94, 103

West, Rebecca, 84

Wharton, Edith, 30

White, Walter, 108, 118

White supremacy: Bontemps and Conroy on, 129; Ellison's *Invisible Man* and, 152; Hurston on, 77; liberalism and, 79; in Wright's *12 Million Black Voices,* 90

Whitman, Walt, 113, 154

Wilson, John Louis, Jr., 60

Winter, Kari J., 139

Wirth, Louis, 83

women: deserving vs. undeserving mothers, 135; in Petry's *The Street,* 135, 137–41; power of, in Hurston's *Moses,* 80; as workers, in Wright's *12 Million Black Voices,* 92

Woodrum, Clifton, 29

Woodson, Carter G., 110

worker alliances, in Wright's *12 Million Black Voices,* 92–93

World's Fair (1939), 61–64, 161

World War II: Bontemps and Conroy on racial equity and, 128; Ottley and, 104–5, 117–19, 121; Wright, Communist Party, and, 98

Wright, Richard: "Big Boy Leaves Home," 84; "Blueprint for Negro Writing," 94–96, 149; communism and, 22, 83–84, 127n91; "The Ethics of Living Jim Crow," 84, 95; FWP and, 82; "How 'Bigger' Was Born," 85n45, 95; Hurston, disagreement with, 69; "I Tried To Be a Communist," 84n43; *Native Son,* 85, 95, 98–99, 110, 111, 129; "Negro Harlem" and, 45–46; Negro History Unit (New York) and, 103–5; *The Negro in New York* and, 108; personal and political life, 82–84; "Portrait of Harlem" and, 1–2, 43–45; South Side Writers Group and, 120; *Uncle Tom's Children,* 84. See also *12 Million Black Voices*

Wurst, Gayle, 141

Yerby, Frank, 122, 127, 144; FWP and, 8

Yezierska, Anzia, 8–9, 41, 162–63

Yiddish Writers Group (YWG) FWP subunit, New York, 100

Printed in the USA
CPSIA information can be obtained
at www.ICGtesting.com
CBHW060302071224
18400CB00008B/26